HAPPY DAYS
& SUNDAYS

ROY CAVANAGH

W0019374

gecko press

First published in Great Britain in 2006
by Gecko Press

www.happydaysandsundays.co.uk

Cover artwork by Ted Andrews
www.tedart.co.uk

Gecko Press
PO Box 6259
Leighton Buzzard
LU7 2WS
www.geckopress.co.uk

ISBN 0-9552796-0-7
Printed and bound in England by Antony Rowe Ltd

For Mum and Dad

ACKNOWLEDGEMENTS

Stockgrove FC and the characters portrayed in this book are fictitious. However, the story was partly inspired by true events and my thanks and appreciation are extended to all the players, officials and supporters of Ashwell Globe FC and to Clive and Trish and all the staff at the Globe. Happy days.

It's been a long and often arduous road from the time those first words were penned sitting in an apartment block in Chiang Mai. My thanks for all those who offered feedback, suggestions, inspiration and encouragement. In particular, Fiona, Shaun, Mark, Simon, John and Jo, Rachel, 'Baghdad' Dave, Robert, Ian, Smithy and Ted.

To the people of Chiang Mai and Thailand thank you for your continuing kindness and hospitality. Finally, thanks to all those I've played football with or against over the years and to all those up and down the country who make the sport what it is.

CHAPTER ONE

'Stroker. You cheating fucking stroker.'

Gary Sweeney had a way with words. Granted, he would never make the Scrabble World Championships. Not that he wanted to. People who played Scrabble were triple word strokers. Stroker was a word Gary Sweeney used a lot. Where other people said tosser, he would say stroker. Often accompanied by the usual masturbatory gesture; the Nescafé handshake as Kevin Hardaker called it, in deference to Gareth Hunt in the coffee adverts of the Seventies and Eighties.

Sammy Koonphool had never heard of Gareth Hunt, but he knew all about strokers and Nescafé handshakes courtesy of his team-mates. The teenager had studied English in his native Thailand, but his first season playing for Stockgrove Football Club had been a remarkable educational experience unlike any of the three previous years he had spent in England. Football has a unique vocabulary and phraseology and it was something that intrigued Sammy Koonphool. The English he learned in the classroom only bore a passing similarity to the strange language spoken in the dressing room at Stockgrove. He could explain some of the phrases to his friends and family in Thailand, but the truth was he

1

didn't understand them all himself. Why did they have to 'get their heads on' before they went on the pitch? How sick can a parrot be? How can anyone possibly give 110% effort when by definition 100% was the maximum? He'd watch television and listen to Hansen and Lineker — the Hansens and Linekers of this world to use true football parlance — and he'd learn more. Then he'd listen to studio experts talking about 'lollipops' and 'giving the goalie the eyes' and he'd be even more confused. Sammy decided that, at the end of the day, it was best to take one cliché at a time. When he first arrived in England he soon learned a multitude of swear words from his school friends, but it was playing Sunday morning football where he realized just how adaptable the 'F' word could be. An amazingly versatile word that footballers and spectators at all levels use. If your team are 3-0 down with a minute left to play, you are fucked. If you have a penalty awarded against you then clearly that decision is a fucking disgrace. After all, the opposition player dived for fuck's sake. It is then suggested to the referee that he buys some fucking glasses. Not just glasses, but fucking glasses. Maybe Ann Summers do a range.

'You fucking cheat,' continued Gary Sweeney, his face now reddened and the vein on the side of his temple throbbing as he thrust forward at the opposition number nine.

'Fuck off, Gary,' was the centre forward's predictably eloquent response to the accusations of diving. The referee interrupted the two protagonists.

'All right, lads, I've given the penalty, now behave yourselves.'

The ref had been officiating at football matches since he finished playing ten years before. He was fifty-two now and carrying a bit of surplus weight around the midriff, but still looked as fit as some of the players he refereed every Sunday.

He was well respected in local league circles by players and officials alike. He had been a reasonable player in his time, but the respect came because he understood what made grown men get out of their bed on a Sunday morning to play football. He had done it himself for many years, shrugging off hangovers, leaving last night's conquest wandering around the flat, scraping frost off the windscreen and joining his mates to play Sunday morning football. Unlike most of the younger refs, he would often ignore the bad language from players and didn't deem it necessary to produce yellow cards. He had no pretensions about refereeing at a higher level and he gave the players plenty of leeway.

There were only two minutes of the match left to play and Gary Sweeney had enjoyed a good morning. His team were leading 3-0 and he had scored the first goal. He was mates with the man he had accused of diving and even shared a drink with him sometimes at Spurs matches.

Gary had been going to White Hart Lane since his dad first took him when he was six years old. His family were all Tottenham, living on The Roundway before moving from London to Bedfordshire when Gary was ten. Ironically, his parents were worried that their son would get into bad company staying in London. He went to his first away game when he was eleven. It was a turning point for the young Gary Sweeney in his duffle coat and Tottenham scarf, as he stood in the away end at Kenilworth Road with his father. The Luton fans hurled coins and abuse and the Spurs fans reciprocated with cans of Special Brew and Hoffmeister. Afterwards, there were running battles in the Arndale Centre and Saturday afternoon shoppers dropped their carrier bags in their haste to avoid the hooligans. Gary's dad was tutting at the idiots who had ruined the day for his son. During the drive back home the young Gary was quiet, not because he was scared, but because he was trying to remember every detail of his adventure so that he could tell the other boys at school on Monday. The football was exciting with two good teams getting the ball on the floor as it should be played. His schoolmates would see that on the *Big Match*, but he wanted to tell them about the things that Brian Moore wouldn't: the swearing, the singing, the smell of cigarettes and roasted peanuts. Being in the away end, Tottenham scoring and Spurs fans celebrating in pockets all around the ground. Sporadic fighting, nothing major, but scuffles here and there. These were all the things that had made the day memorable. He had seen confrontation, a show of strength and a battle of wills both on and off the pitch.

Now as an adult, it wasn't important that there were only two minutes left and his team were winning 3-0. He thought his mate had dived and that was all that mattered. Of course, he would probably see him at Spurs next week, buy him a drink and laugh about it, but not now. Not on the football pitch.

John Woods got a hand to the penalty but could not stop it from going in.

'Unlucky Woodsy,' chirped Neil Roberts.

The unwritten law of football nicknames dictated that John Woods was known as Woodsy and Neil Roberts became Robbo. Nobody knows where the law comes from but everybody who plays football knows it exists. Perhaps God whispered it to Moses as an unofficial Eleventh Commandment.

'Thou shalt give men who play football nicknames,' and Moses, the boy Mozzer, done well and spread the word of Goddo and lo, Woodsy and Robbo appeared.

Sammy Koonphool was familiar with nicknames in his homeland. In Thailand, they would be given to children to confuse evil spirits, but the only spirits the Stockgrove lads were interested in came in bottles. Somsak Koonphool had immediately been renamed Sammy by the other players at Stockgrove. At the private school he attended near Buckingham, he was known by his proper name. His sports teacher there, Neil Roberts, was secretary of Stockgrove. Robbo was thirty-six and as a youngster had excelled at rugby union representing England at under-sixteen level. He was a gifted sportsman who had also played county football as a centre-forward, but as the years advanced he had dropped back into midfield and defence. For the last two seasons, he had played centre-back for Stockgrove. It was whilst playing rugby for Loughborough University that he suffered the knee injury that ended any hopes of a professional sporting career. He now taught the privileged offspring of businessmen, actors and foreign dignitaries in leafy Buckinghamshire.

Somsak Koonphool had been a boarder at Robbo's school since he was fifteen. His father was part owner of the Nok brewery in Thailand and Sammy went back to Thailand three or four times a year whilst his parents would visit England whenever they could. The first time Neil Roberts saw Sammy play he knew the lad had a special talent. Sammy was a natural-born footballer. An overused phrase, but Sammy really was a natural. Everybody at Stockgrove could see that after he had played his first game at the start of the season. Robbo had taken Sammy under his wing. After a Stockgrove match, Robbo's girlfriend would sometimes cook for Sammy; a Sunday roast with all the trimmings. The youngster had grown to love his roast beef and English mustard. Sammy's father had met Neil Roberts a number of times on his visits to England. He had recently arranged for his company to provide a new kit for Stockgrove bearing the name of Nok brewery. Mr Koonphool wanted his son to go on to university and study business before joining him at the brewery. It was Neil Roberts who had impressed on him just how good a player Sammy was. Scouts from Watford had been to see him play for the school team although they hadn't followed up their initial interest. It was Sammy's dream to play professional football in England but even more than that, he wanted to play football for Thailand. No matter how Anglicised Sammy had become, he was still Thai and proud of his country and culture.

Gary Sweeney was calmer now as both teams walked back to the changing rooms. He was still accusing his opponent of diving in the penalty area but there was no malice this time. Stockgrove had won 3-1 with Gary scoring the first goal and Sammy adding the other two. In the last ten years, Stockgrove had won the league six times and finished runners-up twice. As is often the way with good teams at any level, players wanted to play for them and win trophies and especially at Sunday morning level, there are 'pot hunters,' who want to sign for a successful team. But Stockgrove was pretty much a closed shop. Some of the players had been there since the early days when Robbo and Butch formed the club. Naturally, players had come and gone. Players would sign for the team but then gradually drift away, unable to get in the starting line-up and unwilling to give up a Sunday morning to stand on the touchline.

Many of the Stockgrove lads had played Saturday football to a decent level, some semi-pro, and Macca was gracing the lower leagues of professional football before Sammy was even born. As the players got older one game a weekend was quite enough, thank you very much. The bulk of the team had played for Stockgrove for a number of years and they had been in battles and scrapes together on and off the pitch. They had won as a team, lost as a team and socialized as a team. Loyalty and camaraderie. You won't find that in any FA coaching manual. Wenger, Eriksson and Ferguson couldn't coach that, but they all knew the value of it and the importance of nurturing it. Loyalty, camaraderie and understanding are what help make good individuals bond into a good team. Even the Stockgrove wives and girlfriends knew that. They didn't necessarily always appreciate it, but for the most part, they respected it. Their other halves would play football once a week, have a couple of beers after the match, take the piss out of each other and go back home to their loved ones. Every month or so, on a Friday, the lads would have a boys' night out and the women would have a girls' night out. At Christmas and end of season, Robbo would organize a meal, usually at the Globe. Robbo was a natural organizer and he had been secretary of the club since it was founded, attending all the meetings of the league and dealing with the paperwork and the club's finances. He saw Stockgrove as his baby and he took good care of it, even if it did involve dealing with the associated smelly nappies. Sometimes he'd get annoyed, get the hump. Getting money out of the lads was a nightmare. Their subscriptions, their 'subs'. The club had to pay for pitches, referees, match balls and so on. Robbo couldn't believe how difficult it was at times to get a couple of quid each week from men in gainful employment. And Kevin Hardaker was the worst culprit of all, driving to the match in his brand new Range Rover and then revealing he had no money on him this week for subs.

'Fuck me, Kev, only you and the Royal Family don't carry any money. Not related are you?' asked Gary Sweeney.

'Do me a favour Gal, do I look like a Kraut or a Bubble?'

'Well, now that you mention it Zorba . . .'

'Bollocks. I'm more English than anybody in this changing

room.'

Robert Bowles chipped in, 'Sorry Kev, I'm not having that. My forebears fought at the battle of Agincourt.'

Kev responded instantly, 'Fucking hell, Stan. Forebears? Are you sure; who was that then . . . Yogi, BooBoo, Rupert and Paddington?'

Laughter erupted in the changing room. Kev was sharp.

'I'll tell you what Kev, it's a shame you ain't as quick as that on the pitch,' said Woodsy.

'Don't need to be mate. The first two yards are up here,' said Kev, pointing at his head, 'and the third yard . . . well, that's in Butch's shorts!'

Paul Butcher shook his head gently and laughed along with the rest of the team. He was actually surprisingly shy about his appendage. As an adolescent, he had been awkward with girls, self-conscious of his acne. So bad was his acne as a youth that he temporarily acquired the nickname 'Marshes'. Kids can be cruel. In an ageing team of players, Butch was one of the elder statesmen. He had seen his share of nightclubs in his time, usually with Kevin Hardaker. Kev had the gift of the gab, but Paul Butcher was gifted in other areas and when he was in a nightclub, it wasn't just his reputation that went before him. All the girls wanted to know if it was true. It was embarrassing most weekends because Butch didn't even have to try. There were no clever chat-up lines, no need to buy endless drinks and chat nicely to her friends. The girls were brazen. Single, married, engaged, old, young; they were all the same. They would be dancing with Butch, feel his manhood, shriek and that was that. So, the rumours were true. Even in the gents when you were trying to look straight ahead, if you were stood shoulder to shoulder at the urinals with Paul Butcher you couldn't avoid it. It was huge. When God was giving them out he must have misheard Butch, thought he'd said 'socks' and gave him two.

Sammy Koonphool laughed along with the rest of the lads. He didn't pretend to understand everything that was said in the changing room, but his knowledge of rhyming slang was increasing by the week and so was his appreciation of English humour. The way the players talked to each other was vastly different to the conversations Sammy would have at school with his friends. It was at Sammy's first game for Stockgrove where he learned two new essential phrases: 'taking the mickey' and 'taking the piss'. Sammy and his best friend, James Connolly, had joined Stockgrove at the same time. They both played for the school team and Neil Roberts had been very keen to see them sign for Stockgrove. The other players weren't sure at first. Public schoolboys playing for Stockgrove; what was the world coming to? They should have known better than to query Robbo's judgement. James Connolly, JC as he soon became, was an excellent all-round athlete representing his county at football and rugby. He was young, enthusiastic and quick. Sammy shared the same attributes but he looked frail compared to his taller and bulkier friend.

'Fuck me, Robbo, one gust of wind and he'll blow away!' said Kevin Hardaker when he first saw the Thai teenager. But at the end of Sammy's first game when he came on as a second-half substitute, Kev had revised his opinion.

'I've played with some decent players in my time, but that boy is different class. He's too good to be sitting on the Dame Judi; he's got to play every week.'

Neil Roberts already knew that, but he also knew that Sammy and JC had to prove their ability to the rest of the Stockgrove players. Their inclusion in the starting line-up every week would be on merit.

Robert Bowles was the man who had been claiming relations at the Battle of Agincourt. Stan as he was universally known — even his sister had taken to calling him Stan — was indeed a very English Englishman. Holidays at the seaside, fish and chips and real ale. He worked for the local council in the planning department and at thirty-five years old, he had already been married twice and divorced twice. A 100% record as Stan himself called it. He was arguably the least talented member of the team but was probably the fittest. He ran at least fifty miles a week and had clocked up numerous marathons all over the country. Kevin Hardaker commented when he first discovered Stan's passion for running, 'Blimey Stan, marathon running . . . why do you want to smuggle chocolate bars into South America?'

Stan was fiercely competitive on the pitch but quite timid off it. He hadn't enjoyed too much luck in his personal life, but running and football were his true loves. He was a Manchester United supporter, despite the fact that he had lived in or around the Home Counties all his life and his family had no affiliation with the north-west of England. But he liked United when he was a kid and as he grew up he went to see them whenever he could, home or away. The lads at Stockgrove didn't mind Stan's choice of team. Sure, they'd take the mickey, Cockney Red they called him, even though he lived in rural Buckinghamshire, but he went to watch his team and that was the important thing. Stan knew his football and he could talk about United teams from the Busby Babes through to Best, Buchan, Birtles and Barthez. And he talked sense. He acknowledged Arsenal's achievements in the manner that Gary Sweeney never could. Gary and Stan had huge respect for each other, a respect that was borne partly from their knowledge of their respective teams. Gary could talk with authority about any Spurs team from the double winning side onwards. He could also talk with equal alacrity about the darker side of football. Not that he did. The players at Stockgrove knew that Gary had been involved in the occasional fight at Tottenham matches and that he sold knocked-off gear for a living. Even Gary's parents knew their son was no angel, but nobody had any real idea to the extent of Gary's involvement. Nobody, except for Robert 'Stan' Bowles.

Stan was two years older than Gary Sweeney and had known him since Gary first joined Stockgrove as a callow seventeen-year-old. Since then, neither man had played weekend football for any other club. Their mutual knowledge of their respective teams meant they got on well straight away. Despite their different upbringings and outlook on life, or maybe because of it, Stan adopted the role of older brother to Gary. Stan did everything by the book. Rules were there for a reason and without rules and social constraints you would have anarchy. Gary had never seen life's rulebook, but he had his own code of ethics and he had an immense belief in the importance of family and community. His formative years in north London had taught him that. And loyalty. Gary's world revolved around loyalty. To your family, your mates, your football team and your country. Gary wasn't unique in that respect; there were young men like him in every town and city in the United Kingdom. From Sunderland to Swansea, Belfast to Bristol, Hamilton to Halifax . . . everywhere. Young men who sometimes fought with each other at football matches and the media would describe them as mindless thugs. They were anything but mindless. They were young men who had aggression in them, often misplaced, but in another era they would have fought and died for the British Empire. Stan's keen sense of British history meant that he understood this and he could rationalize it. Gary Sweeney couldn't rationalize it in the same way, but he knew that what was inside him didn't make him a bad person. If he had a fight at football, it was with like-minded individuals.

Gary and Stan went to a Tottenham versus United match the season after Gary signed for Stockgrove. They caught the early train to London and were intending to have a couple of beers near where Gary used to live, before meeting some of his friends at the ground. As they walked along the concourse at Euston, a group of six men in their mid-late thirties walked menacingly towards them. As they got closer, the group started humming the theme tune from *The Sweeney*.

'Strokers. Can't you come up with something original?' said Gary, smiling broadly as all the men, including Stan, exchanged handshakes. There were no introductions, just handshakes.

'Anybody about?' asked Gary.

'Dribs and drabs,' replied one of the group. 'Old Bill everywhere but heard reports of a little mob acting-up in Covent Garden last night.'

'Covent Garden? No marks for originality then. Oh, well, could be interesting. See you later lads.'

Stan didn't ask any questions. He didn't need too. He wasn't as streetwise as Gary but he had been to enough football matches to know what was going on.

'Fancy a quick pint up the road?' asked Gary.

Stan looked at his watch but Gary anticipated what he was thinking.

'Never mind that eleven o'clock opening time bollocks. It's the post office club, open twenty-four hours and a great fry-up.'

Lots of the post office boys knew and liked Gary. He had plenty of Spurs mates who worked on the post, but there were men who supported Aston Villa, Coventry and West Ham who all knew and respected Gary Sweeney.

Suitably replenished, they made their way to Wood Green and met Gary's cousin before meeting his other friends near the ground. Stan was introduced as a United fan and it was accepted without any fuss. There were none of the usual questions like, 'Why do you support them, living down here?' Stan was Gary Sweeney's mate and he could hold a conversation about football. That's all people were interested in. The same happened inside the ground when they sat in the East Stand. They all knew Stan was a 'Manc,' but they also knew he was a friend of Gary Sweeney. This was Gary's environment and Stan couldn't help but be impressed by the respect shown to his young friend.

After the match, they ignored the large groups of men waiting on street corners. Just the occasional nod of acknowledgement from Gary as they made the long walk up the Seven Sisters Road towards the tube station, accompanied by the sound of distant police sirens. Stan enjoyed the day out. He hadn't been to see United play for nearly a year and it was good for him to have a day out at football with his mate, but Stan had been acutely aware that the man he regarded as a younger brother, had in fact been looking after him all day. Were Stan not there then Gary's day out would have been very different.

'Enjoy it?' asked Stan on the train home.

'Made a nice change,' smiled Gary.

It was some years later, when Stan travelled with Gary to watch England play in Italy, that he had a better idea of what it was like to live in Gary Sweeney's world.

CHAPTER TWO

Robbo had been enduring a bad day and the phone call from the Football Association was an added burden he could have done without. For the past two seasons, he had been trying to get Stockgrove invited into the prestigious National Cup, a competition that featured the best Sunday morning football teams in England. Winning their fourth County Cup final the season before had clinched Stockgrove's invitation for this year's competition, with the final to be played at Villa Park. Robbo had been delighted to get accepted before his players became too old to do themselves justice. Now as he listened to his answer machine he began to wonder whether it was worth all the hassle. The paperwork for the competition was horrendous. He had already had to re-register details of every Stockgrove player with Soho Square as well as the local FA who administered the league they played in. Now he had received a phone call informing him that the FA could only find registration details for seven of his players. Increasingly harassed, he pulled out his box file with all the players' details and registration numbers. There were only five days left to the first round match and he was still dealing with the bureaucracy of the FA. At least he was more organized, with everything in a box file and on computer as back-up.

Robbo pulled the papers out of the file: Robert Bowles, Paul Butcher, Kevin Hardaker, Neil Roberts, Gary Sweeney, Philip Whitaker and John Woods. The FA held details of these seven. The magnificent seven. Robbo afforded a smile as he pictured himself as Yul Bryner riding with the other six to the aid of Mexican villagers. God help the villagers; between them, these seven were likely to shag all the women and drink all the tequila. These were the seven players who had been with the club the longest. Perhaps he should buy them all a gold watch, no doubt Gary could supply some 'genuine' Rolexes. Robbo was more relaxed now as he extracted the paperwork that he would need to fax through to the FA the following morning. One by one, he pulled out the details of the remaining players. It still seemed strange to Robbo when he saw the players' full names written down when mostly they were referred to by their nicknames. Not a lot of thought went into most of the nicknames, they were just simple derivations from the surnames in most cases, but the nickname law still had certain rules that had to be adhered to. Leon Wilson for instance, had to be called Willo. He couldn't be called Willso or Willsy. It had to be Willo. That's the way it worked. It was the unwritten nickname law that even Isaac Newton would struggle to explain. Robbo pulled out all the registration details. In total, Stockgrove had twenty players signed on. That included six former players, all in their late thirties or early forties, who were retained as emergency cover. At the start of the season, holidays and work commitments meant that Robbo needed to call on the services of his squad players. But when he rang them they had all given reasons or excuses for not being able to play; 'I'm visiting the in-laws/ I can't find my boots/ the dog's sick …' As a consequence, on two occasions Stockgrove fielded ten-man teams. It was after this that Robbo signed-on another two youngsters from his school side. Danny Cartwright and James Lloyd proved more reliable and when required would agree to play at short notice.

With the paperwork taken care of, Robbo went downstairs to call Tommy.

Tommy Boyle was manager of Stockgrove FC. He was fifty-eight and had moved to Bedford when he was twenty-four to work for an engineering company. At the time, it was a huge step for the Scotsman who'd lived all his life in Glasgow and had gone to college there. Tommy was a gregarious young man and instantly made friends in Bedford. He married Sylvia, a secretary at the company when he was twenty-eight and they went on to have three children. They had lived in Milton Keynes for eighteen years and had seen the new town increase rapidly in size. Tommy liked Milton Keynes. It wasn't all concrete cows and roundabouts. It had been a good place to bring up the children and the estate where he now lived had the same sense of community that he had enjoyed in Glasgow. There were plenty of Londoners, who had formed the nucleus of the new town's population in the early days, as well as a smattering of Scots and Geordies.

Tommy retired when he was fifty-four, taking voluntary redundancy from his company. With time on his hands, he could spend more time on the three loves of his life: his grandchildren, his garden and his golf. Tommy would often refer to Sylvia as the fourth love of his life, but never to her face.

Tommy had first seen his new neighbour, Neil Roberts, at the golf driving range soon after Robbo had moved to the estate six years ago. Through golf, they became friends enjoying a round most Sunday afternoons. Tommy started watching Stockgrove on Sunday mornings and with Robbo finding it increasingly frustrating to run the club and manage the team, he asked Tommy to help out.

As a child, Tommy played football with his friends in the street and with the Boys Brigade, but was never good enough for the school team. He didn't mind too much, he played football for fun. He was more of an academic but he still loved to watch football. The lads at Stockgrove didn't know this, they just assumed Tommy had been a good player in his youth. To them, Tommy was fifty-eight and Scottish and therefore he must be a good football manager. Shankly, Stein, Busby, Ferguson . . . Tommy Boyle. Tommy's main asset was his man management skills. Stockgrove had good players but Tommy made them into a better team. He had been manager for four seasons and the club had gone from strength to strength.

The two men discussed the arrangements for Sunday's match with Robbo advising Tommy he would call the coach company in the morning to finalise the details for the trip to Suffolk and the early afternoon kick-off. The team selection took care of itself. Stockgrove had a settled team but Tommy had one important phone call to make to ensure that one of his players was available.

Alan Farley was an apprentice plumber who worked for Kevin Hardaker and at barely seventeen was the youngest player signed on. Inevitably, the older lads had soon dubbed him 'Rusk' and the nickname law meant that this in turn became Rusky. Not Rusko, but Rusky; that's how the law worked. A quiet lad, he was an average footballer but he was a manager's dream. He would turn up every week without fail, knowing that he would be named as substitute. If there was a full side out he'd be nominated as linesman. He never moaned he just got on with it. He enjoyed the banter of the changing room, the mickey-taking, the stories about girls.

The stories; some true but most embellished. Rusky would often be the butt of a joke. Not in a nasty, malicious way but he was the baby of the team, introspective and quiet. When Kev Hardaker took the piss, Rusky would take the piss back. But only with Kev, not with the other lads. Kev liked it when Rusky retaliated to his mickey-taking. It was no good being too quiet and nice. It was a big bad world out there and he'd have to toughen up or people would take advantage. Some of the lads took Rusky for granted knowing he was there to make up the numbers, but not Robbo and Tommy. Players like Rusky were as important as the Colin McSwiggens and Sammy Koonphools of this world. Tommy knew that better than anyone did and that's why he always rang him personally to ensure he was available. Man management; that was Tommy's strength.

CHAPTER THREE

When Neil Roberts pulled into the car park of the Hockey Stadium, his was the last car to arrive.

'Fucking hell Robbo, what time do you call this?' asked Kev Hardaker.

Robbo smiled as he got out of the car. Helen was in the passenger seat and Tommy and Macca were in the back.

'I hope you haven't made him go through ninety minutes and extra-time in the bedroom this morning, Hels,' continued Kev.

Helen blushed slightly and laughed with the others as she got out of the car. Robbo was surprised to be the last arrival.

'I can't believe you lot are all here on time. That's a first this season.'

'Not quite Robbo,' said Butch, 'Kev bought a round in the Globe last week. Now that *was* a first!'

'Cheeky git,' responded Kev instantly. 'If I drank six bottles of Lucozade in ten minutes *that* would be a *thirst*.'

Sometimes Kev was too subtle with his humour and play on words. Only Robbo and Stan got the gag, whilst the others gathered their kit bags as the coach pulled into the car park.

'Pearls before swine,' muttered Kevin Hardaker.

Helen Garner taught English at the same school as Robbo. They had been together four years and lived with each other for three years, Helen moving from her flat in Princes Risborough. They were engaged the previous summer but had not set a firm date for the wedding. Helen's parents still held on to the notion of unmarried couples living in sin. At least now that their daughter was engaged it was just about acceptable. Robbo had never married. He had never been engaged before. Like many men, he was scared to make a commitment. He knew he was scared of the 'C' word but he never admitted it to anybody. Helen was different. This was the woman he wanted to spend the rest of his life with and have children. He had never seriously thought about this before until he met Helen. Robbo would walk naked around the bedroom singing into Helen's hairbrush with a Madness CD on in the background. Singing along to Suggs, *'It must be love, love, love . . .'* Helen telling him to, 'Shut up you daft sod!' But it must be love. As soon as he woke up, every night, every day, it was Helen he needed to chase the blues away. And he liked that. He could open up with Helen; she was his soulmate.

All the women sat together in a group at the front of the coach: Helen, Kimberley Woods, Denise Wilson and Gary Sweeney's girlfriend, Melissa. It was a fifty-six seater coach and was just over half-full. Robbo and Tommy had made sure they had a full team of eleven players and three substitutes. A group of a dozen supporters from the Globe had invited themselves along as well. The Globe was the canalside pub where most of the team would go after a match. They had been going there for the last five seasons after the pub they

20

had previously used, the Stockgrove Arms, was turned into a wine bar by the brewery. Apparently, the pub was attracting the wrong clientele and the brewery decided a change of image was required. All the players had voted to retain the Stockgrove name but find another place to drink. Gary Sweeney captured the mood at the time, 'A poncy wine bar. Strokers. I'd rather drink in an Arsenal pub.'

The Globe was a little bit out of the way, which meant there was the occasional lock-in on a Friday or Saturday night. The landlord, Emlyn, was a genial Welshman. He was a short, stout man with a big belly and a raucous laugh. The lads all liked him. The Globe was a typical country pub. Outside, hanging baskets brimming with flowers festooned the whitewashed walls. Inside, there was a small bar area with a slate floor, wooden beams and a real log fire. A small archway led through to a large restaurant area. The pub had an excellent reputation for food and it was here where the team would have their Christmas and end of season get-togethers. After the match on a Sunday, Emlyn would lay on baskets of chips, and ham sandwiches for the Stockgrove players.

The supporters from the Globe strung out along the back few rows of the coach and a big cross of Saint George flag was draped from the back window. Emlyn couldn't make the trip but had provided two cases of lager. Robbo told his players, 'Look lads, I don't want to get heavy, but this is the biggest match in the club's history. Have a laugh, have a sing-song, but no drinking.' The players didn't need to be told. Sure, this was all a good laugh, a bit of an adventure and vastly different to their normal pre-match routine, but they were there to play football. The National Cup. They had all arrived early at the meeting point, they had all cleaned their boots and nobody had been for a drink on Saturday night.

Most of the team had even abstained from sex the previous night, not by choice and not that they admitted it, and now Robbo was giving them a team-talk on the bus. This was the big time. This is how the pros do it. Well, not quite, as the hiss, fizz and ping of lager cans being opened echoed from the back seats.

'Where's the porn on the TV?' asked Big Frank, a barman at the Globe.

'Don't worry about the Frankie Vaughan,' said Kev as he handed Robbo an audio-cassette to give to the driver. Kev Hardaker had made a compilation tape of his favourite songs: The Undertones, The Jam, Elvis Costello and Oasis amongst others. Most of the players and supporters were in their thirties. Bollocks to all that techno and speed garage nonsense. This is the stuff. The coach was soon reverberating to Feargal blasting out 'Teenage Kicks'. The younger lads shook their heads.

Halfway into the journey the coach pulled into a roadside café. Whilst the supporters from the Globe tucked into their full English, Tommy ordered scrambled eggs on toast for all members of the squad. Kevin Hardaker's request for a bottle of the house red received short shrift.

An hour before kick-off, the coach pulled into the car park at Woodbridge. It was a mild day for the middle of January, almost spring-like, and the pitch was in good condition. There was one main stand that could seat just over two hundred people and opposite, in splendid isolation, were two concrete dug-outs. There were six seats for the home officials and substitutes and five seats and one broken one for the away team. A small caravan sited at the entrance to the main stand served tea and hot pies. The group from the Globe headed straight for the pies, whilst the rest, including the four women, went into the clubhouse where officials from Green Man FC welcomed them. The Green Man, much like Stockgrove, had dominated their league for the last five seasons, winning the title on four occasions. Most of their players were in their mid-twenties and half a dozen played Saturday football to a good standard in the Jewson League. This was the National Cup and there would be no easy matches for Stockgrove.

Tommy led his team into the away dressing room. It was a fairly typical changing room but in better condition than the ones they were used to, with plain white walls and four rows of slatted wooden benches. Above each row of benches there were metal hooks and, luxury of luxuries, a coat hanger. Like most changing rooms the shower had two settings; too hot and too cold. The familiar scent of liniment, body odour and air freshener filled the air. It doesn't matter how many air fresheners you put into a football changing room, a heady mixture of liniment and body odour will always prevail.

'Settle down lads,' began Tommy, 'I don't want to hear anybody else's voice for the next five minutes.'

Like nervous schoolchildren, the players sat quietly on the benches. Robbo, Butch, Willo, JC and Sammy maintained eye contact with Tommy as he spoke. The others mainly leant forward, hands clasped on their knees staring at the floor. Phil Whitaker was gazing at the wall opposite, fixed in concentration. Tommy always gave a pre-match team talk, but today was different. He still wore his familiar Harris Tweed flat cap as he spoke, but there wasn't the usual humour in his voice. The 'Jock-ularity' as Kev called it, was gone. Often he would have to talk quite loudly to make himself heard above the idle chit-chat and puerile jokes of the team, as they discussed who did what and with whom the previous night. But not today. Tommy spoke quietly and deliberately.

'You are a good team, but this competition is full of good teams. Neil Roberts has been trying to get you in this competition for the last two seasons because you all pestered him to enter it. So today, you prove yourselves worthy of being invited. In the league, you can coast in some games and still win. We all know that. Anybody coasting today will be off the park and replaced. Simple as that. Your reputation means fuck all here. *FUCK ALL!*'

Tommy shouted the expletive. The players exchanged glances. Tommy Boyle rarely swore. Crap was usually as strong as it got with Tommy. He'd say shit or bollocks when he was very angry, but this was a different Tommy. Sammy and JC looked at each other, stunned. Robbo, Butch and Willo maintained eye contact with their manager. Willo gulped as Tommy held his gaze for a couple of seconds. There was total silence for what seemed an eternity before Tommy spoke again, pulling out a sheet of paper from his shirt pocket. A few of the players took the opportunity to cough and clear their throats. Tommy spoke quietly again.

'This is the team that will start. In goals …' It was always in goals with Tommy, never in goal or goalkeeper. 'In goals, John Woods. At the back: Kevin Hardaker, Neil Roberts, Paul Butcher, Philip Whitaker. Right midfield James Connolly, left midfield Leon Wilson. Robert Bowles and Colin McSwiggen in the middle. Up front, Gary Sweeney and Somsak Koonphool. Starting on the bench will be Alan Farley, James Lloyd and Daniel Cartwright. Nobody get changed yet. Go for a walk, look at the pitch, stretch your legs, go to the toilet. Get changed in fifteen minutes and we'll have a proper warm up.'

Tommy turned and walked slowly out of the dressing room. Normally, Tommy would use the players' first names or nicknames when announcing the team, even though the team was more or less the same every week. But today Tommy had used full names. Today was different. Tommy was different. It was Neil Roberts who broke the silence.

'Well, you heard the man, have a pitch then have a look at the piss.'

Laughter echoed around the changing room. Robbo was the only man in the room who hadn't realized what he had said.

'Mr Roberts, that is a classic,' said Butch shaking his head, a big toothy grin illuminating his unshaven face. Robbo still looked blankly as Butch revealed the spoonerism that had made the team laugh.

'Oh, shit, you're joking? I'll never hear the last of this will I?'

As Robbo walked out with Butch to look at the pitch and walk round, the other players were already in a huddle talking loudly enough for Robbo and Butch to hear.

'So, Woodsy, do you think the piss will take a stud?' asked Macca.

'Reckon so mate,' replied Woodsy.

'All right lads that's enough,' declared Kevin Hardaker, 'anybody can make a slip of the tongue. No need to take the pitch.'

Leon Wilson launched into an uncannily accurate impersonation of Chris Eubank.

'Yesth. Do not take the pitch out of the skipper.'

'You stroker, Robbo,' added Gary Sweeney for good measure.

Tommy Boyle had met the match officials and exchanged pleasantries. The referee and the two linesmen had all travelled together from Ipswich but arrived just fifteen minutes before kick-off complaining about a flat battery. At least they were here. It was a rare privilege to have bona fide linesmen. This was only usually granted for league and County Cup finals.

The Stockgrove team changed into their pristine new kit supplied by Sammy's father; navy blue shirt with white lettering depicting the name 'Nok Brewery', white shorts and red socks. Colin McSwiggen, a fervent Celtic fan, was mortified when he saw the new kit. Previously, Stockgrove had played in all blue, which was just about acceptable for Macca. But red, white and blue . . .

'I cannae wear that!' exclaimed Macca, sounding more Scottish than at any time since the rest of the team had known him. 'For Christ's sake, you'll have me playing a flute and singing "God Save The Queen" next week.'

'But Colin, it's the national colours of Thailand,' explained Tommy gently. 'You wouldn't want to offend young Sammy and his father would you?'

Macca laughed, 'Well, as it's Thailand that's OK.' He smiled at Sammy and winked as he changed into the kit. But Macca had not been entirely joking. He didn't want to wear red, white and blue. Football rivalries and bigotries can, and do, run deep.

Stockgrove were outplayed for the first twenty minutes of the match. The Green Man were a very good side who played one- and two-touch football. John Woods pulled off three saves to keep the game scoreless. From the third save, the ball fell to Phil Whitaker who swung his left foot at the ball. His sliced clearance was brought down on his chest by Colin McSwiggen. Macca looked up and played a simple ball that bisected the two opposition centre-backs. Sammy Koonphool had started his run from just inside his own half and as the home defence appealed in vain for offside, the Thai teenager raced on to the ball and into the penalty area. As the goalkeeper advanced, Sammy caressed the ball into the bottom corner. Against the run of play, Stockgrove were one-nil up. The increasingly boisterous band of fans from the Globe started dancing a conga in front of the incredulous small knot of home supporters. The goal clearly unsettled the Green Man, who began conceding a rash of free kicks. Stockgrove enjoyed more possession and gradually began to dominate the half.

At half-time, the players retreated to the dressing rooms. Tommy Boyle waited patiently for his players to stop jabbering. They spoke excitedly, adrenaline flowing and were full of praise and self-congratulations, 'Well done Woodsy . . . Sammy, quality son . . . Macca, fucking top drawer, you never lose it mate . . .'

'OK lads,' interjected Tommy after a minute or two. He wanted the players to talk. They were excited and morale was good.

'OK lads,' he said again, as the players began to quieten down. Speaking in staccato sentences, he continued, 'Good half. No changes yet. Don't let them settle on the ball. Same again this half.' And that was Tommy Boyle's half-time team-talk. No clever stuff about tactics. Man management, that was Tommy's forte. Why use a thousand words when a dozen were more effective. The players were up for the game and the team spirit fostered from off the field friendships was there for all to see. Tommy left the players alone in the changing room for the next ten minutes. He walked to the small caravan, bought a cup of tea with three sugars and sat alone in the dug-out, waiting for the second half.

Two minutes into the second period, James Connolly broke free on the right hand side. He pushed the ball past the opposing left-back and crossed to the penalty spot where

Gary Sweeney rose unchallenged to head the ball straight at the goalkeeper. It was an easy save at any level but the ball bounced off the keeper's chest and out of his hands. Sammy latched on to the loose ball in a flash for a simple tap-in. Two-nil. Gary Sweeney was relieved. The team were ecstatic. Belatedly, the supporters from the Globe ran out from the clubhouse with pints still in hand. Not one of them had seen the goal, but the groans from the glass collector had them tripping over themselves in the race to get outside. Perhaps they thought they would be able to see the replay on the big screen. Perhaps not. There was no conga this time, but a rendition of *'Tommy Boyle's Stockgrove Army'* sufficed for a moment or two until the allure of the Cornish pasties proved too much to resist.

The Green Man battled gamely but were unable to recapture their passing game from the opening twenty minutes. The Stockgrove goal was never really under threat despite a good period of Green Man pressure in the last ten minutes of the match.

A small buffet was laid on after the game. Robbo made a short speech heeding Kevin Hardaker's advice not to get his 'wucking mords fuddled.' He thanked the home team for their hospitality and Gary Sweeney muttered under his breath, 'And thank you to the keeper for the second goal.'

The team and supporters clambered aboard the coach for the journey back to Milton Keynes. The original plan was to go straight to the Hockey Stadium to pick up the cars, but after a swift whip-round the coach driver agreed to take those that wanted to go, to the Globe.

'Righto, now let's have some music,' said Robert Bowles.

'Oi, oi, Stan, are you going to sing?' asked Phil.

'Where's that tape, Kev?' said Woodsy.

The first few bars of 'Wonderwall' were soon cascading

out of the speaker. The lads from the Globe crashed the vocal coming in too early with, '*Today is gonna be the day . . .*'

'Easy boys!' exclaimed Kev Hardaker. 'If we're going to do this let's do it right.' He rewound the tape and this time everybody got the cue right. Even the girls joined in. If Tommy Boyle had known the words, he would have joined in. The journey seemed to fly by. There were no stops on the way back but fortunately, there was a toilet on the coach. A very smelly, lager stained toilet. Music blasted out: 'A Town Called Malice'; 'Down In The Tube Station'; 'Jimmy Jimmy' and 'Oliver's Army', which soon became '*Tommy Boyle's Army*', as the words were changed from Declan MacManus's original.

There was a burst of laughter from the back seats. Then, quietly at first, a rendition of 'Wonderwall'. There was more laughter as other people picked up the new song and joined in. Kev walked to the front of the coach and stopped the tape, cutting Paul Weller off in his prime. Now he could hear a lusty rendition, '*. . . And all the runs that JC makes are winding, and all the goals that Sweeney scores are blinding . . . and Sammy Koonphool, you are* WONDERFUL*!*' More words were added, '*Woodsy . . . are you gonna be the one that saves me . . .*' Frank the barman and Tony Smith, a regular at the Globe, had been responsible for the song that was to become the club anthem for the rest of the season and beyond.

The coach pulled into a small lay-by near the entrance to the Globe. Those staying on board said goodbye to the others. The coach was too big to go down the narrow lane that led over a humpback bridge to the canalside pub. Butch, Phil, Stan and Gary Sweeney led the walk down the lane towards the Globe. They were followed by Kev, Rusky, Danny and Lloydy with Big Frank and his group straggling further behind. The motley crew was singing the new version of 'Wonderwall' as they staggered down the lane. There had been no booze ban for the players on the return journey home and they took full advantage, stocking up with cans from the clubhouse in Woodbridge. The Globe bar was busy and a big cheer went up when the group entered. Frank had rang Emlyn straight after the match with the result.

'Marvellous, boys. Absolutely marvellous.' Emlyn shook hands with everyone and went behind the bar himself to ensure each of the group had a free beer.

'I know you want to celebrate lads but I've still got a lot of families eating next door, so no singing and keep the language down.'

It was a reasonable request. The man had a business to run and he had bought them all a drink, not to mention two crates for the coach down to the game. But the group were in party mood and wanted to sing.

'Miserable git,' said Kev. 'It was never like that in the Stockgrove.'

'No, you're right Kev. We never got free beer in the Stockgrove,' said Stan.

'All right, fair enough,' conceded Kev.

But Stan, like the others, shared a small sense of anti-climax. They'd had a great day and wanted to continue the festivities. It was a bit like being invited to a party only to find out it was being hosted by the Temperance Society.

At the Hockey Stadium, Robbo and Helen were the last two to disembark. Meticulous as ever, Robbo had been double-checking nothing had been left behind. He noticed the state of the toilet floor, which was awash with lager where a can had been dropped. The driver told him not to worry; he'd clear up the mess, informing Robbo the coach was in worse states after doing the school run. Besides, he had enjoyed driving the team. The people on board had been generous with their whip-round and the cash presented to the driver was a very pleasant bonus. He wished Robbo good luck for the next round and hoped he could drive the team again.

The coach driver would have his wish granted. Later in the week, the FA would inform Robbo that Stockgrove had been drawn away again in the next round and would play Marlborough Wanderers from Diss in Norfolk.

CHAPTER FOUR

It was raining heavily on Monday morning as Robbo and Helen drove to school. The previous day's promise of spring had been replaced with a chilly reminder of winter. Robbo and Helen weren't complaining. They had enjoyed their weekend and Helen was pleased for Neil. She knew how much time and effort he put into running 'that bloody club,' as she would sometimes call it. More than that though, she wasn't just pleased for her fiancé and his friends, she too had enjoyed the whole day; the football, the singing on the coach, Helen had enjoyed it all. She had been given an insight to why Neil would get out of a nice warm bed on a Sunday morning to kick a ball around with men who were old enough to know better. When it came to football, Helen was ambivalent. She had grown up with two older brothers and a father who would watch any match that came on the television. Helen watched England matches but she never had any club allegiance, despite her family all being West Ham fans. Robbo was West Ham too, although he had only been to see them a handful of times in the flesh. Growing up, Robbo was always playing football or rugby at the weekends and usually both. And when the football and rugby seasons finished it was cricket. These days Robbo made do with Sky television. Sky TV was a boon for people like Neil Roberts, but Gary Sweeney hated it; football should kick-off at three o'clock on a Saturday afternoon. End of. Television had neglected the paying spectator in favour of the armchair fan. Gary was no fool, he knew how much money had been introduced into the game and how the general standard had improved as a consequence. But had it improved the standard at Spurs? It may have done down the road in N5, but where were the players of the past . . . Perryman, Mabbutt, Hoddle. The Perrymans, Mabbutts and Hoddles of this world. And there was certainly no improvement for the English national side. No, for Gary television and the gentrification of football had been at the expense of the most loyal supporters. He resented having to choose between Spurs or Stockgrove matches on a Sunday.

Helen enjoyed watching England matches on Sky and could never understand why so many people would want to spend all that money watching England play abroad. Going to Japan like Gary Sweeney had just to watch football. Must be bloody mad. More money than sense. But yesterday she had really got involved, jumping up and down when Sammy scored. All the women: Helen, Denise, Kimberley and Melissa had enjoyed the day out.

Denise would sometimes go with Leon to QPR. They would leave their son with Leon's mum and dad in Harlesden and then meet Leon's mates in the Bushranger for a few drinks before the match. Afterwards, they'd be treated to some great West Indian food when they returned to Leon's parents. But Helen had never experienced a day out at football and she was surprised at just how much she had enjoyed it. Christ, she thought, she'd be setting the video for *Soccer AM* next!

'What are you smiling at?' Neil asked his fiancée as he

drove towards Buckingham.

'Just thinking about yesterday.'

'*Sanuk mai*?' asked Neil.

'*Sanuk mak*!' replied Helen.

They both laughed. It had been great fun yesterday. They had picked up a few words of Thai from Sammy and were planning to go to Thailand for their honeymoon as and when they married. They were still laughing when Robbo switched the radio from Talk Sport to Horizon Radio, who were playing 'Wonderwall'. It was a perfect moment. Helen was singing the few words she could remember from the Stockgrove version, whilst Robbo was wiping tears of laughter away from his eyes. No other woman had made Robbo laugh the way that Helen did. It was a cold Monday morning in January as they happily drove to work. You weren't meant to be this happy on a Monday morning. The Robbos and the Helens of this world weren't meant to be this happy. And the phone call Robbo was to receive later that morning would make the weekend complete

Helen spoke to JC and Sammy before her English class and said how much she had enjoyed the match. The youngsters had enjoyed it too, not just the match, the whole day. The same as Helen, they had enjoyed the singing on the coach, the mickey-taking and the supporters doing a conga.

Sammy had already telephoned his father in Thailand and described, in excited tones, what the day was like. Mr Koonphool was pleased for his son but had to admit he was not familiar with the conga. He'd watch the satellite feeds of Premiership football in Thailand every week and he'd see Shearer, Owen, Giggs . . . but no conga. His son was happy in England and had adapted well to life there. Sammy was academically gifted, an outstanding footballer and was well-liked at school. He was very easy going and nothing perturbed him too much. But he missed his family. Sammy was an only child but it wasn't just his mother and his father he missed, but his grandparents, aunts, uncles; his extended family and the childhood friends he had in Thailand. He still kept in touch with some of his friends by email. Some were at college and others were working full time. Sammy missed other things about Thailand, particularly his mother's cooking, although he appreciated the Sunday roasts cooked by Helen. There was a good Thai restaurant a half-hour drive from the school and Sammy would go there at least once a month with JC and his family or Helen and Neil.

At first, Sammy hated the English weather. It had been February when he first arrived as a fifteen-year-old, and Arctic winds and sub-zero temperatures greeted him at Heathrow. The longer he stayed though, the more he enjoyed the change of seasons. Spring was his favourite, enjoying bicycle rides through the Chiltern countryside. He couldn't drive, but his father had promised to pay for lessons when Sammy finished school in the summer. The summer seemed a long way off for Sammy. His father was keen for him to study for a business degree at university but Sammy still harboured dreams of becoming a professional footballer. He was small at five foot six and slightly built, but he was very strong. Sammy was as intelligent on the pitch as he was off it. Anticipation, speed and finishing were his strengths. Gary Sweeney's father had seen Sammy play twice and had called him an 'Oriental Jimmy Greaves.' The players had to assure a bemused Sammy this was indeed a compliment.

On Saturday, Neil Roberts's school team were to play an inter-schools cup match against a side from Aylesbury Grammar. Robbo was giving no thought to that match as he entered his office, his legs mud-splattered from the cross-country run he had just made his third year students endure. Robbo only did a little running himself, mainly chasing up the stragglers and looking for smart-arses taking short-cuts or enjoying a sneaky cigarette. Some things remain constant over the years and it doesn't matter if it's a comprehensive or a public school; adolescent boys hate cross-country running. There was a note on Robbo's desk with a number to ring. He dialled the number and almost immediately the phone was answered.

'Good morning, Reading Football Club, how can I help you?'

'Good morning. George Fielding please.'

'Certainly, sir. One moment . . .'

George Fielding introduced himself to Neil Roberts. He was a member of the coaching staff at Reading and wanted to come and watch Sammy play for the school this coming Saturday morning. He explained that one of the club's scouts had enthused about Sammy. Robbo hadn't even been aware that Sammy had been watched. The man from Reading asked Robbo not to tell Sammy he was coming. In his experience when young lads knew football clubs were watching they tended to try too hard.

That evening, driving back home to Milton Keynes, Robbo told Helen about the phone call. She could hardly contain her excitement.

'All right, calm down sweetheart,' said Robbo, 'he's just coming to have a look at Sammy play that's all.'

'But that's good. He's from the coaching staff, right? They must be really interested, yeah?'

Robbo knew Helen was right but tried to play it down and made Helen promise she wouldn't tell anybody else. Nobody in the staff room and especially not Sammy.

'I'm serious, Helen. Not a word to anyone. Not just Sammy. None of the other teachers or Kimberley Woods, Denise, Melissa —'

'All right, Neil,' interrupted Helen abruptly. 'God, what do you take me for?'

Robbo had made his point but he wondered if he had been too harsh with Helen. It was a very quiet journey home. He knew Helen was no gossip merchant. In fact, in his experience, the people who could least keep a secret and liked to gossip most, were the lads at Stockgrove. They'd describe it as banter, but more often than not it was idle gossip;

'Saw that Paul Johnstone down the Globe last night. Never guess whose wife he's shagging . . . Didn't she have an affair with . . . I shouldn't be telling you this but . . .'

If it was in a football dressing room it was banter, that was OK, but if it was a group of women in an office or at the hairdressers', that was gossip. It was another example of the unwritten rules of the male football environment; the banter and nicknames of this world.

Neil Roberts drove alone to school on Saturday morning. Helen's mum was coming over for the day and the two women were going shopping. Occasionally, Helen would go with Neil when the school had a home match. She really wanted to go today to see Sammy do well but she had butterflies in her stomach as it was. What would it be like if she was actually there?

As kick-off time approached, Robbo was anxious too. Would George Fielding show up? How would Sammy play? Would the team win? Robbo announced the starting line-up and gave a brief team-talk to his players. They were a good set of kids, no backchat, respectful of their elders — blimey, they were a lot more mature than the players of Stockgrove!

There were no special words of encouragement for Sammy, quite the opposite, Robbo hardly spoke to the lad.

The match was fifteen minutes old when a man in his early forties walked up to Neil Roberts, shook hands and introduced himself as George Fielding.

'Got the right one this time,' he said, explaining to Robbo how he had introduced himself to the sports teacher from Aylesbury Grammar. Robbo smiled as he shook hands. When Robbo had spoken on the phone two days before, he had built up a very different mental image of the man from Reading. He pictured a tall man, maybe fifty, grey hair, tracksuit — but George Fielding was forty-two and had a full head of thick black hair. He was lightly tanned and wore a Stone Island jacket, dark jeans and Timberland shoes. Robbo half expected him to pull out a wad of tickets '. . . I'll buy or sell. What are you after, halfway line? No problem.' He could easily have passed for one of Gary Sweeney's business contacts, but George Fielding was no ticket tout. He made a bit of small talk and Robbo confirmed the young man in white, wearing the number nine shirt was Somsak Koonphool. The man from Reading's mobile phone rang and he walked slowly around the pitch to the opposite touchline.

The match was a dour affair. All kick and rush with neither side playing well. Then, just on half-time, Sammy played a neat one-two with JC on the edge of the box. Robbo watched in disbelief as Sammy shot tamely at the Aylesbury goalkeeper. Shit. He never misses those. Shit, shit, shit. Had Helen told Sammy he was being watched? Shit. Almost as an afterthought, he looked for George Fielding. Had he gone already? Did he see . . . ? Robbo saw the Reading man walking towards the car park.

Twenty minutes into the second period Sammy received the ball with his back to goal, just inside the Aylesbury half and near the touchline. A neat drag back left one opponent floundering. Sammy raced towards goal and feinted to cross with his left foot. As the fullback lunged in, Sammy flicked it over the defender's leg and cut a perfect ball back to the advancing James Connolly who side-footed the ball into the net. With ten minutes left to play Aylesbury equalized from a penalty. There was more drama with a minute left as a ball was played into the Aylesbury box and Sammy met it perfectly on the volley. The keeper had no chance, but watched as the ball crashed against the crossbar. From the resulting breakaway Aylesbury went straight up the other end of the pitch and scored the winner. It was a very cruel way to lose a football match.

As the teams were walking back to get changed, Robbo was surprised to see George Fielding approach him.

'Unlucky. Not the best of games but a nice goal by your lads. I thought you were the better team. Sorry I've got to shoot off but I'll be in touch.' That was all he said. He gave Robbo a firm handshake and he was off, walking towards his car. Robbo couldn't believe it. Where was the man from Del Monte when you needed him? The man from Reading, he say no!

'Sorry, Mr Roberts,' said Sammy. The lads at Stockgrove would ridicule Sammy, JC, Danny and Lloydy when they called Robbo, sir or Mr Roberts on a Sunday morning. After a few games, the youngsters were soon calling their sports teacher Robbo. But only on Sundays.

'What are you sorry for, Sammy?'

'We didn't play very well today, sir'

'No we didn't but —' Robbo's mobile was ringing. 'Excuse me, Sammy.' He walked outside to answer Helen's call.

'No, lost 2-1 . . . No, not really . . . JC scored . . . Yes . . . Not sure . . . Of course he'll have other chances . . . About two o'clock, just got to clear up here . . . OK, love. Bye.'

Neil Roberts was in his office when the phone rang Monday lunchtime.

'Hello, Neil, it's George Fielding. Sorry I didn't have much of a talk after the game, but the youth team were playing in Greenford at one o'clock.'

'No, no, of course,' replied Robbo, surprised by the call.

'So what's the set-up with Somsak? His parents are in Thailand, right?'

Robbo explained the situation to the Reading man.

'Look Neil, the lad had a quiet game on Saturday, that can happen. My scout here, Steve Palmer, has seen him a few times now, was even at that match in Woodbridge the other week . . .'

Robbo almost dropped the phone. George Fielding sensed the surprise.

'Thought that would shock you. Steve's a big fan of your lad, that's why I wanted to see what all the fuss was about. If it hadn't of been for Steve talking about him all the time I would have gone when he missed that sitter on half-time.'

Oh shit, thought Robbo, he had seen it.

'But that moment for the goal and the volley near the end were quality. The boy's got ability, there's no doubt about that. I want to invite him for a trial, but I'd like to speak to his parents first.'

Neil Roberts thanked George Fielding and promised to call him tomorrow after speaking with Somsak. After school, Robbo called Sammy into his office and broke the news. The Thai youngster could hardly contain his excitement. Robbo handed Sammy the phone to call his parents. There was no reply at his parents' home so he tried his father's work number. Mr Koonphool was surprised to hear from his son at that time of the day and immediately asked what was wrong. Had his son been in an accident or trouble at school? Sammy allayed his father's worries.

'No Dad, nothing's wrong. Quite the opposite.' His father listened quietly as his son explained about the man from Reading.

'OK, Somsak, I will speak with your mother tonight and then I'll call Mr Fielding tomorrow.'

Sammy passed the phone back to his sports teacher.

'Hello, Mr Koonphool . . . yes sorry, hello Joe, how are you?'

Sammy's father, Narong, liked to be called Joe. As a teenager, he had worked as a bellboy in a Bangkok hotel. A long-term American resident at the hotel always referred to Narong as Joe, and the name had stuck. The other hotel staff even started calling him Joe.

'Yes, Somsak did very well . . . Of course you have to discuss the matter with your wife . . . Yes . . . Helen's very well, thank you. Of course I will . . . Tomorrow? Yes, that's fine . . . OK, I will . . . and you Joe. Yes, he's still here.'

Robbo handed the phone back to Somsak and walked outside to the playing fields, leaving the boy alone to speak privately with his father. Not that it would have mattered, Robbo only understood the few basic words of Thai that Sammy had taught him and Helen, but it was still nice for the youngster to have some privacy. A few minutes later Sammy walked outside and joined Robbo.

'What do you think, sir?' asked Sammy.

'I think it's a great opportunity,' replied Neil Roberts.

'That's what my father says. I know he wants me to continue my studies, but if I became a professional footballer he'd be over the moon!'

They both laughed. If Sammy made it as a footballer, he

vowed never to use football clichés in any interviews. But at the end of the day, he had a long way to go before that happened and he wouldn't be able to do it without the help of the rest of the lads. I mean, you know, he was fortunate really Brian, but he would love it, really love it, to make it as a pro. Yes, Sammy found football clichés very amusing.

When Joe Koonphool broke the news to his wife Ladawan, she cried with joy. Joe had to explain to her that their son would only be going to Reading to try out with a host of other young hopefuls. Ladawan Koonphool knew how much Somsak's dream meant to him. Of course he could go to Reading. Then a string of babbled questions. 'Where is Reading? Who plays for them? What league are they in? Will we be able to watch him on television?' The excitement had overtaken Ladawan Koonphool. Joe laughed and told her to calm down. Their son would merely be trying out at Reading, not playing for the first team. Joe didn't want to raise his wife's expectations or hopes too much, but inwardly he was as excited, more excited, than his wife. He kept his emotions in check nearly all the time. Never too angry or over-excited. *Jai yen* the Thais called it; cool heart.

CHAPTER FIVE

It was six in the evening in Thailand when Joe Koonphool rang Reading Football Club. George Fielding had only been in his office for twenty minutes and was still sorting out the morning's post. The nature of the job meant unsocial hours with evening matches to watch and youth team and school fixtures at weekends. Then there was the paperwork to deal with which seemed to increase year by year as the FA brought out more directives and edicts. Every one of these seemed to have some sort of course attached that he was obliged to attend. He disliked most of the instruction courses, which seemed to be more about accounting than football, but he loved his job and attended them grudgingly.

Joe Koonphool and George Fielding spoke for nearly fifteen minutes. The man from Reading addressed all of Joe's questions and concerns. Mr Koonphool was delighted his son was being given a chance to prove himself and was impressed by his first conversation with George Fielding. The Thai man considered himself a good judge of character. His instincts were seldom wrong in this respect and it was a trait that had helped him throughout his business career. He knew a charlatan when he spoke to one, Thai or Westerner.

The conversation had set Joe's mind at rest. Within minutes of speaking to the Reading man, he was leaving a message on the voicemail of his son's mobile phone. After returning his father's call, Sammy waited until the end of the school day before visiting Neil Roberts's office. Despite being a sports teacher, Robbo still had some reports to file. He never had as many as his fiancée though, a fact that he took great delight in teasing her with. The youngster's trial at Reading would take place the following Wednesday. Joe Koonphool was happy for George Fielding to liaise directly with Neil Roberts. Joe trusted Neil implicitly. Both Neil and Helen had taken Sammy to their hearts; he was a young man who was a real credit to his parents. Like most of the boarders at the school, Sammy was impeccably mannered and smart in appearance. But above and beyond that, he showed immense respect for his elders. Not in a fawning, sycophantic manner, but in a discreet fashion which even impressed his peers. Sammy had no enemies at the school. He was studious and quietly spoken, but had a ready wit and sense of fun and gained kudos for his football ability. He was a good all-round sportsman except for cricket. It was the one sport he had never taken to, despite his excellent hand-eye co-ordination. In the few years he had spent in England, he never appreciated the subtleties of the game, preferring to devote his time to honing his football skills.

There would be no football for Sammy this weekend. The school had no match on the Saturday, only playing as they did, once every two or three weeks and Robbo had already decided not to play Sammy in Stockgrove's league match on the Sunday. If the lad got injured Robbo would never forgive himself. Sammy couldn't see the problem but accepted Neil Roberts's decision without question.

That Sunday, Stockgrove produced their worst performance

in two seasons in losing 3-1 to a team third from bottom of the table. Tommy Boyle was distinctly unimpressed. He threatened changes for the following Sunday's trip to Norfolk in the National Cup, but secretly he just hoped his team had got a bad performance out of the way and would return to form the following week. Robbo had a personal shocker in the match. An own goal in the first half was followed shortly after half-time by a clumsy challenge to concede a penalty. John Woods made a fine save but the ball rebounded kindly to the penalty taker to make it 2-0. In making the challenge, Robbo had hurt his ankle and was forced to hobble off. 'Rusky' Farley replaced Robbo in defence and the young man put in a steadfast performance that was the one bright spot of the day for Stockgrove.

Robbo's ankle was still troubling him on Wednesday afternoon, as he set off with Sammy in the passenger seat, for the trip from Buckingham to Reading. The directions from George Fielding were clear and concise and Neil Roberts had no trouble finding the training ground. Robbo hobbled off to find a cup of tea whilst the Reading officials spoke to Sammy and the other trialists at length, before the young hopefuls changed and warmed-up prior to a practice match. Sammy was handed a yellow training bib that swamped his small frame, but worse than that, it had a red number four on the back and front. Sammy wanted to change the number but was reluctant to speak up. No, he'd just have to forget about the number and show the officials what he could do. The match was over in what seemed no time at all. Sammy had played for thirty minutes in a match that lasted forty minutes in total. He had barely touched the ball. As Sammy was getting changed, George Fielding spoke with Neil Roberts.

'I'm sorry Neil but not this time. He's a terrific little player, but at the moment we think he's just a bit too small and will get knocked off the ball too easily.'

Robbo thought that was bollocks. He had seen Sammy playing against Sunday League cloggers and he could hold his own and give some back. Small in stature he may be, but Sammy was no lightweight. Robbo gave a small sigh and thanked the Reading man.

'Look, Neil, sometimes I'm right about players and sometimes I'm wrong. It doesn't mean the boy isn't good enough. He just isn't right for us at the moment. If it was down to Steve Palmer, he'd give him a contract here and now, but at the end of the day it's my decision, not Steve's.'

At the end of the day! George Fielding really was a football man. The official took time to speak to each of the trialists. It was no consolation to Sammy that nobody else would be invited back for further trials either. Neil Roberts seemed more disappointed than the Thai teenager did. Sammy remained phlegmatic. If it wasn't meant to be this time, then so be it. That was his Buddhist belief.

'Never mind, sir, there'll be other chances.'

Hold on, thought Robbo to himself, isn't that what I should be saying? The truth was, Neil Roberts was investing some of his unfulfilled dreams in Sammy. When Robbo was injured at university, his hopes of playing rugby for England at senior level were gone. His parents still had the scrapbooks full of local newspaper cuttings and photos of him at Twickenham, playing for England under-sixteens versus France.

'Of course there will be other chances Sammy,' he concurred as they walked back to the car.

'But I am a bit gutted,' said Sammy with a smile in his voice.

Neil Roberts laughed at the boy's wit. No, not boy any more. This was a young man with great composure, on and off the pitch.

That night, Helen answered the phone when Joe Koonphool rang. George Fielding had already rang him in Thailand and told him Somsak was a good player, but Reading could not offer him a contract. Mr Koonphool had appreciated George Fielding's call. It was a sign of good manners and respect. His initial judgement of the football man's character was correct. Joe spoke at length with Helen. He was a bit of a charmer and he reminded Helen in many ways of her late grandfather. Joe then thanked Neil for all his help. Somsak really was a chip off the old block.

'He'll have other opportunities. No problem — *mai pen rai*,' Joe said, 'but he won't wear the number four shirt next time. That's bad luck for Thai people. Next time I've told him to get the number nine shirt, that's for good luck!'

He wished Stockgrove well for Sunday's match in the National Cup and said he looked forward to seeing the young couple when he came over to England in two weeks' time.

CHAPTER SIX

It was 9 a.m. when the coach pulled out of the Hockey Stadium car park at Milton Keynes for the journey to Diss. This time there were only twelve spare seats on the fifty-six seater coach. It was the same squad of players from the previous round and Colin McSwiggen's wife, Wendy, joined the four women from the previous trip. Supporters from the Globe occupied the rest of the seats. After the previous round's match, many of the Globe regulars decided this would be a great day out.

The week before the match was Big Frank's birthday. Frank Marinelli wasn't particularly tall at five foot nine, but it was fair to say he was no stranger to the dessert trolley. He was a barman at the Globe and worked in a shoe factory during the day. Franco Roberto Marinelli was second generation Italian and had lived in Milton Keynes all his life. He didn't speak Italian but supported Italy in all sporting matters, especially against England. This led to plenty of good-natured abuse from the regulars at the Globe. It was Frank on his birthday who suggested the supporters should go in fancy dress for the following week's trip to Norfolk. What a great idea everybody agreed.

Big Frank boarded the coach to the accompaniment of wolf-whistles and laughter as his ample girth waddled down the aisle in his Biggles costume: black boots, leather flying jacket, flying helmet, goggles and long white scarf. A stick-on handlebar moustache topped off the look. Fair play to Frank, the lads all agreed. He could easily have changed into his civvies, which were in his car.

'All right, all right, I'll pass out the needle and cotton; great stitch boys,' said Frank.

He had been well and truly stitched up by the lads from the Globe and he knew that, perversely, the only way to save face was to wear the costume for the rest of the day.

Neil Roberts sat alongside Tommy Boyle at the front of the coach. Robbo's ankle had improved greatly but he had declared himself unfit to play. Tommy had already decided that young Alan Farley would take his place. However, Rusky would play at right-back with Kevin Hardaker moving into the middle of defence to pair with Butch. Robbo saw the sense in having a more experienced centre-half partnership. Apart from that, the team was unchanged from the previous round. The main thing that had changed was the atmosphere on board the coach. After the initial mickey-taking out of Big Frank, the coach soon settled down and about thirty minutes into the journey most people were having a snooze. There was no heavy drinking this time and no loud music. The coach pulled into a roadside diner at Thetford forest. The weary group disembarked and as in the previous round, Tommy ordered scrambled eggs on toast for all the players. After breakfast, Gary Sweeney was stretching his legs when he spotted a recently dead pheasant. The opportunity was too good to miss. He walked over to Kev Hardaker and whispered in his ear. Kev approached the coach driver explaining he needed his asthma inhaler from his kit bag. The luggage hold was obligingly opened. Leon Wilson had heard Kev's request and smiled. If Kev suffered from asthma, then it had developed that week.

'What are you up to?' asked Willo, pulling Kev to one side. Just as he did, Gary Sweeney emerged furtively from the bushes holding a carrier bag with the dead pheasant inside. He found John Woods's kit bag and the pheasant was soon sharing his new home tucked in between a pair of size nine Puma King boots and a large pair of Sondico gloves.

Willo looked on incredulously. 'I don't want to know,' he said.

Gary and Kev grinned like naughty schoolboys. Kevin Hardaker winked at Leon Wilson and Willo could not help but laugh at the two men behaving like a couple of kids. In a team where mickey-taking and practical jokes were the norm, Gary and Kev were the unsurpassed masters. Putting Ralgex spray into an unsuspecting player's underwear whilst he was in the shower was passé for them. They had moved on to bigger and better things and Woodsy was often on the receiving end. At the end of last season they had superglued Woodsy's boots to the changing room ceiling. The season before that, they had pulled off a stunt that the SAS would have been proud of. As Woodsy and his wife were having a meal at the Globe, the pair removed all four wheels from his car leaving a set of bricks in their place. Woodsy could take a joke. He was pretty much unflappable and would take everything in his stride. After the car incident his wife was furious, but Woodsy knew who was behind it straight away. He retrieved his car the following day with all the tyres duly replaced by the offending duo. When they found out how angry Kimberley Woods had been, Gary and Kev arranged for a big bouquet of flowers and Gary acquired two tickets for the couple to watch *Les Miserables* in the West End. Gary and Kev liked a practical joke but nothing malicious. The young Sammy and James Connolly were amazed at some of the things these supposed adults would get up to. Sammy particularly enjoyed it. In his homeland, they had a word for it — *sanuk*. In the changing room, the other players had two words for it.

After the breakfast stop the coach became livelier. The players started to talk about the game and a card school started on the back seats amongst the supporters from the Globe. Big Frank passed round some cans of lager. Biggles had removed his flying jacket but everything else remained intact. He had drawn double looks from many motorists as they passed the coach, with Big Frank waving regally to the bemused car passengers as they overtook.

The ground at Diss was bigger than the one at Woodbridge and had an excellent playing surface. The supporters didn't care about that as they made immediately for the bar. The two bar staff on duty were overwhelmed as a large group, headed by Biggles, flew into the small clubhouse. They didn't have this many people at the Saturday matches. The players meanwhile, were about to get changed.

'What the fuck . . . !' exclaimed a startled John Woods as he opened his kit bag. As the offending article was removed, gales of laughter emanated from the changing room. This was vintage Sweeney/Hardaker. Even Tommy Boyle was laughing loudly. Gary Sweeney and Kevin Hardaker were both close to tears as they developed a fit of the giggles. Kevin Hardaker fought back the giggles long enough to say, 'There you are Woodsy, that's the new goalkeeper Tommy's signed on . . . Dave Pheasant.'

That was too much for Gary Sweeney as he sunk to his knees clutching his stomach. He was laughing so much it actually hurt.

'Dave fucking Pheasant,' chuckled Woodsy.

The entire team were still laughing about the incident when they went out to warm up.

The linesman jumped back in shock when he checked the netting shortly before kick-off. The unfortunate bird was nestled in one corner.

'What is that?' he said to John Woods.

'What's what?' replied Woodsy, innocently.

'*THAT*!' shouted the official.

'Oh, that. Yeah, it's Dave the club's mascot. Wonderful plumage.'

'Well, what's it doing there?'

'Not a lot really. It's bereft of life, passed on, gone to meet its maker, it is an ex-pheasant . . .' Woodsy could see the linesman was not sharing the joke. 'I'll tell you what, I'll put it in that clearing over there for now,' said a deadpan Woodsy.

'You do that,' replied the official.

The match itself was surprisingly one-sided. Stockgrove won 3-0 with all the goals coming in the first half. Macca notched twice and Gary Sweeney scored with a rare header.

The home team had arranged a buffet lunch at a local village pub about fifteen minutes drive from the ground. The Sunday afternoon quiet of the country pub was soon shattered by the coach-load from Stockgrove arriving. The landlord's face lit up and the pound signs registered in his eyes. Ker-ching! He had been expecting the players from Diss Wanderers plus their opponents and a few officials, but the large group of beer-hungry supporters was a bonus. It would be record trade for a Sunday. He even had to call in two more bar staff.

Big Frank was talking to Phil Whitaker and was trying to

make himself heard above the hubbub.

'Look, karaoke.'

'Who's Gary Oakey?' replied Phil.

'No, you knob, karaoke. Look, over there.'

Sunday night was karaoke night at the Anglers' Retreat and it always started at seven o'clock, but today it started at 4.34 p.m. precisely when Frank 'Biggles' Marinelli grabbed the microphone. He was soon joined by Tony Smith, the co-collaborator on the Stockgrove version of 'Wonderwall'. There was no music and the microphone was switched off but they were mere details. The players and supporters were soon in full voice, '. . . *and all the runs that JC makes are winding . . .*'

The team from Diss watched impassively. Pheasants, Biggles and Gallagher Brothers. It sounded like a firm of accountants. And to think people from Norfolk were meant to be the country bumpkins. The landlord was forced to open the karaoke proper, shortly after five o'clock to prevent a riot breaking out. Gary Sweeney had seized the microphone and was launching into his party-piece.

'*Two little boys had two little toys, each had a wooden horse . . .*'

It was real pub singer material, but Gary was singing with gusto and nobody was going to stop him. As the evening wore on, more locals entered the pub and one by one, they were invited to join the Stockgrove singers. The coach was due to leave at six o'clock, but a whip-round produced fifty pound, which kept the driver happy enough, sitting on the coach having a nap.

Neil Roberts brought an end to proceedings just before nine. Everybody was rounded up, including two of the group from the Globe who were fostering close relations with a couple of Norfolk lovelies in the car park.

'Coitus interruptus,' declared Tommy as the two sheepishly

boarded the coach.

'Was that Russell Crowe's character in *Gladiator*?' cracked Kevin Hardaker.

'I believe it was, Kevin,' laughed Tommy.

Kev produced his compilation tape and the singing continued for another thirty minutes before people started to slowly fall asleep as the coach trundled back to Buckinghamshire.

CHAPTER SEVEN

Tuesday was Helen's birthday and Robbo had reserved a table at the Italian restaurant in town. When he got in from work that night, he checked his answerphone as usual. At last, a home match in the next round of the National Cup. Stockgrove would face Erdington Casuals from Birmingham. There would be no transport to organize this time, but he would have to liaise with the good people at Leighton Town Football Club who would host the match. It was a stipulation of the competition that each ground must have seating for at least one hundred people and must have separate changing rooms for each team. The local council pitches where Stockgrove played their home games failed miserably on both counts. Under normal circumstances, Robbo would have been making phone calls immediately. But not tonight. The table was booked for seven o'clock and it was gone six already. Helen was running a bath and was undressing in the bedroom when Robbo walked up the stairs. Helen was completely naked and Robbo paused for a moment in the open doorway.

'I love you Helen Garner.'

'You daft bugger,' laughed his fiancée.

'Helen, I'm serious. I don't say it often enough.'

Helen walked over to her boyfriend and kissed him lightly on the lips.

'I love you too darling, but if I don't turn that tap off you might stop loving me when the bathroom's flooded.'

The meal was superb. They had taken a cab to the restaurant so they could both enjoy a drink. The second bottle of Chianti was half-empty on the table. Helen insisted it was half-full and that was the difference between an optimist and a pessimist. Except, she couldn't say optimist or pessimist properly, the words tumbling out of her mouth sounding like, 'opteemish and peshimish.' She giggled girlishly at her pronunciation.

'God Almighty! And me an English teacher.' She giggled again in between mouthfuls of wine. Putting her hand to the side of her mouth she beckoned Robbo to move closer as she whispered, 'I think I'm a bit tipsy.'

'I think you are, love,' agreed her fiancé, confirming the obvious.

Neil Roberts pulled out a small box from his jacket pocket.

'What's this Mr Roberts, another present for Miss Garner?' Helen was wearing the dress from Next that Robbo had given her that morning. He had surprised Helen because she had been in the shop two weeks before with Neil's mum and remarked how nice it looked. Mrs Roberts pointed it out in the catalogue to her son, suggesting it would make a good birthday present. When Helen opened up her present that morning, Neil Roberts earned double Brownie points.

He handed a small blue box to his girlfriend. Helen opened the box and pulled out the silver eternity ring.

'I love you Helen Garner and I want to spend the rest of

my life with you.' Robbo had never been one for extravagant gestures or romantic sweet-talk, but with Helen everything was right. Helen half-smiled and bit her lip slightly in her attempt to stop herself from crying. 'You soppy sod . . . You lovely, lovely, soppy sod.'

The following morning's journey to school was very quiet. They were both tired and Helen was slightly hungover. Neither of them were accustomed to going out during the week, opting instead for cosy nights in front of the telly. Helen would mark some essays and then settle in to watch the soaps. *EastEnders* was her favourite, but Robbo would usually be in the kitchen cooking dinner. He was a competent cook — years of practice as a single man — but not as good as Helen. He would often venture from the kitchen into the front room watching snippets of television and annoying Helen with his questions.

'I thought he'd died . . . How long's she been back in Albert Square? . . . Is that whats-his-name's girlfriend?'

'Crikey Neil, for someone who's not interested in the programme you do ask a lot of questions.'

'Just taking an interest, love,' Robbo would say.

At school that lunch-time, Sammy confirmed to Robbo that his parents were coming to England a week on Saturday, the day before the match with Erdington Casuals. Sammy had told his father all about the National Cup adventures and Mr Koonphool was looking forward to seeing how the team sponsored by his company were progressing. The visit was a business trip for Joe Koonphool. Nok brewery were looking to promote Lanna Beer in Europe with major supermarkets. Tesco had expressed a firm interest. Lanna Beer was selling well in their stores in Thailand and it seemed logical to extend sales to Europe. Tesco had many outlets in cities and resort areas throughout Thailand where they were known as Tesco Lotus.

Thailand is an increasingly popular destination with many British people: from backpackers in Khao San Road and Ko Phan Ngan; package tourists in Pattaya and Hua Hin; honeymooners in Ko Samui and Phuket. Many small towns in Britain have a Thai restaurant nowadays and most supermarkets stock a range of Thai food. The world was a smaller place with cheaper flights, and Nok brewery were confident there was a market for their beer in the United Kingdom and the rest of Europe.

Joe Koonphool was a good businessman. He had provided Stockgrove with a new kit bearing the logo of his brewery. The resulting exposure in Sunday League football was hardly likely to set the share price of the brewery rising, but Joe was a believer in the adage, 'from little acorns mighty oak trees grow.' He had dozens of Thai sayings stored up, often producing them in business meetings with Western counterparts. He would make his sales pitch in English and interject it with the occasional Thai proverb. Western business people seemed to be suckers for this form of Oriental wisdom and Joe Koonphool knew how to play to the gallery. To Nok brewery, it didn't matter how small their initial market share was. Just get a toehold and you have the chance to grow the business from there. '*Kam kii dii kwaa kam tod,*' Joe would say with a twinkle in his eye; 'It was better to hold a shit than a fart.'

Joe had deliberately scheduled his visit to coincide with school half-term. The delegation from Nok were staying at a Bicester hotel which gave them easy access to the M40 for their series of meetings in London and the Midlands. Joe Koonphool also had a proposition to put to Neil Roberts.

* * *

JC drove Sammy to Heathrow to meet his parents' flight from Thailand. Taxis had already been pre-booked to take the Nok brewery delegation to their hotel in Bicester. Sammy thanked JC for the lift and headed to the arrival lounge. The youngster had an hour to wait, so he bought a coffee and a copy of the *Evening Standard* and made himself as comfortable as anyone can make themselves in an airport. Every now and then, he'd look up from his newspaper and watch people go by. People of all ages, all body shapes and all nationalities. He saw nuns in black and white, African women in colourful tribal costume, people carrying skis, parents carrying children, policemen carrying guns and one middle-aged man carrying a surfboard. Sammy thought to himself that Heathrow must be one of the most cosmopolitan places on the planet. He was accustomed to airports, travelling many times, usually alone, to and from Thailand. The world really was becoming a smaller place. Cut price airlines, package deals and the spread of the Internet meant booking air travel was becoming easier and cheaper. Whereas people once holidayed in France, Spain or Greece they were equally as likely now to spend a fortnight in Mexico, Dubai or Thailand.

Sammy *waied* to the delegation from Nok brewery in traditional Thai fashion, pressing his hands together in front of his chin and lowering his head slightly. The group, including his father, all *waied* back but Mrs Koonphool just hugged her son.

Sammy was an only child and Ladawan Koonphool had wanted him to continue his education in Thailand. Her husband had convinced her that a private school education in England would help their son's all-round development. There were plenty of quality international schools in Thailand but

59

Joe felt he was doing the best for his son's future. It didn't take Sammy too long to adapt to life in England. His English was already perfect when he arrived, but he had picked up many more colloquial words and phrases from the players at Stockgrove.

'Are you eating properly, son? I've brought some food from home,' said Mrs Koonphool as she checked that her son wasn't wasting away. Ladawan Koonphool had packed chillies, noodles, spices, fish sauce and sundry other reminders of home. 'Does he look thin to you Narong? He looks thin to me —'

'Stop fussing,' interjected Joe Koonphool, 'he's fine. Look at him, quite the man.' Joe put his arm around his son's shoulders. They were both small at five foot six or so, but Joe was well-rounded these days, the result of too many business lunches. Sammy's father had been a good athlete as a youngster and a very good *takraw* player. This is a game played with a rattan ball that has to be kept off the floor using any part of the body, except for the hands. It is usually played over a volleyball net between two teams with three players on each side. The game is acrobatic with participants leaping to perform scissor kicks and overhead kicks. Joe's *takraw* days were in the dim and distant past, but his son had inherited his father's ability with a ball at his feet.

Just as they were getting in the taxi, Joe handed his son a copy of the previous week's *Bangkok Post,* a well-respected English language broadsheet. 'Page sixteen and don't laugh at the photo.'

Sammy thumbed his way through the newspaper until he saw his father's picture beaming back at him under the headline, '*Nok Targets Europe*'.

It was a full-page article about the continued success of Nok brewery and Joe Koonphool's own personal rise to business stardom. Sammy smiled as he read the newspaper, intermittently looking up at his parents. Towards the end of the article, Sammy started laughing. He read aloud the part that amused him. 'Nok brewery are involved in a sponsorship deal with amateur football club Stockgrove FC in England. Narong Koonphool's son, Somsak, a student in England, stars for the team and has attracted interest from a number of professional English League clubs.'

Sammy looked at his parents who were smiling broadly. The Thai youngster couldn't wait to show this to Robbo and the rest of the lads. Stockgrove FC mentioned in a Thai national newspaper. Then he thought again. Perhaps they would think he was being flash. After all, the article mentions him by name and suggests he was on the verge of becoming a professional footballer. No, no it doesn't suggest that, it just says he's attracted interest from clubs, nothing more. Conflicting thoughts crossed in Sammy's head. He was still smiling and thinking about whether to show the article to his team-mates when his father said to him, 'You'll have to show that to Neil and Helen.'

Joe Koonphool was a modest man. He was extremely successful but he had worked hard all his life. As a child, he worked on his parents' farm near Kanchanaburi, toiling for hours in the heat working in the rice fields. Then, when he was fourteen, he left school, his parents unable to pay for his education beyond that. Against his parents' wishes, he moved to Bangkok to seek his fortune in the capital. He found work as a bellboy in a hotel, surviving on the meagre wage he was paid and sending the money he gleaned from tips back home to support his parents.

The long-term American resident who had taken to calling Narong Koonphool, 'Joe', helped him with his English and the young Narong Koonphool was a fast learner. He was a natural with the hotel's customers and when he was seventeen, he began a training course to enable him to work on reception. The hotel paid for his English lessons at night school and then, later on, his business management course. At the age of twenty-six, he became manager of the hotel, the youngest hotel manager in Bangkok. The American resident had long since left the hotel. He had been on a one-year contract for an American investment company assisting a fledgling business in Thailand.

The name of the American was Patrick Hannity, and fifteen years after his first visit to the hotel, he returned with his wife. Narong Koonphool instantly recognized the man who had christened him Joe and helped him with his English. 'Welcome back, Mr Hannity,' said Joe, as he *waied* and then walked round from the front desk to shake hands warmly with the non-plussed American. Responding to the look of bemusement on Patrick Hannity's face, he added, 'You don't recognize me do you? It's me, Joe . . . the bellboy.'

'Well, I'll be . . . Joe my boy!' The American was laughing now and embraced Joe Koonphool. When he stayed at the hotel fifteen years before he had treated Joe almost like the son he didn't have. Patrick and Letitia Hannity had never been blessed with children but now here was the former bellboy stood in front of a very proud Pat Hannity. The bellboy who had worked and worked and become manager of the hotel. As the Hannitys had walked into the hotel, Pat had wondered if he would recognize anybody from his first visit. Fifteen years was a long time although the hotel itself was just as he remembered it.

After they had unpacked and freshened up, the Hannitys joined Joe for a drink in the Lounge Bar. Joe insisted that the American couple join him at his home that night for dinner.

Ladawan was a wonderful cook and had been married to Joe for three years. The Thai man wanted to thank the American for the kindness he had shown to him before. Pat Hannity was humbled and Letitia Hannity had to fight back tears as Joe recounted his story of progress from bellboy to manager. In turn, Pat told an enquiring Joe the reason for his return to Thailand. The American was recruiting staff. The fledgling company he had helped fifteen years ago was Nok brewery. The brewery had been successful and was looking to expand further with the aid of their American backers. Pat Hannity was looking for management people at a new brewery in Chiang Mai, which had been experiencing start-up problems. Patrick Hannity knew he had to have a long chat with Joe Koonphool, but now was not the time or place. In the coming days however, he had extensive talks with the Thai man. Pat had to convince Joe he was the man he had been looking for. Joe loved working in the hotel and besides, what did he know about the brewing industry? Pat Hannity allayed Joe's fears and when he presented details of the remuneration package, Joe's jaw actually dropped open for a fleeting moment. Any doubts Joe Koonphool had about his ability to do the job disappeared in that moment. He was a married man now with a one-year-old son, Somsak, and this new job could secure his family's financial future as well as that of his parents and his wife's parents.

The Chiang Mai brewery thrived and Joe was promoted twice in as many years. He worked on short-term contracts in Hong Kong and Singapore establishing Nok's interest in those two countries. After returning to Thailand, he was involved in a management buyout that led to him becoming part owner. Joe Koonphool was very much the public face of the brewery. A charming family man with a classic rags to riches story.

Somsak Koonphool had never wanted for anything in his young life, but his parents had taught him the value of money from an early age. They had also instilled in him humility and respect for his elders.

As Sammy sat in the taxi en-route from Heathrow to Bicester, he again wondered whether he should show the article to the lads at Stockgrove. I'll show it to Mr Roberts as Dad had suggested, thought Sammy, he'll know what to do. Of course, if Sammy showed the article to the other players they would give him a bit of ribbing, take the piss; that's what they did in the changing room. But every member of Stockgrove liked the unassuming Thai youngster. 'Somsak Koonphool is a class act on and off the pitch,' Tommy Boyle would comment at the end of season presentation awards later that year.

CHAPTER EIGHT

As requested, all of the Stockgrove players were at the ground before twelve-thirty. It was the first Sunday of March but spring seemed a long way off. The sky was slate-grey and the temperature was barely above freezing. A strong northerly wind blew crisp packets and McDonald's cartons around the car park at Leighton Town's ground.

Inside the home changing room, Tommy Boyle clicked on another bar of the electric heater.

'What's the matter, Tom? I thought you Sweaties were used to the cold,' joked Gary Sweeney.

'Yeah, 'kin 'ell Tom. You Jocks are all a bunch of tarts ain't yer,' responded Colin McSwiggen in an accent that even Dick Van Dyke would be ashamed of. But the Scotsman's impersonation had the desired effect, bringing howls of laughter from the other players, including Gary Sweeney. The dressing room banter is a part of all football teams and Colin McSwiggen often commented that the team spirit at Stockgrove was the best he had ever encountered.

As usual, Tommy announced the team. Robbo's ankle was fine now and he had played a full ninety minutes the week before with no aftereffects, so Rusky was again on the bench.

Helen drove Mr and Mrs Koonphool to the ground, arriving twenty minutes before kick-off. Much like his son, Joe Koonphool was well used to the weather in Europe and particularly in England, on his frequent visits. But Ladawan Koonphool was shivering despite wearing two jumpers below her thick winter coat. In her country, when the temperature dropped below seventy-five degrees at night, taxi drivers would be huddled around fires waiting for fares as amused expats walked around in T-shirts and shorts.

As kick-off approached, a crowd of two hundred had braved the wintry weather. There was a large contingent from the Globe and a number of players from the other clubs in Stockgrove's league had come along to watch. The crowd stood huddled in the two stands sheltering from the biting wind. A group of eight supporters had travelled from Birmingham with Erdington Casuals. They were all wives or girlfriends of the Erdington players, and shortly after kick-off they were treated to Big Frank leading a rendition of, *'Is that all you take away?'*

The strong wind and bumpy pitch suited Erdington more than Stockgrove. The Birmingham side were a physical team who got the ball forward to their two front men as quickly as they could. The Erdington number nine was providing real problems in the first twenty minutes for the Stockgrove defence.

What Robbo and Butch lacked in pace they made up for with experience and they knew that if they didn't make their mark soon, they would be in for a torrid ninety minutes. Butch was the first to make his mark. A high ball was pumped upfield towards the Erdington striker. Butch won the header cleanly, but as he came down his studs landed firmly on his opponent's boot. Play continued as the Birmingham man lay in a crumpled heap on the floor. Butch had been so subtle nobody knew it had been deliberate, not even the unfortunate player on the receiving end. As play continued, Butch went to his opponent's aid. 'Sorry mate, I must have caught you when I landed,' the Stockgrove player said, sincerely. Butch then shouted for Phil Whitaker to kick the ball out of play so that the Erdington player's injury could be treated. Paul Butcher even helped to carry the injured player from the pitch, winking at Neil Roberts as he did so. The ref commended Butch on his sportsmanship. The Erdington substitute was smaller and slower than the man he had replaced and did not have as good an understanding with his fellow forward. In an instant, life had become easier for the Stockgrove defence. The match was goalless at half-time, as the players hurried to the warmth of the changing room.

The players emerged for the second half to be greeted by flurries of snow sweeping across the ground. Ladawan Koonphool and Helen had decided it would be sensible to remain in the clubhouse for the remainder of the match. Joe Koonphool had met the group from the Globe at half-time and was invited to join them as they sat in the stand for the second half. Joe was a gregarious individual and would strike up conversation readily. In the short space of the half-time interval, the lads from the Globe were treating him like a long lost brother.

'Bit different to Bangkok then, Joe,' said Big Frank as he pointed up to the sky and the snow falling.

'Not really,' replied the Thai man, adding with a completely deadpan delivery, 'sometimes we have freak cold spells in Bangkok. Sometimes the temperature can plummet to eighty degrees and I have to put on a long-sleeve shirt.' There was a slight pause before Big Frank and the others began to laugh. The lads all agreed Joe was 'top man'. Joe was not familiar with this expression but decided he liked it, and later that day when Sammy explained the meaning, Joe liked it even more.

The match continued in stalemate until ten minutes from time when JC crossed a ball into a crowded penalty area. The Erdington keeper caught the ball in midair but as he landed, he collided with his own defender and the ball fell obligingly to the feet of Gary Sweeney who swung instinctively at the ball. Gary didn't connect cleanly and the ball was stopped on the goal line by the Erdington right-back. The ball broke free again and in the mêlée that ensued, Robert 'Stan' Bowles latched on to the loose ball and drove it into the bottom corner of the net. Stan looked the most surprised player on the pitch for a moment. It was his first goal of the season and he wasn't sure how to celebrate. He ran towards the clubhouse and around the back of the goal to the corner flag. He stopped briefly to pull his shirt over his head and then continued his run along the touchline in front of the main stand. A couple of Stockgrove players had chased him for a short distance to congratulate him, but Stan was away. He was used to running long distances, but not with his shirt over his head. It was a ridiculous celebration and one that Stan would be rightly embarrassed about after the match. True to form, he was ridiculed by the other players in the changing room for his over the top celebration. At the end of the season he would win the hotly contested, Gary Sweeney sponsored, 'Stroker of the Year' award; a small engraved trophy presented every year to the player responsible for the most ridiculous act of the season. The previous year it had been won by Leon Wilson. The unfortunate Willo had gone to a QPR home game and ended up having one too many beers in the Bushranger after the match. Coming out of the pub, he tripped and split his forehead, which meant he was unable to play for three weeks.

Stan wasn't concerned about all that now and nor were the rest of the Stockgrove players. The snow, which had been intermittent, was beginning to fall again and was settling on the pitch. It didn't appear to matter as the match moved into injury time. The supporters from the Globe were already on their way to the bar when the Erdington captain struck a shot from twenty-five yards that flew into the Stockgrove net. It was a fantastic strike the equal of anything you would see in the Premiership. Every Erdington player converged on their skipper. As Stockgrove kicked off for the restart, the ref blew the final whistle. The Stockgrove players sunk to their knees. The lads from the Globe couldn't believe it, an Edward Woodward — the equalizer — with the last kick of the match. But not even that was going to stop them from getting a beer. Joe Koonphool had already joined his wife and Helen in the clubhouse and through a misted-up window and a flurry of snow, had just about seen the ball go into the net.

The ref insisted on a quick resumption for the extra-time period fearing the snow may begin to settle rapidly. He gave the teams just two minutes and then they would restart. Stockgrove were deflated. Tommy Boyle tried to rally his team but they sat on their haunches, dejected. There was no time for Tommy to make inspired speeches or talk tactics. A few swigs of water, a couple of segments of orange and Stockgrove were kicking off again in a match they thought they had won. The men from the Midlands were buoyant and within a minute of the resumption, Woodsy had tipped another long-range effort around the post. Stockgrove were in danger of buckling under the pressure being exerted by Erdington. Tommy instructed Gary Sweeney to drop back into midfield. It was an inspired move. Gradually, Stockgrove began to control the game. Erdington still had four players at the back despite Sammy being the only Stockgrove forward.

In the second period of extra-time the snow was beginning to fall again, this time heavier and more persistent. The home side were now dominating the midfield and Sammy Koonphool was making intelligent runs pulling defenders out of position. The ref was looking with concern, as the snow was showing no signs of abating. The touchlines were becoming as difficult to see as the match ball. Where was the orange coloured ball when you needed it, thought the match official. With three minutes left to play, JC won a tackle in the middle of the pitch. He collected the loose ball and jinked past the Erdington captain. As so often in the past, he instinctively looked up for his friend and team-mate. Sammy was already running away from his marker when the ball was played through by JC. The Thai youngster took one touch with his left foot and with his right foot struck an unstoppable shot high into the right hand corner of the goal. There were no elaborate celebrations this time, just firm handshakes and smiles of relief. A cry of 'come on boys' came from Butch as he clenched his fists and urged his team-mates on for the remaining minutes.

Erdington were beaten. The final whistle blew and Joe Koonphool's newfound friends were shaking him by the hand. 'He's some player that son of yours,' commented Emlyn the landlord. 'Too good for this team; should be playing at a higher level,' the Welshman continued.

Joe was proud of his son. He had watched the last period of extra-time stood in front of the clubhouse and behind the goal where Sammy had scored. Emlyn was right, thought Joe, his son should be playing at a higher level. But he wasn't too good for the team. No player is too good for a team. Emlyn hadn't meant it in that context and Joe realized that. Joe had seen it often enough in the business world. You can have a team of talented individuals, but it doesn't always mean you have a talented team, he would say at his sales meetings. It was something Joe firmly believed in and taught his son from an early age; the importance of teamwork and helping others. Ladawan Koonphool emerged from the clubhouse for a brief moment to join her husband and applaud their son, as he made his way off the pitch and towards the changing rooms.

As in previous rounds, a buffet was provided by the home team but the officials from Erdington declined the offer of refreshments. It had stopped snowing for the time being but the visitors decided it would be prudent to set off as soon as the players were showered and changed. The journey back to Birmingham would probably take an hour and a half. With the match going into extra-time, it would be getting dark soon and the roads could become icy. Tommy and Robbo agreed it was a sensible decision and didn't consider it a snub. The food didn't go to waste, there were enough hungry supporters to ensure that. A group of about sixty, including the Stockgrove players, stayed in the clubhouse celebrating the victory.

Emlyn was the first to leave, saying everybody was welcome back at the pub. Two minutes later Emlyn was back in the clubhouse. He had slipped over on black ice in the car park and had come back to warn everybody to be careful. 'It's like a bloody skating rink out there.' Helen and Robbo walked outside to check on the weather. It was starting to snow again and nobody would be joining Emlyn back at the Globe tonight. Helen said she'd drive the Koonphools back to Bicester straight away. 'Drive carefully, love,' Robbo told his fiancée.

'You too, sweetheart.'

As Helen and the Koonphools said their goodbyes, more

people agreed that it would be a good time to go, and steadily the players and supporters left the clubhouse for the short journey home. Within forty minutes, everybody had left. Kevin Hardaker and Stan were the last to leave.

'Come on Stan, time to do the Pickfords. Let's make a move.'

'Do you want me to talk you through it again, Kev? I was twenty yards out, beat three players, juggled with it for a minute and then lashed it into the top corner. Quality. You can't coach that.'

Both men laughed. Each time Stan had described his goal he was two yards further back and had beaten one more player. Stan didn't score very often these days, on or off the pitch, as Kev was quick to remind him. 'No wonder you can't get a bird Stan, never mind the goal, talk me through the celebration. What the fuck was that all about?'

Stan could only laugh and shake his head.

CHAPTER NINE

Neil and Helen enjoyed a lie-in on Monday morning. It was half-term and when Helen went down to make a cup of tea, she opened the kitchen blind to reveal a glistening carpet of snow. The sky was clear blue and the sun shone brightly, reflecting off the snow.

In Bicester, the Koonphool family were treated to the same sight as they ate breakfast. The manicured gardens of the hotel were enveloped by an inch of pristine snow. Birds hopped around looking for food and a squirrel scurried along a tree branch. The match the previous afternoon had been Ladawan Koonphool's first experience of snow and she didn't like it, but today was different. Sat inside in the warmth, looking out on to a beautiful English country garden the whole scene was quite enchanting. 'I'll get the camera when we've finished breakfast,' she said. 'It really is beautiful.'

It was only the second time Sammy had seen snow during his stay in England. Joe Koonphool had experienced snow in New York and Chicago on previous business trips. He agreed with his wife that it did look beautiful, before talking to his son about the proposition he had for Neil Roberts. When he finished talking, Joe asked his son's opinion.

'I think he'll love it, Dad. Everyone will,' said Sammy. 'In July you think?'

'We're not certain yet son, but July looks probable. Head office in Bangkok will be finalising details in the next few weeks once we know what Neil's decision is.'

The hotel concierge approached Joe. 'Excuse me, sir, your car has arrived.'

'Ah, good. Thank you very much,' replied the Thai man. Joe had arranged for a hire car to be delivered. The delegation from Nok brewery would travel by limousines to their business meetings, but there would still be plenty of free time for Joe and his family, and a hire car would give them more freedom to explore the surrounding towns and countryside.

That night, Joe, Ladawan and Sammy joined Helen and Neil for dinner. The snow had already melted as Joe drove his family to the Thai restaurant near Milton Keynes. The owners were an English man and his Thai wife who had met when he was the head chef at a hotel in Phuket and she was a receptionist. Neil, Helen and Sammy were all regular customers and were warmly welcomed by the owners. Sammy introduced his parents and within minutes, the owners and Sammy's parents were all conversing in Thai like old friends.

Neil and Helen noticed how much spicier the food was. Joe had asked for the food to be cooked 'traditional Thai style,' and he smiled as Neil — in between mouthfuls of rice to quench the fire in his mouth — agreed it certainly was spicier than usual. 'You'll have to get used to that Neil when you come to Thailand,' laughed Joe.

'Once we've set a date for the wedding Joe, then we'll sort out the honeymoon, but we've both set our hearts on Thailand.' Neil smiled as he looked across at his fiancée.

'How about this July?' enquired Joe.

Neil nearly choked on a piece of fish. 'Slow down Joe, we're not thinking about getting married until next year!'

Joe grinned. 'Who's talking about marriage? I'm talking about coming to Thailand in July.'

Neil and Helen looked at each other quizzically. Joe continued, 'Nok brewery is arranging a football competition back home. It's an opportunity to get all our branches together and at the same time promote Lanna Beer. There will be a competition for children and one for adults. We're already publicising the tournament in Thailand and the interest nationwide is huge. We'll be arranging a series of regional qualifiers with the top teams progressing to the grand tournament in Chiang Mai in July. As an aside, there will be a separate in-house tournament for Nok employees and associates.'

Neil and Helen sat passively listening to Joe.

'The in-house tournament will involve two teams from our head office in Bangkok plus one each from our breweries in Chiang Mai and Surat Thani. Our sister breweries in Singapore and Hong Kong have also confirmed they will each send a team. We've also invited our investment company in America and today, I'm formally inviting Stockgrove Football Club.' Joe stopped talking and waited for Neil's response. Neil Roberts sat for a moment without speaking, taking in everything Joe Koonphool had said.

'Joe, I'm flattered, the whole team will be. It's a long way to go for a game of football but I'll ask the lads and see whether we can get enough people to go,' said Robbo, still visibly surprised by the offer.

'Of course,' replied the Thai man, 'they have to arrange leave dates with work and discuss it with their partners, I understand that. Nok are arranging all the transport and accommodation for the overseas teams and that will obviously extend to Stockgrove as well. We will pay all the expenses for thirteen players and their partners; flights, hotels et cetera. The only cost your players and guests will incur will be for food, drink and their entertainment. Naturally, Sammy will be staying with us and I'll meet the cost of his plane ticket personally, so that leaves you to choose the other thirteen people you wish to take.'

Robbo was stunned. A free holiday for thirteen people plus their wives and girlfriends; he'd have no difficulty getting volunteers for this. The only difficulty he might have is in deciding who not to take. He was already visualizing his team playing in Thailand. It would be a far cry from their only previous excursion. The players from Stockgrove had played in a summer seven-a-side tournament at Butlins in Skegness five years ago. They were on Stan's second stag weekend. Indeed, with Stan's matrimonial record, another stag weekend was long overdue. They hadn't known about the football until they arrived and decided it would be a good laugh to enter the competition. And so it was that the seven least hungover players emerged from their caravans on Sunday morning in borrowed football kits. They were amazed to reach the semi-finals before the previous night's drinking finally took its toll.

A free trip to Thailand or two weeks spent decorating the house — that was the choice now for Neil and Helen. They hadn't intended to have a holiday this summer, instead saving their money for their future wedding. The paintbrushes and tins of Dulux could wait, but the young couple were still feeling quite emulsional. This was almost too good to be true. When Joe had finished outlining the offer, Neil thanked him.

'Joe I don't know what to say, it's such a generous

invitation. I'll speak with everyone as soon as I can, but I don't think there'll be much of a problem in getting a team together! Thank you Joe.'

'No problem Neil. It's good publicity for us as well. The money we spend will come out of our advertising budget. With Somsak playing for you, an English team already sponsored by us, we'll generate lots of interest in the media back home. The whole thing makes good business sense from Nok's point of view.'

Helen drove back from the restaurant that night with Robbo sat in the passenger seat talking excitedly into his mobile phone, first to Butch and then Kev and Phil. Each time the conversation followed a similar pattern, 'Yes, I know it's late . . . No, I'm not pissed . . . That's right, Thailand . . . Yes, that Thailand where Sammy comes from . . . No, it's not a wind-up . . .' and so the conversation went on.

Robbo would speak to each and every one of his players the following day but tonight he was going home to celebrate, in very intimate fashion, with his girlfriend.

That Sunday it was a full strength Stockgrove side that won their league match 6-2. It was also the first time that season, including the National Cup games, when every player that was signed on for Stockgrove turned up to watch the match. Good news travels fast. It didn't surprise Robbo, but it did amuse him to see so many people trying to ingratiate themselves.

After the match, everybody returned to the Globe where Robbo convened an official club meeting to discuss in detail the invitation to travel to Thailand. Helen acted as secretary taking notes of what was discussed. Robbo again relayed, almost verbatim, the conversation he'd had over dinner with Joe Koonphool. 'So there you have it gentlemen. If anybody feels they can't go for whatever reason, please let me know as soon as you can.' There was a brief pause before Kev Hardaker tentatively raised his hand like a schoolboy who wanted to go to the toilet, but was embarrassed he'd be laughed at by the rest of the class. Without hesitation Robbo said, 'Kev it's all right mate you really don't have to put your hands in your pocket, the flights and accommodation are all paid for.' The group laughed as one. Kevin Hardaker's 'short arms and long pockets syndrome' was part of Stockgrove folklore.

'No Robbo seriously, I can't go. I can't fly,' responded Kev in a low, quiet voice.

'That's all right Kev, we'll get the plane,' interjected Willo, anticipating what was going to be a very weak and predictable gag by Kev Hardaker's high standards. Again the assembled group laughed.

'I'm being serious lads, I'm shit scared of flying.'

Robbo was still half expecting a wisecrack. The group were deadly quiet now, Kev had reeled them in and now he'd deliver a killer gag, it was all about the delivery . . . but not this time. Robbo realized Kev was being quite serious. Butch was the first to speak, still at the back of his mind thinking that once he had spoken, Kev would then crack the joke at his expense. 'Fuck me Kev, you kept that quiet.'

'It's not the sort of thing you brag about Butch,' replied Kev quietly.

Butch was racking his brains. This can't be right; Kev must have flown before. Paul Butcher started going back in his memory. Lads' holidays in Spain, stag-dos in Dublin and Prague; Kev had been invited on all of these and declined. Too busy with work was his usual reason for not going. Nobody really queried it at the time. He was self-employed and had a business to run. Now it all made sense to Butch.

Missing Stan's first stag-do in Dublin because he was working. At the time, Butch had thought that was a bit lame. Lack of money would have been one thing, but Kev was minted. So it was true, somebody he had known for over twenty-five years and not once had he known his friend had a phobia about flying. Butch was still amazed, 'All the years I've known you mate and I didn't have a Scooby.'

'The full Denis Bergkamp mate, that's me,' replied Kev with a rueful smile.

Willo tried to convince Kev it would be no problem. 'Look mate, I know it's a twelve-hour flight, but that's twelve hours of free drinking. You don't even need to leave your seat, just press the button and of those lovely trolley-dollies will be over with a vodka and coke. Turn on the old Hardaker charm and bish, bash, bosh, before you know it you'll be joining the Mile High Club.' The assembled crowd rocked with laughter except for Denise Wilson, who punched her husband in the thigh.

'Cheers mate, but seriously I get really claustrophobic. I had a bad experience flying to France when I was younger and I just can't face it now,' said Kev.

He didn't elaborate any further, but as a teenager his family were on a flight from Heathrow to Paris that was involved in an emergency landing. The landing gear on the plane wasn't working properly and as it came into Charles de Gaulle airport, the passengers were warned to brace themselves. From his window seat, Kevin Hardaker could see row upon row of fire engines and ambulances waiting near the runway. The landing was still firmly entrenched in his memory. The sparks mixing with the foam on the tarmac as the aircraft landed. The screams and panic as the plane skidded along the runway. Bags falling from overhead compartments, his dad's head bloodied from a bottle of duty free which now lay broken in the aisle its contents staining the aircraft floor and the smell of whisky permeating the air.

Kev's father and sister flew back to France the following year despite their trepidation. 'Get back on the horse Kevin, that's what we've got to do,' his dad kept telling him. He knew his dad was right, but the young Kevin had a panic attack trying to get on that second flight and was unable to fly. His mum had to drive him back home with Kevin crying most of the way, a mixture of embarrassment and shame that he wasn't able to conquer his fear.

Kevin had never told anyone about this when it happened and he wasn't about to start now. He just told the other lads that he was scared and suffered from claustrophobia. There was no need for everybody to know the full details. His revelation had put a temporary dampener on the meeting. It was left to Kev himself to lift the mood. 'Well that's the bad news. The good news is there's an extra place for somebody.'

When the trip was first mentioned, Joe said Nok would meet the costs of thirteen players excluding Sammy. Robbo had his regular ten starters plus Rusky — that was eleven — and Tommy would fill the twelfth space. Joe had already confirmed that was no problem, it was entirely up to Robbo which thirteen people he chose. That would have left the eight other squad players vying with each other for the one remaining place on the Thailand trip, but now with Kev's bombshell there were two places up for grabs. The next question for Robbo was how would he decide who would go. Perhaps it should be decided on seniority; who had been with the club the longest. Neil Roberts wasn't a vindictive man, but he thought back to all the phone calls he had made earlier in the season to some of the older lads when he was short of a player for the match on Sunday. The same players he had signed on who would make an excuse for not being able to play at such short notice, but who were all here now sat in the Globe pleading their case for why they should go to Thailand. Then there were the two youngsters from his school, Danny Cartwright and James Lloyd, friends of JC and Sammy who played in the same school team. They were signed on as emergency cover and had never let Robbo down when he had rung them. When required they always turned up on time on Sunday morning and Robbo had included them in his National Cup squads. If he took them to Thailand, he would be accused of favouritism. It was a no win situation for Robbo and even with Kev ruling himself out, it meant six players were going to be very disappointed not to mention the wives and girlfriends who'd be missing out on a free holiday. Neil Roberts decided to seek advice from Tommy Boyle and Paul Butcher.

'Aye, it's a tough one Neil. Sleep on it for a few days,' was the sum total of Tommy's advice. Robbo stepped outside and sat alone for a moment before Butch joined him.

'What do you reckon I should do mate?' asked Robbo.

'Tommy's right, sleep on it for a few days. Whatever happens somebody's gonna have the arsehole about it. Just remember, everybody who really deserves to go will be there. Except for Kev of course. Fuck me, I still can't get over that. Christ, I've known him — well we've both known him — since we were kids, but I never knew that.'

A free holiday to Thailand, but Robbo's initial joy had been tempered by Kevin Hardaker's news plus the realisation that he was going to have to find a way of allocating the spare places. Butch left Robbo alone again to contemplate his decision. As Butch stepped back into the pub, Phil Whitaker passed him on the way out. Phil sat next to Robbo on the wooden bench outside. 'All right mate, glad I've caught you alone.'

'Shit, don't tell me you're scared of flying too!' said Robbo.

'In a manner of speaking . . .' Phil paused to check Robbo's expression.

'This is a wind-up isn't it? What's going on?' asked a slightly confused Neil Roberts.

'No Robbo, seriously, I don't think I'll be able to make it. Michelle's pregnant and the baby is due in October. We're both worried about flying all that way so close to the birth and it would be no fun for 'Chelle in the heat over there. She's said I can go by myself but I can't, it wouldn't be right.'

'Ah mate that's great news, about the baby I mean, not the bit about not coming to Thailand. Congratulations mate.' Robbo shook his friend's hand and slapped him on the back.

'Cheers mate. We didn't want to say anything until we were sure everything was all right and that. Michelle's not quite two months gone and we haven't told anybody yet, not even our parents, so mum's the word, no pun intended.'

'Of course, Phil. I won't say anything to Helen and when you announce the news I'll act all surprised.'

'Nice one Robbo. I'm sorry to let you down mate.'

With his last comment, Phil Whitaker had summed up the camaraderie the team had built up over the years. He had just announced he was to become a father for the first time — the greatest moment of a man's life — and he was apologizing for letting his mate down because he couldn't play in a football match. Neil Roberts was delighted for Phil and Michelle, but it now meant that two of Stockgrove's longest serving players and two of his closest friends, were going to miss this fantastic trip.

Neil had already discussed the possibility of starting a

family with Helen. They had agreed to wait until after they were married. It was bad enough for Helen's old-fashioned parents that their daughter was living in sin. Having a baby out of wedlock would give Robbo's in-laws a coronary.

Once Stockgrove had been invited into the National Cup, there was nothing left for them to achieve. They of course had the possibility of winning the Cup, but Robbo was a realist and knew how difficult that would be. Ten years ago and even five years ago, they could have won it, especially if they had a player like Sammy in their line-up then. But now the players were growing old collectively. In the National Cup, the old hands had excelled themselves and with JC and Sammy in the side, they had real pace and quality to go with experience. They had reached the fourth round with a mixture of experience, ability and above all else, a team spirit built up over many years. If they were to win their fourth round match, they would be into the quarter-finals. The last sixteen teams with the final at Villa Park a real possibility. In the next round, Stockgrove faced a daunting trip to Liverpool to play last season's runners-up, Bootle Corinthians.

CHAPTER TEN

Sammy always enjoyed his parents' visits. This time he was particularly happy that his mum and dad could see him playing alongside his friends at Stockgrove. Sammy loved playing Sunday football for Stockgrove but he knew this would be his first and last season playing for them. Colin McSwiggen, Paul Butcher, Gary Sweeney and of course Neil Roberts, had all urged Sammy to play semi-professionally on Saturdays. He had to test himself at a higher level and give himself the best possible chance of being signed up by a League club. Macca had used his contacts at Chesham United to get them to come and watch Sammy play. After one look at the Thai youngster playing against Erdington, Chesham were keen to sign him immediately. After discussing it with his father, Sammy advised Chesham he was going to wait until the summer before deciding what to do next season. Joe and Ladawan knew their son had his heart set on becoming a professional footballer and they were going to give him their full backing. Sammy had promised his father he would obtain his business degree. The original plan was for Sammy to go to university, but if he got a chance with a League club Sammy would take it and continue his studies at night school if necessary. Joe Koonphool had now spoken to people from Chesham and Reading as well as the players at Stockgrove, and they had all sung the praises of his son. Sammy had always been a good footballer and on this visit, Joe had seen glimpses of just how good he was.

The invitation for Stockgrove to play in Thailand was as much a surprise for Sammy as it was for Robbo. Not once had Joe Koonphool mentioned the tournament to his son until they sat at breakfast that snowy morning two weeks ago. His parents were back in Thailand now but before they left, Sammy was delighted, although not surprised, when Neil Roberts confirmed to Joe Koonphool that Stockgrove would be honoured to compete in the Nok brewery tournament. Robbo had decided the only fair way to fill the remaining places for the trip was to put everybody's name into a hat and pull out two names. That way everybody had an equal chance. Tommy Boyle would make the draw at the Globe on Wednesday night.

The canalside pub was already packed when Tommy Boyle entered with his wife, Sylvia. Once Tommy had made the draw, the Scottish couple would dine with Neil and Helen in the Globe restaurant. It would give Tommy and Neil the chance to discuss the forthcoming match in Liverpool. It would also provide an opportunity for Neil to tell Tommy about a decision he had been putting off for a while.

A cheer went up when Tommy entered the pub and a brief rendition of *'Tommy Boyle's Stockgrove Army,'* momentarily startled diners in the adjoining room. The Globe regulars had gathered to talk about the plans for the weekend trip to Merseyside. A car-load of four were going up on Friday morning and spending the night in Blackpool. They would then drive across to meet the others on Saturday. Robbo had made a booking with the Holiday Inn at Haydock for the players and supporters, obtaining a considerable discount for the block booking. A friend of Emlyn's ran a pub in St Helens and he had arranged for the coach to stop there after the game. Frank had already picked up his Biggles costume from the fancy dress shop, going along with three others as they collected theirs to ensure he would not be the solitary supporter in costume. At least a dozen people had promised to come in fancy dress on the day of the match, but Frank still expected many to bottle out. All mouth and no action; that's what Big Frank thought about his mates in the Globe. He had been asking all week what costumes the others had. The stock response was, 'Not sure yet, going down Friday to see what they've got.'

It was time for the names of the lucky two players to be drawn from the hat. The hat itself had been purchased by Emlyn some years before at Twickenham when he had seen his Welsh compatriots defeated by England. It was basically a jester's hat, fourteen inches tall with a wide brim. Red, white and green in colour and made of fake fur, it had six prongs protruding from the top with small bells attached. Emlyn had been very drunk when he bought the thing and it now sat on a shelf next to the optics, serving as a reminder to the foolish things man can do when alcohol takes hold.

The hat was removed from its shelf in ceremonial fashion by Emlyn and, playing to the crowd, he walked slowly towards Tommy. The landlord of the Globe was holding the hat in front of him on a drinks tray mimicking a Royal Coronation.

'Where do you think you are Taff, bloody Westminster Abbey? Get on with it!' cried an anonymous voice from the restaurant. Even the diners had stopped to watch what was going on. Emlyn stifled a chuckle. Big Frank led a few bars of the 'Funeral March'. Kevin Hardaker began to commentate in hushed, reverential tones.

'And here we have Archbishop Emlyn of Eisteddfod approaching Lord Thomas of Sweaty Sock.' Emlyn heard and was trying hard not to laugh with everybody else, the effort making his hands shake with the hat vibrating on top of the tray. Kev hadn't finished yet. He was sounding more like David Attenborough than Jenny Bond as he continued, 'Lady Sylvia of the Glen resplendent in fuchsia, smiles benignly as the portly custodian of the Coronation Crown approaches. The assembled massed ranks of foreign dignitaries and media having just one thing to say to Archbishop Emlyn . . . *Who ate all the pies, who ate all the pies . . . ?*' Emlyn could no longer contain his laughter and the hat fell off the tray. People were walking over to the Globe's new royal correspondent and complementing him on his commentary skills.

'You loon Hardaker,' said Gary Sweeney. Emlyn picked the hat up and handed it to Tommy. Sylvia Boyle neatly folded the eight pieces of paper with the names on. Having folded them twice, they were placed into the hat and Sylvia gave it a little shake for good measure. Looking away, Tommy placed his arm into the hat and pulled out the first name.

'Steven Bennett.'

Steve was thirty-nine and had stopped playing two years before. He was still reasonably fit but had stopped playing simply because the enjoyment had gone out of the game for him. The season he had retired, he was beginning to resent getting out of bed on cold Sunday mornings. He had told Robbo he'd give it to the end of the season and that's what he did. At school, his nickname had been 'Gordon' but it never really stuck and his mates would just call him Steve. Following the strict rules of football nicknames, he should have been called 'Benno', or at a push, 'Benny', but he was the exception to the rule and unusually, he was referred to as Steve.

Vicky Bennett hugged her husband when his name was called out. Robbo shook hands with Steve. He was still signed on for Stockgrove but Steve told Robbo only to call him as a last resort. Neil Roberts had done that early in the season when Stockgrove only had ten players. On one occasion, Robbo had left messages on his answerphone and on the voicemail of his mobile, but Steve hadn't got back to him. On the second occasion when Robbo rang on the Saturday evening before the match, Steve had told him he 'had a family do to go to in London.' Maybe he did or maybe he didn't. Robbo later found out it was the latter. It was after this that Robbo signed on Danny and Lloydy from his school as cover. Secretly, Robbo hoped that the two young lads would be the names pulled out of the hat. They were good kids and a trip to the Far East would be educational for them. Not that Robbo really resented Steve and Vicky going. They were a pleasant enough couple and over the years Steve had done his bit for the club. It wasn't that Robbo disliked Steve, but he couldn't help but think about Kevin Hardaker already missing the trip and the imminent withdrawal of Phil Whitaker. If Phil had withdrawn earlier in the bedroom he might still have been going to Thailand thought Robbo. Kev and Phil were two far more deserving cases than Steve Bennett. That wasn't Steve's fault and the players at Stockgrove congratulated him and his wife on their good fortune.

Tommy pulled out a second piece of paper. The room was quiet now, nobody ordering drinks or talking. As Tommy opened the piece of paper, Kev Hardaker resisted the urge to say, '. . . will play number twenty-seven, Bristol City.'

Robbo was pleased to hear the name 'Daniel Cartwright.' Young Danny wasn't at the pub to hear his name. None of the teenagers were, with the exception of Rusky, but Robbo would see Danny at school the following day. He'd also see James Lloyd at school and tell him he'd miss out on the trip that his friends were going on. The other five players whose names were in the hat were present at the Globe and tried to make light of their disappointment. Two of them were booked on the trip to Liverpool and with talk of Thailand, it would be a long coach journey for the two men.

As the assembled crowd began to disperse Robbo shouted out, 'Hold on. We're going to pull out one more name as a sort of reserve in case anybody else drops out.' The crowd gathered round again, but this time it was Robbo who pulled out the third name.

'James Lloyd,' announced Robbo.

There are times in life where a man has to distort the truth for the greater good; 'the cheque's in the post', 'of course I love you', 'no, your bum doesn't look big in that'. Robbo felt no pangs of guilt as he announced Lloydy's name. Lloydy, Danny and Rusky never moaned about being on the bench, were always punctual for matches and would tell Robbo well in advance if they were unavailable. A club secretary's and a manager's dream; the Dannys, Lloydys and Ruskys of this world. Now they would all be going to Thailand. James Lloyd wouldn't know it yet, thinking he was down as first reserve, but when Phil Whitaker broke the news of Michelle's pregnancy then Lloydy could start stocking up on the suntan lotion.

The jester's hat was returned to its usual resting place and the pub reverted to some normality. Drinks were ordered and players and supporters alike chatted about Thailand and more importantly for now, the trip to Merseyside.

Neil, Helen, Tommy and Sylvia walked through the archway that separated the dining area from the rest of the pub. The women sat at the table whilst the men stood at the small bar and ordered drinks. 'Tom, I've talked it through with Helen and I'm not going to change my mind.'

Tommy patted Robbo on the back, 'That's fair enough laddie, I understand. Sylvia will be pleased; she reckons I've been neglecting the garden.'

Neil Roberts had spoken to Tommy Boyle at the end of the previous season, announcing his intention to stop playing and finish his role as club secretary. Tommy had talked him out of it using an old football cliché, 'You're a long time retired. Give it some more thought, one more season, eh?'

Tommy and Sylvia had always been good neighbours and when Helen moved in with Robbo, she had an instant rapport with Sylvia. The two men would go off to play golf and gradually Tommy's involvement with Stockgrove grew from spectator to manager. All the lads respected Tommy and none more so than the club secretary. Robbo was pleased that Tommy talked him out of a premature retirement but now things had changed. Helen was the most important thing in his life now. Not work or football, but Helen Garner. They were going to get married and have children. Robbo had made the commitment to Helen that he had been unable to make to any other woman. His fiancée didn't want him to stop his involvement with Stockgrove; she enjoyed the social aspect of the football club. Robbo wasn't using Helen as an excuse for retiring. It was just that the timing was right. The team were getting older and some of the enjoyment of playing was going out of it. Players he used to play against were retiring and were being replaced by youngsters who were quick and energetic. Even the referees were starting to look younger. Then there was the paperwork from the FA, the forms to fill out and the phone calls to make. 'The truth is Tom, it's just too much of a pain in the arse now; I've lost my enthusiasm.'

Tommy Boyle smiled at Robbo's succinct appraisal. 'That's understandable Neil. You said this would be your last season.'

Robbo's decision to retire was not made lightly. With Robbo retiring, Butch and Phil would almost certainly follow suit. Both men had already talked about packing up playing. Ironically, Robbo had talked them out of it saying he himself would be giving it one more season and it would be good to have at least one crack at the National Cup. With three of the stalwarts of the club gone, players like Woodsy and Kev would probably consider hanging up their boots. Of course new players could be signed on, but the heart of the club would be gone. Who would take over Robbo's duties as club secretary? Tommy had already indicated he wouldn't do it. He had seen the time and effort Robbo put in. When Robbo left, Tommy would be calling it a day as well. Robbo knew that when he announced his decision it would, effectively, be the end of the club. It would be a sad moment but all good things come to an end. They'd still keep in touch with one another, the senior players at least, and there'd still be nights at the Globe. There just wouldn't be so many.

For the time being, Neil and Tommy would not say anything to the rest of the team. Although he had nearly retired the previous year, the other players just took it for granted that Robbo would keep on running the club. All they had to do was turn up each Sunday where and when Robbo told them, and pay their subs. They didn't even have to worry about washing the kits. Neil Roberts had done that for the last four seasons. At one time the players were taking it in turns, but when the weather turned bad and the kits were thick with mud, the excuses started coming in. 'The washing machine's on the blink Robbo, I'll do it next week mate, all right?' Or,

'Me and the missus ain't getting on too well at the minute. If I bring that lot home she'll go Garrity and I don't know how to use the bloody machine.' And when the players washed their own kits it was fine until they rang on Friday to say they couldn't play on Sunday and Robbo had to drive round and collect the kit. Robbo had bitten his tongue and said nothing. Eventually, he said he'd do the washing himself each week, it just made things easier. All he asked was that at the end of the match the kit be turned round the right way and placed in one pile on the floor. Only half the team seemed capable of understanding this simple request.

Helen said he was soft and she was right. And then there were the subscriptions. Every week the same performance to get money from everybody to pay the pitch and referee. In seasons gone by Robbo would have laughed at each new excuse from the players explaining the reason for having no money on them this week. They would all pay eventually, but that wasn't the point. It was a pain in the arse and the players took too many things for granted. But then Robbo would go to the Globe after the match and the banter would start up again and he had to laugh. The team spirit really was superb, but increasingly this season, washing the kits and collecting the subs had irked Neil Roberts. He was resenting doing it each week and he would go home to Helen and whinge about it.

'Oh for God's sake Neil, don't bloody do it then! Get the lazy sods to wash their own kits and if they don't pay their money, they don't play. Simple,' was Helen's response. 'And another thing,' she'd continue, 'why do you have to ring everybody each week? They should be ringing *you* to find out the arrangements. You spend enough money on that bloody club as it is.' His girlfriend was right; perhaps she should be club secretary. When it came to Stockgrove, Helen could see things in clear lines. Black and white, no ambiguity. It wasn't the same for Robbo, the lines were more blurred. He had helped form the club all those years ago and it was still his baby. That's why he pampered it and cleaned up after it; washed the dirty nappies and winded the little darling in a manner of speaking. Well now baby Stockgrove had grown up and was a young adult. It was time for Daddy Robbo to wave goodbye to his offspring.

CHAPTER ELEVEN

The trip to Liverpool had brought about a change to Stockgrove's National Cup away game routine. Firstly, it was eleven o'clock on Saturday when they all met up. Secondly, the meeting place was the Globe.

Emlyn arranged a cup of tea and a bacon roll for everybody and many of the lads had a pint. It was a pleasant spring morning and most of the group sat outside. The people aboard the narrow boats that cruised along the canal were pondering why so many people would be sat outside a pub at that time of the morning. Then they would see the eight-foot Cross of Saint George flag which now had the words 'STOCKGROVE F.C.' emblazoned upon it, suspended from the humpback bridge.

Woodsy started an unlikely conversation with Stan as they watched the barges drift idly by.

'Stan, do you reckon it's possible to go from here all the way to Liverpool by canal?'

'I would think so mate. Grand Union up to Brum and the Black Country. Then there must be some network or other that'll get you on to the Manchester Ship Canal and across. Wonder how long it would take.'

'And how many locks you would have to navigate,' countered Woodsy.

Gary Sweeney heard the conversation.

'What a pair of strokers. Have you been on the gear?'

Woodsy was not put off his train of thought. 'No, think about it Gary. Just think about all those pubs you'd pass on the way up. Mind-blowing really.'

Gary was not convinced. 'You loon, Woodsy. I'm off to talk to the geese, they make more sense. And you two had better stock up on the Mars bars judging by that conversation. We don't want you getting the munchies halfway up the motorway.'

Just before midday, the group of fifty-five walked over the narrow bridge and up the small lane to the lay-by where the coach was waiting. It was the same coach and the same driver from the previous trips. The driver had actually requested the job. He had enjoyed the previous days out almost as much as the players and supporters and the lads had been generous with their whip-rounds to thank the man driving the coach. This weekend would be a good earner for him, and the players saw it as a good omen to have the same driver. There would only be one spare seat on the coach this time and that was soon occupied by five crates of beer.

Leon Wilson was the first to notice the new adornment at the front of the coach. 'That's quality!' he exclaimed, 'I feel like a pro now.'

People behind Willo waiting to board looked at where he was pointing. There, wedged on the dashboard against the windscreen for passing motorists to see, a large piece of white card with the words 'STOCKGROVE F.C.' written in bold black print.

The two local newspapers had carried articles on the

team's progress in the National Cup, printing a team photo and an interview with Neil Roberts. Three Counties Radio and Horizon Radio had picked up on the articles and also interviewed Robbo.

Willo continued, 'I see we're getting the VIP treatment now that you're a famous celebrity Robbo.'

Initially, it was a quiet journey on the way up. The women were chatting amongst themselves and the players and supporters were cracking jokes and enjoying a few drinks. For the first time in the competition, all the wives and girlfriends were able to make the trip: Kimberley Woods, Denise Wilson, Wendy McSwiggen, Sylvia Boyle, Helen, Michelle and Melissa.

Kev had his compilation tape, but the video was working and the driver put on an *Only Fools and Horses* tape. It was the perfect choice of viewing; the Christmas special with Del Boy and Rodney dressed up as Batman and Robin. The comedy was timeless. A lot of the lads had seen some of the episodes that many times they knew all the dialogue. It was a testimony to the quality of the writing and acting that the nation as a whole had taken the series to their hearts. When the tape came on, the people on the back seats were singing along to the theme tune. The co-producers of the Stockgrove version of 'Wonderwall', Frank Marinelli and Tony Smith, had collaborated to produce a song-sheet especially for the weekend. Tony had typed it all out on his computer and produced thirty copies. Clearly, some people have too much time on their hands. Now was the perfect time to pass the song-sheets around the coach. The barman and the Globe regular had surpassed themselves. Gilbert and Sullivan, Rodgers and Hammerstein, McCartney and Lennon and now Marinelli and Smith. The first song on the sheet was 'Wonderwall', the song that had become the Stockgrove standard. In honour of the trip to Liverpool, 'Ferry Cross the Mersey' had become *'Throw Tommy in the Mersey'*. The eponymous Sixties song, 'Hey, Hey We're the Monkees', had become:

'Hey, hey we're the Stockgrove
So don't come drinking with us
'Cos we'll drink you under the table
Without any fuss.'

It was inspired stuff and the coach became more animated as people laughed and sang. 'D.I.S.C.O.' by Ottowan had become:

'G-L-O-B-E
We are G-L-O-B-E
We are G, we are glorious
We are L, we are lunatics
We are O, we're outrageous
We are B, we're ballistic
We are E, everyeeewhere!
G-L-O-B-E
G-L-O-B-E'

There was even a tribute to Gary Sweeney's lifestyle to the theme tune from the video they had just been watching:

'He's got defenders in his pocket
He's got a suitcase from Milan
And where it all comes from is a mystery
But Spurs are on their way to Division Three
Upset him once and he'll go berserk
Gary is a loon and he doesn't work
La la la la, la la la la laaa, la la la la . . .'

Gary Sweeney was a real life Del Boy. No income tax, no VAT, no money back, no guarantee. He made his living from the black economy. He was a rogue but he was also one of the best and most loyal mates you could wish to have. A gentleman in his business dealings, he'd buy or sell pretty much anything, but never drugs. That was definitely off limits. The low-life who dealt drugs were scum in Gary's eyes. Messing up kids in the playground with Es and charlie was beneath contempt.

The coach arrived in Haydock just after half-past three having encountered the usual traffic delays on the M6 near Birmingham. They passed the racecourse near the hotel and some of the supporters were asking Phil and Michelle if they had any tips.

'Don't eat yellow snow,' said Phil.

'And don't tie-up your shoelaces in a revolving door,' added Michelle.

It was a well-rehearsed response to the question they were always asked when people found out they worked in a bookmaker's office.

At the hotel, people checked-in and went to their rooms. Some watched television and rested, whilst others showered and changed, eager to make the most out of the weekend. Big Frank, Tony, Butch, Stan and Rusky were the first to return downstairs having merely deposited their bags in their rooms. They were on to their second pint in the hotel lounge before some of the other lads from the Globe joined them. When Tommy and Sylvia arrived, Stan immediately got up and bought the couple a drink.

'Don't worry boss,' said Stan, 'we won't go silly. We've only had a couple on the coach and at these hotel prices we won't be having many here.'

Tommy chuckled. That morning at the Globe, he had asked the players to go easy on the beer. Tommy hadn't got all heavy over the matter, the players were all adults and it was up to them if they wanted to drink, so long as they were fit to play the following Sunday afternoon. The players knew how important a game this was and they didn't want to let anybody down — themselves or Tommy. They also didn't want to let Robbo down. Nobody had actually said as much, but they all knew without Robbo they wouldn't be in the competition. He had done all the organizing: the FA, the transport, the hotel. The whole weekend had a sense of occasion about it; staying at a hotel the night before the game, the shirts and ties the players would wear on the way to the game, the travelling support. The players didn't want their cup run to end. Win the match tomorrow and it would be the quarter-finals. Two matches away from the final at Villa Park, the ground they had passed on the way up that afternoon.

When Tommy finished his drink, he suggested that those who wanted to, should meet in the restaurant at half-past six. There was a carvery and an à la carte menu, and the regulars from the Globe had just discovered it was happy hour in the bar between five and six. Perfect. They could enjoy a drink or two, have dinner and board the coach at seven-thirty. The coach was booked to go into Wigan town centre for those that wished to go and would return to the hotel leaving Wigan at midnight. Thanks to the ever reliable planning and organizational skills of Neil Roberts, everything had been pre-arranged and taken care of.

After dinner, the players and the wives and girlfriends all retired to the hotel lounge bar. They were joined by a dozen of the supporters who were not interested in a tour of the fleshpots of Wigan. That left an all male group of twenty-one to board the coach for Wigan. The driver agreed to drop off and pick-up at one meeting place. Anybody not there at midnight, then tough they'd have to find their own way back to the hotel. The coach drove into Wigan town centre and the driver designated the Spinners' Arms as the meeting point. The pub was central and had a sign declaring 'coaches welcome.' As the group disembarked, the driver reminded them, 'Twelve o'clock lads and then I'm gone. I'll stay here now and have a kip. See you later.'

The landlord looked up when the group walked in. He quickly assessed they'd be no trouble. The pub was used to rugby and football supporters and they were never any problem. The occasional stag or hen-do would come in, but always early before going on to a club or a pub-crawl and similarly they were no hassle. There was no need for bouncers here, or rather door staff or security, as they like to be called to heighten their importance. In the landlord's opinion, it was the bouncers who invariably caused the trouble.

'Good evening gentlemen, what can I get you?' The landlord welcomed the group warmly. As the orders came in, two barmaids came across to help serve.

'What's the occasion lads, stag-do?' The landlord could see the group were a mixture of ages and were not an obvious collection of drinking companions, so he was confident his guess was correct. He was very surprised and interested when Emlyn told him about Stockgrove and the National Cup.

Some of the group sat down en masse at a couple of tables near the window. It was quite a big pub, bigger than the Globe, but with no separate dining area. They did food: sandwiches, burger and chips, bangers and mash, shepherds pie. Standard pub food you'd call it; 'Traditional Pub Fayre' the sign outside proclaimed. There were half a dozen people in the pub when they arrived; two young couples sat in an alcove and two men in their thirties stood at the bar. The young couples sat down acknowledged the group with a friendly 'good evening.' The two local men stood at the bar were speaking to Big Frank and Tony. They had heard Emlyn's conversation with the landlord and were similarly interested.

'So you've come all the way from Milton Keynes to watch a football match in Liverpool tomorrow?' The two men weren't usually interested in football. They took an interest in England matches and liked to see Wigan Athletic do well, but Wigan was traditionally a rugby league town and that was where their main interest was. Some of the group were chatting to the bar staff and the lads had soon settled into the friendly environment. Small groups of men and women started to come into the pub ready for a night on the town. The women were in high heels, shiny dresses and make-up. The men wore the standard uniform of any young buck out on the town: dark trousers, shirts untucked and too much hair gel. The group from Milton Keynes commented to each other on how feminine the women looked. Many of the women were drinking pints, but they still appeared more glamorous than the women down south. They just seemed to have made more of an effort with their appearance. There was some element of truth in the observation, but the main reason the girls looked different was that they were different. They weren't the same faces the Globe lads were used to seeing each week. One thing everybody agreed on was that everybody was friendlier 'up north.' It may have been a bit of a cliché but it was definitely true here. If a group of twenty-one northerners had walked into the Globe, they would have been eyed with some caution. The local men would have taken umbrage and the local women wouldn't have been too friendly either. Not in Wigan. Perhaps it was because the Globe group were fortified by alcohol and had an 'I'm on holiday' good feeling about the weekend. It was great to have conversations with the Wigan women who didn't automatically think you were trying to chat them up and get into their knickers, even though some of the lads were. Old

101

habits die hard. This was a great pub and they stayed there longer than they anticipated.

When Frank Marinelli looked at his watch, it was ten-thirty. He spoke to the rest of the group to see what they wanted to do. Only four of the men suggested moving on to another pub and then a club. The rest were quite happy to stay where they were. They had been drinking virtually all day, and tomorrow would be the same. If they stayed in the Spinners' Arms until closing time, they only had to stagger to the car park and the coach would be ready and waiting to take them back to their hotel. They had all enjoyed their night in the Spinners' with the friendly locals, but Big Frank and the other four agreed it was time to say their goodbyes and hit the bright lights of Wigan.

Tony Smith had been talking to a group of girls in the pub who had suggested the lads should try Wetherspoon's before moving on to Stringers nightclub. The girls themselves would be in there later. Tony had bought them all a drink to say thank you. Smithy saw himself as a smooth operator. He really fancied one of the girls, but didn't want to blow his chances too early. The night was young and he'd see her in Stringers later. He had done the groundwork as he called it, laid the foundations. Give it three hours and he'd be laying more than foundations, he thought to himself. Smithy was a painter and decorator and good friends with Butch and Kev. He was a regular at the Globe and had been going out with his girlfriend for over a year. Smithy was what the other lads called a 'player', but not in the football sense. He was seeing two other women behind his girlfriend's back. Smithy claimed he couldn't help it.

'It's just the way I am. Must be in my genes,' he would say.

'That's the trouble Smithy, you can't keep it in your jeans!' Kev would tell him.

Frank and all of the regulars at the Globe knew about Smithy's infidelities, but it was none of their business. As far as they were concerned, Smithy was all right. He liked a drink and a laugh and he had an eye for the ladies. In many ways, he was similar to his friend Kev Hardaker. The main difference — apart from Kev's superior bank balance — was that Kev had more charm about him. Kev may have been a bit of a tart who slept around, but never when he had a girlfriend. When he was in a relationship, Kev was one hundred per cent faithful. One hundred and ten per cent. Tony Smith was different in that respect and some of the players' wives thought Smithy was smarmy, not like Kev who could get away with murder. Kev would always be making cheeky comments to Helen, Kimberley and Denise. That's all it ever was with Kev, a bit of innocent fun. He'd flirt with grannies in the supermarket and the middle-aged women at the petrol station, bringing smiles to their faces.

'When are you going to find a nice girl and settle down?' Helen would say to Kev.

'Wouldn't be fair on all the other women, Hels,' would be Kev's reply, although secretly that was all he wanted. Find a nice girl, get married and have children. It was only in the last year or so that Kev had really begun to think along these lines. He still enjoyed going to clubs, but it wasn't the same anymore. He had seen the shit that Butch had to go through when he split up from his wife. It had nearly tipped Butch over the edge, sending him to drink wildly and neglect work. Better to stay single Kev had thought at the time, nobody needs that sort of grief. In the last year though, he had really noticed how happy Robbo and Helen were together and Phil with Michelle. That's all Kev wanted for himself now, a bit of domestic bliss and two point four children.

Tony Smith wasn't concerned about domestic bliss. All he

was interested in was a few more beers and trying his luck in Stringers. He waited with Frank outside the front of the Spinners' Arms whilst the other three men who were joining them went to the toilet. Following the gentlemen's law at the urinals, the three men all stood a comfortable distance apart as they took care of business. A bit of idle chatter amongst themselves, but no eye contact; eyes had to be firmly fixed on the wall in front. These were the unwritten rules. They had all been drinking pints and they found it easy to relieve themselves. There was no 'stage-fright,' that awkward moment when you want to piss, but when you're in there stood at the urinal, nothing happens. The trio finished simultaneously. If there was synchronized pissing at the Olympic Games then these men would bring home gold for Great Britain. A couple of shakes, tuck it back in and zip up. They all washed their hands, being amongst the fifty per cent of well brought-up men who actually bothered no matter how drunk they were. They had all seen Tony Smith in the Globe on Sunday lunchtimes, having a piss, not washing his hands and then helping himself to the peanuts on the bar counter. Dirty git. Needless to say, they didn't eat any peanuts at the Globe.

Matt Baker, Shaun 'Jonjo' O'Neill and Pete Woods joined Frank and Tony outside. Pete was the younger brother of the Stockgrove goalkeeper. Frank had already stopped one taxi only to be informed by the cab driver he could only take four passengers. He advised the group they may be better off to take a bus from just up the road. The five men stood alone at the bus stop for just a few minutes before a bus approached. Frank flagged it down and asked if he was going anywhere near Wetherspoon's or Stringers. The driver said he was, albeit via the bus depot. The lads jumped on, paid their money and collected their ticket. The five men began talking loudly. They weren't talking loudly deliberately, but the diesel engine of the bus was noisy. In addition, they had consumed a lot of drink and like many men, they had a tendency to talk louder the more they drank. As they talked, the two elderly ladies who were sat a few rows behind them, heard their southern accents and began a conversation.

'Off for a night on the town lads?'

'That's right love. Just the five of us now, the others have gone to get their beauty sleep,' replied Jonjo.

'The others? How many of you are there?' enquired the old lady, clutching her tartan shopping trolley for balance as the bus turned right.

'Well all together there's about sixty.'

'Oh my goodness! You're not from Wigan though are you?'

'No love, we've all come up from Milton Keynes,' said Jonjo.

The other lads had all turned round by now and were taking it in turns to add bits of information about the weekend: the football match in Liverpool, the hotel in Haydock, the others still in the Spinners' Arms. The women were intrigued.

'Playing tomorrow you say. Will it be on the telly?' the other lady asked, innocently.

Jonjo laughed. 'No unfortunately not,' but then he noticed a slight smile on the woman's face. Was the old girl having a bit of fun at Jonjo's expense? Jonjo wasn't sure, but he did know that these two elderly women were a couple of characters.

'I'll tell you what,' he continued, 'if you like, I'll get you a couple of match tickets and get the coach to pick you up on the way.'

Quick as a flash the feisty pensioner replied, 'I'd love to but my boyfriend might be upset.'

'And I'm washing my hair tomorrow,' added the other woman.

The men laughed heartily and introduced themselves properly to their new friends, Gladys and Betty. The conversation continued with the men talking about previous matches in the National Cup. They treated Gladys and Betty to a rendition of *'Hey, hey we're the Stockgrove,'* with the women joining in the second time.

The bus pulled into the depot and the old women gathered their shopping trolleys, wished the men good luck for the match and thanked them for the entertainment on the bus. As the ladies boarded another bus, they were still waving. Jonjo blew them a kiss and the old girls reciprocated. Within a few minutes the bus with the five men was on its way again.

'Absolute quality,' said Matt.

'Wigan, what a top place,' added Smithy.

'I'll tell you what lads, a few more minutes and I reckon I might have been in there,' said Jonjo.

'Don't worry mate,' said Pete, 'they'll probably be in Stringers later dancing round their shopping trolleys.'

The bus pulled to a halt. The driver turned around and called back, 'That's Wetherspoon's just over there lads, and Stringers is about fifty yards further on round the corner,' pointing the direction as he spoke.

The men each thanked the driver and disembarked the now empty bus. They headed straight into Wetherspoon's. The pub was busy without being packed and they were served almost immediately. The group were still talking about the pensioners on the bus. It had been a good day and it seemed like just a few hours since they were sat outside at the Globe eating their bacon rolls and supping their pints. Twelve hours had passed since then and they had been drinking steadily throughout. They had all been eating at regular intervals and none of them were drunk, but they were merry. They were in high spirits and were enjoying their stay in what they had already dubbed, 'Wigan — Party Capital of Europe.' Who needs Amsterdam, Prague, Dublin or Ibiza? 'Keep it real, keep it Wigan,' was their new motto.

Matt and Frank began talking to a local man and his girlfriend, asking them what Stringers was like. The young couple said it was OK. A mixed crowd went in there: teenagers, single mums, lads and lasses on the pull. The young girl, who looked no older than nineteen, said the music was good.

'A bit of garage, R and B, Northern Soul, that type of thing. They usually play some cheesy tunes too; some old stuff for people like you,' she joked.

'Bloody cheek!' replied the thirty-five-year-old Frank, 'I'm only twenty-two, I've just had a hard life.'

The young couple laughed because Frank had taken the comment in good spirit. He actually looked older than he was. He was overweight, balding prematurely and his fashion sense was more Millets than Max Mara. None of this bothered Big Frank. He was an effervescent character that people warmed to easily. 'A real people person,' the brewery had described him as at Christmas when he was presented with the Employee of the Year Award. Frank was single, but was not without female admirers. 'For a bald fat bloke, I do better than I should,' Frank would say.

Matt Baker was the quietest of the group, but on nights out like this he was always good company. He didn't say too much, but when he did speak it was usually worth listening to. He was softly spoken and had a dry wit, which the lads liked. Matt called Jonjo, Pete and Tony across.

'Apparently, Stringers is all right. Shall we finish these and do the off?'

107

'Yeah, don't want to keep the ladies waiting too long, it just wouldn't be fair,' commented Tony Smith.

'Leave it out Smithy,' said Jonjo, 'It's grab-a-granny night in Stringers and you missed your best opportunity on the bus.'

'You're only jealous Jonjo 'cos Gladys fancied me more than you. Imagine that blue rinse bobbing up and down on your chap as she's giving you a nosh!'

Jonjo shook his head at the imagery. Tony Smith had a unique ability to bring any conversation round to sex.

'That's right, Smithy, you old pervert, talk to her nicely she might even put her teeth in for you,' added Matt.

'Better still if she doesn't,' replied Smithy.

The five men decided to split into two groups in case the bouncers weren't letting groups of men in. As it turned out, there caution was misplaced. There was no queue at the door and when Matt, Jonjo and Pete went in, they were immediately beginning to wonder if it was a good idea.

The entrance was gloomy and the walls were painted purple. The doors were canary-yellow with black frames. It looked like Laurence Llewelyn-Bowen had been given free rein. It was horrendous. If Carol Smilie saw this, she wouldn't be smiley anymore. The nightmare continued inside with Formica tables, smoked glass and psychedelic lighting. Silver glitter balls dangled from the ceiling. Jonjo looked round surveying the scene, half-expecting Austin Powers to pop out from behind a pillar at any moment. The club was virtually empty and the DJ was playing Bobby Brown, 'My Prerogative.' Pete looked at the other two and was the first to say what they all were thinking.

'Well we're here now. Let's get a drink and wait for the other two.'

Frank and Smithy arrived whilst Pete was ordering the

drinks. They had no trouble locating each other in the near-empty club. Smithy was shaking his head as he approached the others.

'Stringers? More like fucking mingers.'

Pete came back with five bottles of Carlsberg. 'Quick, move away from the bar before she realizes she's undercharged me. That was only a fiver.'

The other four men burst into laughter. Jonjo pointed to a fifteen-foot banner suspended over the bar announcing: 'CARLSBERG — £1 A BOTTLE.'

Pete had to laugh at his faux pas. How could he have failed to see the banner? He looked around again in disbelief, shaking his head as he did so.

'At least the Seventies theme's extending to the drinks prices,' commented Frank cheerily.

The group's initial misgivings began to recede as the club slowly began to fill up. The music was best described as eclectic, but the dance floor was soon crowded, mainly with women of varying ages, so the DJ obviously knew his stuff. Small knots of men were dotted around the dance area supping pints and clutching bottles, unwilling to relinquish their drink for the sake of five minutes of feeble chat-up attempts.

'I'm off for a walk round,' said Smithy abruptly.

'Fair enough. See you later,' replied Frank.

Nobody else was interested in wandering around the club and even if they had been, the manner of Smithy's announcement indicated he intended it to be a solo expedition.

When Smithy was out of earshot, Frank began singing the Bobby Brown song that was playing when the lads first entered the club.

'*Smithy's going walking, to ladies he'll be talking . . . that's his*

109

prerogative.'

Big Frank was obviously in the wrong job. His ability to take a song and change the lyrics to amusing effect was rapidly becoming an art form.

The four friends continued to talk and joke in Smithy's absence. Matt felt a hand squeeze his bottom and a voice whisper in his ear.

'Hello sexy, great arse.'

Matt turned round and was startled to see the woman from the Spinners' Arms, the one that Smithy had been talking to.

'Where's your friend?' enquired the girl.

'Who? Smithy? He's just gone for a walk round. Probably be back in a minute,' replied Matt.

'He fancies himself a bit your mate doesn't he?' said the girl.

Typical, thought Matt, just when he thought he had half a chance, all she wanted to do was talk about bloody Smithy.

'No, he's all right, he's a nice bloke, just the way he comes across sometimes,' replied Matt, resisting the temptation to put the knife in by saying, 'Oh yeah he fancies himself all right, more than he fancies his girlfriend or the other two girls he's been shagging behind his girlfriend's back.' That would be bad form to say that about your mate.

Frank, Jonjo and Pete were talking to the other four women as Matt stood with the other girl.

'My name's Caroline, by the way.'

Matt placed his bottle on the shelf near his elbow and wiped his hand dry on the back of his trousers. He shook the girl's hand lightly.

'I'm Matt, very nice to meet you Caroline.'

The girl laughed, genuinely pleased with Matt's manners. 'Well, aren't you going to introduce me to your friends?'

'Of course,' said Matt.

As the men and women were being introduced to each other, Smithy returned. Without acknowledging the other women, he walked straight over to Caroline, gave her a kiss on the cheek and said, 'Nice to meet you again.'

'And you must be Smithy,' said Caroline.

'That's right, Tony Smith.'

'OK, Tony Smith, well I'm Caroline and us girls want to buy you all a drink, seeing as you bought us one in the Spinners'.'

'No, that's all right Caroline I'll get —'

'We insist,' interrupted Caroline.

'Fair enough, I'll give you a hand at the bar.'

Caroline and Smithy walked to the bar as the four girls chatted to the three other lads. Matt was standing alone now having been usurped by Smithy. Jonjo had seen what happened and called to Matt.

'Over here mate, you'll never guess what happened after we left the boozer.'

At that precise moment in time, Matt couldn't give a monkey's what happened in the pub. Typical, bloody typical he thought. For the first time in ages, an attractive girl starts talking to him and she's only interested in one of his mates. Ah well, bollocks to it, he must have been stupid to think she'd be interested in him. Matt walked across to the others and listened as Jonjo began to tell his story.

'Ten minutes after we left, Joe Mortimer had a piss in the ladies toilets, and I mean *really* had a piss. He must have been so drunk. Apparently he just walked in, bold as brass like, stood against the wall and relieved himself. How steaming must he have been? I mean, the fact that there were no urinals would have been a clue, that and the two women adjusting their make-up in the mirror. For God's sake, he could have at least made it to the cubicle.'

Matt had cheered up on hearing the story. 'How do you know it was Joe?' he asked.

'Sandra here, was in the loo at the time and she described him perfectly; little bloke, mid-fifties, grey hair, wearing a yellow round-neck sweater . . .'

'That'll be Joe then,' confirmed Matt, smiling broadly.

'And it gets better Matt. As he's having a slash, he only starts singing 'Danny Boy'. He finishes off, goes back to the others, sits down and carries on drinking as if nothing's happened. Fucking classic. Sorry girls, excuse my language.' Jonjo was practically in tears as he laughed and recounted the story.

'What did the landlord say?' asked Matt, by now thoughts of Smithy and Caroline a distant memory.

'He pissed himself.' Jonjo corrected himself in between laughs, 'Bad choice of phrase there in the circumstances, but apparently he thought it was hysterical. Emlyn and a few of the others offered to clear up the mess, which they did. Emlyn was mortified. Sandra said he gave twenty quid to the landlord for the charity box. Sandra used to work there and says the guvnor's president of the Lancashire Publicans' Association. Wait till he tells the boys that story at the next meeting; he'll be dining out on that for years. Unbelievable, plus he's probably had the best night's takings since Christmas. The girls here said Joe was even waving to everybody as he left, totally oblivious.'

Jonjo revelled in recounting the events and the girls were laughing even more now than they were at the time. The girls' laughter was infectious and Matt, Frank, Jonjo and Pete were laughing along, and the more they thought about the whole Joe Mortimer scenario, the funnier it became.

Caroline and Smithy returned with the drinks. Smithy was put out that he had missed out on something.

112

'Must have been funny whatever it was,' he said brusquely.

None of the group acknowledged Smithy, they just continued to laugh. Caroline just shrugged her shoulders as Smithy looked at her. Caroline had guessed what the others were laughing at, but she wasn't going to tell Smithy.

As many men do, Smithy felt the need to inform everybody of his movements. 'I'm off to the loo, back in a minute.'

This had the others laughing again as they were reminded of the unfortunate Joe Mortimer. Smithy was annoyed that he hadn't been let in on the joke and he sulked off to the toilet. Whilst Tony was gone, Jonjo spoke with Matt.

'Don't get wound up over Smithy, you know what he's like with women.'

'Yeah I know, Jonjo, but I really thought . . . ah never mind. Here's to Stockgrove.' Matt clinked his bottle with Jonjo's. For the second time in the evening, Matt felt a hand on his bottom.

'Come on sexy, on the dance floor now. Let's see what you've got!'

Matt turned around to see Caroline walking slowly towards the dance floor, beckoning him seductively with her right index finger. He wasn't sure what was going on. Was this a wind-up? He hesitated for a moment until Jonjo said, 'What are you waiting for mate, you're in there. Go on son, go and cut some carpet. Show her that old Matt Baker magic.'

Matt Baker magic, he thought to himself. Oh yeah, that's where he dances with a bird and she disappears. No, come on be positive, perhaps Jonjo was right. Matt walked towards Caroline who took his hand and led him to the dance area.

'Come on,' she said, 'I love this song.'

They danced and talked for twenty minutes. Matt couldn't believe how well they were getting on.

'What about Smithy?' asked Matt, repeating the question twice to make himself heard above the music.

'What about him?' Caroline replied.

'I think he likes you.'

'He likes me all right. When we were at the bar he said we should go to another club, just me and him.'

'What did you say?'

'I told him to piss off, I was out with my friends and my friends came first. Besides, he may be good looking but he's a smarmy bastard. Reminds me of my ex. He was a two-timing low-life, wouldn't be surprised if your friend was the same. No offence Matt, I know he's your friend.'

'None taken. Sounds like you've got him sussed.'

'Yeah, I'm a good judge of character. I had him sussed at the Spinners'. I told him we'd come in here later knowing that he'd turn up and hoping that you'd be with him.'

Matt was really confused. He had never been good at reading signals given by women, it might as well have been Morse code for all the sense it made. But even Matt Baker realized this woman was flirting with him. That'll be it, he thought, just a bit of harmless flirtation. He was out with his mates, she was out with hers, and they were all having a good time. The couple danced and chatted like old friends as Matt lost his inhibitions.

Tony Smith was talking to Jonjo and suggesting they move to another club.

'No way, Smithy. We're getting on well with the girls here and I reckon Matt's cracked it with your bird.' Jonjo couldn't resist teasing Smithy. It wasn't often Matt struck lucky with the ladies and if he did it at Smithy's expense, then so much the better. Jonjo knew how far to push things. They'd had a good day and he didn't want it ruined by Smithy acting like a child who'd just been told he can't have an ice cream. He called Smithy closer and put his hand on his shoulder.

''Ere mate, listen. This is why we were all laughing before . . .' Jonjo told the story again of Joe Mortimer in the ladies, this time embellishing it with a few more expletives and details for maximum comedic effect. The story did the trick with Tony Smith laughing in the same fashion as everybody else had the first time Jonjo had told it. Smithy forgot about Caroline and Matt and was happy drinking and chatting with the others.

The night flew by and everybody was enjoying themselves. Eventually, Matt and Caroline rejoined the rest of the group. The man playing the music was more Smashy and Nicey than Ministry of Sound but in fairness, the music had people dancing. You can only play to the room you're in and he knew his audience. He had played Maze, Madness and Madonna at various points in the evening, so eclectic was definitely the word. His teachers at the DJ training school would have been proud as he moved close to the microphone and whispered.

'Now for the last ten minutes here at Stringers we slow it right down, so find that lovely lady or handsome man as we move smoothly into the erection section.'

He played The Commodores, 'Three Times a Lady'. This was reviving memories of school discos. Caroline again took Matt's hand and they moved on to the dance floor, followed closely by Jonjo and Sandra. The others looked on; they had got on well but not that well. Big Frank and Pete were very drunk by this stage, the day's alcohol consumption finally catching up on them, and Tony Smith had decided none of the girls came up to his usual high standards. By the time the last bars of Take That, 'Back for Good' were fading away, Jonjo and Sandra were indulging in a spot of tonsil tennis. Caroline and Matt were smiling as they looked on at their friends snogging like a couple of teenagers on their first date.

'OK, boys and girls, we look forward to seeing you at Stringers, Wigan's premier nightspot next weekend and remember . . . if you can't be good, be careful,' announced the DJ.

Caroline kissed Matt on the right cheek and then again, ever so lightly, on the lips.

'Thank you Matt for restoring my faith in men. I've had a really great night.'

'I have as well,' was all Matt could say in response, his heart sinking as he realized the night was over. Too much of a gentleman Matt Baker, that's your problem, he thought to himself. Caroline interrupted Sandra and Jonjo's snog-fest to tell her friend the girls were leaving.

'I'm not going anywhere without this gorgeous hunk of a man,' said Sandra. She really was pissed. Jonjo had been called a few things in his time, but at five-foot seven and eight stone wet through, 'gorgeous hunk of a man,' wasn't one of them.

'Look Jonjo, me and the boys are gonna get a cab back to the hotel. We'll see you later mate.'

'Oh no you won't Matt,' corrected Caroline. 'You and lover boy here are coming back to my place with the rest of the girls.'

Matt could hardly believe his ears. He didn't say another word until he left the club. Caroline did all the talking.

'Nice meeting you fellers,' she told the three remaining lads. Frank and Pete were drunkenly propping each other up and Smithy was looking on jealously as Jonjo and Matt left with the girls, Caroline adding, 'We'll be gentle with them. Byeee!'

CHAPTER TWELVE

Neil Roberts was having breakfast by himself at seven-thirty on Sunday morning. Helen was having a lie-in and was nursing a hangover. The night before had developed into quite a session. Robbo had gone to his room just after ten. He had watched the news and the football highlights before slowly drifting off to sleep. He was woken up at 1 a.m. by Helen returning to the room. She had been fairly quiet up until the point when she came out of the bathroom.

'Owww, shit!'

'Helen? What's the matter?' asked Robbo, as he fumbled for the switch for the bedside lamp.

'Sorry darling, I just stubbed my toe.'

Helen climbed into bed and cuddled up to Robbo.

'I'm horny,' she whispered.

'You're pissed,' responded Robbo. 'Who's still down in the bar?'

'Quite a few. All the girls are still there and a few of the Globe lot, but most of your players have been good boys like you and gone to bed early. Only Butch, Stan, Kevin and Tommy are still there . . . oh, and Stan as well.'

Helen was clearly drunk and Robbo couldn't resist teasing

117

her.

'I thought Stan might have still been there.'

Helen paused for a moment, 'Yes Stan's still there. Didn't I say?' Once more, she cuddled up to her fiancé kissing him on his chest and stroking her hand on his thigh.

'Darling . . .' began Helen.

Robbo interrupted his girlfriend.

'Big game tomorrow, I'd better get some sleep. Goodnight love.'

He gave Helen a quick kiss and switched off the light.

Now sitting at the table by himself, Robbo was feeling tired. No matter he thought, he'd have breakfast and go back to bed for a few hours. The coach wasn't leaving until midday and he could have a couple of hours kip, freshen up and then go for a walk around the hotel grounds to stretch his legs. He was pleased when Helen told him that most of the players had not stayed in the bar all night. Only Butch, Stan and Kevin were still drinking . . . oh, and of course, Stan, as Helen had drunkenly pointed out. Robbo wasn't unduly concerned by this, but he was surprised to hear that Tommy and Sylvia were still there.

As Robbo was going up to his room, he met Woodsy and Macca in the foyer.

'Bloody hell, you two look terrible. I thought you went to bed early.'

'We did Robbo,' explained Macca. 'We both went up just after you to watch the football and get some zeds. Wendy's come into the room about two o'clock in the morning singing, *Hey, hey we're the Stockgrove*. Bloody funny now thinking about it, but I wasn't impressed at the time.'

Woodsy added, 'At least Kimberley wasn't singing, she was too busy being sick in the toilet. I was awake till gone three o'clock making sure she was all right. To top it all she woke me up half an hour ago asking me to get some paracetamols. I've left her alone to suffer while I get some brekkie.'

Robbo had to smile as he pictured Wendy singing. He told the duo about his own lack of sleep courtesy of Helen.

'Blimey boys, we'd have been better off staying in the bar,' observed Woodsy.

From eleven-thirty onwards a steady stream of players and supporters began checking out at reception, swapping stories about the previous day and night. Tommy and Sylvia looked and felt terrible. They had both been drinking whisky for much of the night and Robbo took great delight in teasing the elderly couple about the perils of alcohol. The trio of single men: Butch, Stan and Kev, all looked remarkably well. They had finished drinking at 2.30 a.m., went to bed and slept solidly. All three had enjoyed a hearty breakfast and were raring to go for the match. Before the weekend, Robbo was apprehensive. It was the biggest match in the club's history and with so many supporters coming up and socializing with the players, there was a temptation for some of the lads to forget what they were there for. That hadn't happened. They had all had a drink and enjoyed themselves, but all the players were now looking forward to the match in Bootle. Ironically, the one man who wasn't fully focused on the match was Tommy Boyle, who was borrowing some paracetamols from Kimberley Woods. Tommy must have thought he was still drunk for a moment, when he heard roars of laughter and he turned round to see a group of men in fancy dress.

The players were the first to board the coach. As instructed by Tommy, they all wore black shoes, black trousers and white long sleeve shirts. Gary Sweeney — who else — had supplied identical plain burgundy-coloured silk ties. Robbo had asked no questions about where the ties had come from, although he suspected that Gary didn't have a receipt for his 'purchases'. They all sat together in the front rows of the coach, again as instructed by Tommy who was dressed the same as the players. The wives and girlfriends were next to board, sitting in the seats behind the players. Then came the supporters in various states of sobriety. As Joe Mortimer got on, a chorus of 'Danny Boy' rang out. Joe — bless him — even joined in thinking they were paying homage to young Danny Cartwright. He still didn't remember his actions in the ladies toilets at the Spinners' Arms and nobody had the heart to tell him, at least not yet anyway. There was no sign of either Jonjo or Matt and nobody had spoken to them or heard from them, although Big Frank had relayed the details of the previous night in Stringers and the flirtatious senior citizens on the bus. The fancy dress brigade were last to board the coach and were greeted by loud cheers as they did so.

The coach, closely followed by the Blackpool four, arrived at the car park of the ground in Bootle. The players disembarked first, looking and feeling professional. There was just under an hour to kick-off and Tommy escorted his players to the away dressing room. He wanted them changed early and going through a proper warm up. It had only been a short journey today from Haydock to Liverpool, but yesterday had been a long day and Tommy wanted clear heads and loose limbs for the match.

As the supporters were getting off the coach some of the officials from the home side were driving into the car park. Looks were exchanged but no words and then startled looks as the last twelve men got off the coach. Biggles, Postman Pat, Napoleon, Bugs Bunny and a nun were the first to get off. There was then a brief hiatus because the Pope had tripped over his robes and spilt his can of John Smith's. The Vatican would not have been too impressed by the Pontiff's blaspheming. Fortunately, Bashful, Happy and Grumpy were on hand to help his Holiness to his feet. The Pope gave the dwarves a quick blessing by way of a thank you, anointing them with the Holy Water from the Tadcaster Brewery. Three men dressed in shell-suits, curly black wigs and stick-on moustaches were imploring everybody to 'calm down, calm down.' Frank 'Biggles' Marinelli was delighted that the chaps from the Globe had been true to their word and turned up in fancy dress. The Blackpool four added to the surreal scene as they got out of their car: the Blues Brothers, Elvis and Julius Caesar. The Roman Emperor rebuffing insults about his footwear, insisting that Reeboks were de rigeur at the Senate these days.

The wives and girlfriends, together with some of the other supporters, headed to the clubhouse. Meanwhile, the Pope led his flock to The Rocket, the Beefeater pub directly opposite the football ground car park. The locals watched in stunned silence for a few moments as the procession made its way into the pub. The Blues Brothers were shaking hands with bemused drinkers and children were rushing over excitedly to greet Postman Pat.

'No I haven't got Jess,' Postman Pat told the kids. 'Jess is at home with Mrs Pat while I have a beer with the lads.'

Grumpy, Bashful and a not very Happy, were having an argument about whose round it was. An unshaven nun finally settled the dispute by declaring, 'For fuck's sake I'll get them in.' Not a phrase you hear everyday in the convent. Napoleon had chalked his name up to play pool claiming to be so good he could beat anybody with one arm tied behind his back. Elvis and the Harry Enfield Scousers were sat down at a table looking at the menu, whilst Julius Caesar and Bugs Bunny

121

were out the back having a smoke. Biggles was chatting to the barman.

'Pretty much your usual Sunday lunchtime crowd then,' said a deadpan Biggles.

'Yeah pretty much,' replied the barman, 'but his Holiness doesn't usually come in until after evening mass.'

The supporters who weren't in fancy dress were beginning to wish they were. When they all left to go to the match, everybody in the pub gave them a round of applause. Outside, the Pope walked into the middle of the road and acted as lollipop man as the group crossed. A small line of traffic built up as they waited for Postman Pat, who had been signing some autographs for the kids. The Pope blessed the motorists for their patience and they in turn beeped their horns and laughed.

The players from both sides were already out on the pitch warming-up. With the arrival of the fancy dress brigade, it meant that support for the two teams was more or less equally divided. Biggles led the way as they walked in single file in front of the solitary stand, acknowledging the cheers and wolf-whistles from both sets of supporters. The Bootle players watched the procession marching its way behind the goal where their goalkeeper was stood. The Bootle captain approached the referee. That famous Liverpudlian sense of humour was missing as he said, 'Oh, ay ref, you can't let them stand there.' The ref seemed at a loss as to what action to take. They didn't teach you this on the referee training course. Neil Roberts hadn't seen the Bootle captain approach the ref. He was already jogging towards Big Frank's fancy dress group.

'Look lads, fantastic support and everything, but it's not really fair if you stand behind the goal. If we win they'll only complain about unsportsmanlike behaviour.'

Frank accepted that Robbo was right and the Harry Enfield Scousers were reinforcing his point by talking to the home team's goalkeeper.

'All right, all right, all right . . . they do though, ah they do though don't they . . . calm down . . . are you telling me to calm down . . . ?' The home keeper was not amused. Robbo offered his apology for the behaviour of the supporters.

'Sorry about that mate, they're just having a bit of fun.'

'Fucking Cockney twats,' was the keeper's surly response to Robbo's olive branch. Fair enough, thought Robbo, who raised his eyebrows but said nothing.

Stockgrove had the same starting line-up as in previous rounds, with the three teenagers, Rusky, Danny Cartwright and Lloydy on the bench. Tommy Boyle had recovered sufficiently from the previous night to give the team a rousing team talk. The Stockgrove players were fired up and the large contingent of travelling support had given them a boost. There was a mixture of nerves and excitement as they had taken the pitch. They could win this match and progress to the quarter-final. They were even more confident than they had been in previous rounds.

Bootle started the match well. They were a very good team who were favourites to win the Cup this year. All of the Bootle team played semi-professionally on Saturdays. Two players in midfield had League experience with Tranmere and Oldham Athletic and were soon showing their class and experience. Willo, Stan and JC were being hustled off the ball. Only Macca was holding his own in the Stockgrove midfield. Gary Sweeney and Sammy hadn't even touched the ball when Bootle scored the first goal of the match after just twelve minutes. The home goalkeeper celebrated by running out of his box and giving a one fingered gesture to the fancy dress brigade on the touchline. This time Big Frank really did have to get the Harry Enfield Scousers to calm down. Stockgrove were being outclassed and the game was less than fifteen minutes old. As he had done in the previous round, Tommy instructed Gary Sweeney to drop back into midfield, leaving Sammy alone up front. When Tommy had issued the instruction in the previous round, the match was in extra-time. Here it had barely started. It was a stark admission by Tommy that his team were being swamped. As before, the tactical switch brought results. Now Macca and Gary were both winning balls and JC, Willo and Stan were becoming more involved. Sammy Koonphool was working his socks off, closing down defenders and making runs to create space for his team-mates.

With thirty-five minutes gone, Macca played a long cross-field ball to JC on the right wing. The youngster ran at the Bootle left-back, pushing the ball into space behind the defender. The teenager from Stockgrove was too quick for the fullback, but the Bootle centre-half was covering and scythed JC down just outside the penalty area. It was a horrendous looking foul that left the youngster lying motionless on the floor. Gary Sweeney was enraged as he ran over to the Bootle player.

'You fucking animal!' he shouted.

'Fuck off divvy.' The Liverpudlian pushed Gary in the chest. Three Bootle players plus Stan and Willo ran in to separate the two. Butch, Robbo and Phil got there just as the referee and one of the linesmen were stepping in. Tommy Boyle was fuming as he attended to the gash on JC's leg. The tackle had split the lad's shin pad and left a gaping wound on the calf where the metal studs had ripped the skin. The home goalkeeper was taunting Phil Whitaker.

'What's the matter ugly, can't you southern fairies take a

few tackles?'

Phil smiled at the man doing the taunting and patted him on the head.

'You go back to your goal sonny. Let the grown-ups deal with this.' Phil was a big man in every sense and the home keeper scuttled away. Order was restored after a few minutes and the referee and linesman began talking to one another. With a blast on his whistle the referee summoned the Bootle centre-back and Leon Wilson. Willo couldn't believe it, looking around and then pointing at himself, 'What? Me?' The linesman ran to the referee again. Another blast on his whistle and he was beckoning Gary Sweeney who began walking slowly towards the official. By this time, Willo was baffled and was jogging towards the ref. He was stopped halfway as the man in black waved him away, pointed at Gary and shouted, 'You, number eight. Come here and hurry up!' The Stockgrove players shook their heads. How could he have mixed up Gary and Willo?

Gary and the perpetrator of the foul stood either side of the ref, looking down at the pitch as they were spoken to. They were each shown a yellow card and were instructed to shake hands. Both men refused and Gary Sweeney left, shaking his head in disgust.

'That's a joke ref!' an angry Scottish voice cried. 'Look at this wee boy's leg and you end up booking one of my players.' Tommy's voice was crackling with anger.

'Any more from you and you'll be getting a red card, manager or not.' Tommy was now incensed and Robbo had to stop his manager from running over to the official. Robbo and Tommy helped carry JC from the pitch.

'Bloody disgrace,' said Tommy loudly as he passed the referee. The man in black hesitated for a moment as he caught sight of the blood gushing from the Stockgrove player's leg.

He decided not to carry out his threat of further action against Tommy Boyle. The teenager received a sympathetic round of applause from both sets of supporters as he left the pitch.

Wendy McSwiggen and Helen were waiting by the touchline as JC was carried off. Wendy, in her professional guise of nurse, cleaned some of the blood away and just said, 'That needs stitching, he'll have to go to casualty.' An official from the home team had joined the cluster and kindly volunteered to drive the injured player to hospital. Wendy offered to go as well but Helen said she would go, feeling an obligation as his schoolteacher. She didn't actually say that, simply stating, 'I'll go Wendy, you spend all week in a hospital, you don't want to be spending your day off in one.'

Tommy brought in Danny Cartwright for JC in a straight swap. Finally, Stockgrove took the free kick they had been awarded for the foul on JC, but Macca drove his shot straight into the home side's defensive wall. The ball rebounded to Gary Sweeney who sliced his shot horribly wide. The centre-back who had been antagonizing Gary gave a derisory 'Ee-ore'. Gary gave his tormentor the Nescafé handshake, telling the man with the donkey impression, 'All mouth, you fucking mug.' There were still ten minutes until half-time and Gary had been riled. Robbo caught Tommy's attention, gesturing in the same way that Lineker had done to Bobby Robson in the World Cup semi-final in Turin, when Gazza had just been booked and was in danger of losing control. 'Keep an eye on him,' Robbo mouthed to Tommy.

Tommy Boyle was relieved when the half-time whistle came. Stockgrove had been outplayed for much of the half and they were rattled. He himself needed to calm down and the interval was welcome. He was thankful his team were only one-nil down at half-time. Gary Sweeney was involved in further altercations with the Bootle centre-back as the players headed for the changing rooms.

Tommy had regained his composure and was his normal self as he addressed the team.

'Don't let them bully you. You've got to start dominating that midfield . . . Macca, good half. Gary, don't let them wind you up . . .' He issued words of encouragement and advice, carefully going round to each player in turn. There wasn't too much for Tommy to say. The players were motivated before the match and the foul on JC had served to add some niggle in the game, both verbal and physical. Tommy just had to make sure his players harnessed their aggression positively.

Five minutes into the second half, a cheer went up from the Stockgrove supporters. Matt and Jonjo had been spotted walking along the touchline, Matt rather sheepishly, but Jonjo was milking the applause and waving to the stand. The home supporters were as baffled as the players and officials by the sudden burst of noise. Frank 'Biggles' Marinelli welcomed the conquering heroes with a handshake.

'Well done boys. Good of you to make it.'

Jonjo and Matt had been unaware, like everybody else, that so many people were going to be in fancy dress. Frank himself had been surprised by the turnout. The two men were a bit overwhelmed as the Pope, Elvis and all the others crowded round, eagerly wanting to know what had happened the night before. Tony Smith had joined the throng now and was as keen as anybody to hear the story.

'So it was you two with five birds. Result. I want you to deliver all the details,' said Postman Pat, 'the more sordid and kinky the better.'

The nun added, 'That's right, we want a full confession.'

Matt disappointed the group by saying, 'No it wasn't like

that. We just went back to Caroline's house, had something to eat, a few glasses of wine and everybody gradually fell asleep.'

Elvis had a suspicious mind. 'I'm not having that. You had five birds gagging for it and you all fell asleep?'

Matt was smiling coyly, 'A gentleman never tells.'

Jonjo added quickly, 'That's right Matt, but I'm no gentleman. What a fantastic shag!'

The group were laughing now as they listened intently to Jonjo. Bugs Bunny was all ears. They knew you had to take some of Jonjo's stories with a large pinch of salt, but it made them all the more amusing. He was a typical bloke in the sense that he liked nothing more than to brag about his sexual conquests. If Jonjo had sex the night before then all the lads would hear about it, in explicit detail, the following day. Matt wasn't like that, partly because it wasn't very often he had something to brag about, but more because he genuinely thought it wasn't very gentlemanly to talk about any girl he had slept with. The lads knew they wouldn't get much out of Matt, but Jonjo was a different proposition and he was relishing telling the story. Jonjo knew very well that it had been the girls doing the pulling, but he wouldn't mention that in his story.

'What a night boys. Matt's hiding his light under a bushel. He pulled the best looking one, Caroline.' Frank and Pete Woods confirmed Caroline was an extremely attractive girl. Big Frank, lacking the poetic ability of Keats or Wordsworth described Caroline as, 'fit as fuck'. High praise indeed.

Jonjo continued, 'So I'm with Sandra, no stunner but a great laugh.' The irony was deliberate on Jonjo's part, himself no Brad Pitt. 'Not up to my usual supermodel standard but I had to help my wing man out.' Jonjo was now pointing at Matt. 'So we get a minibus taxi back to Caroline's gaff and she starts cooking some pizza. I'm in the front room having a fumble with Sandra and the other three birds are all chatting away with Matt telling him how cute he is. I tell you boys, the man was on top form. If he'd been playing poker he'd have been on for the full house!' The group acknowledged Matt as Jonjo continued. 'Anyway, cut a long story short, the three girls have a bit of pizza and some wine and all crash out in the spare room. Casanova here disappears upstairs with Caroline and I give Sandra the best two minutes of her life on the living room floor. I can still feel the carpet burns. This morning, Sandra takes the other three back home leaving Caroline to cook a fry-up for me and Matt. The full Montgomery; black pudding, the works. The two lovebirds disappear upstairs again to work off the cholesterol and Billy-no-mates here is left watching poxy *Hollyoaks*. Eventually they surface and Caroline gives us a lift over here. It's a wonder she had any energy left. Matt rang Helen to find out where the ground was and here we are. What's the score?'

The lads were happy that two of their group had enjoyed carnal relations. Matt was happy too. Caroline was a lovely girl who he would see again. His ego had been given a boost by her and the way Jonjo told the story. It was also one in the eye for the Tony Smiths of this world.

Focus soon settled back on to the match. Bootle had started the second half much in the same way they had started the first. They were showing why they were favourites to win the competition. Physically strong, they also had plenty of skill, particularly in midfield. Like Stockgrove, many of the Bootle team had played together for a number of years and they weren't about to let a load of southern poofs come to Liverpool and win.

Midway into the second period the home side scored

again. A corner kick was floated high towards the back post, where the Bootle number eleven rose unchallenged to head the ball past a helpless Woodsy. Recriminations began amongst the Stockgrove players. Woodsy was blaming Phil who in turn was reproaching Kev. Robbo was asking Woodsy why he didn't come off his line to catch the high ball when it was played in. It didn't matter who was at fault, they were two-nil down. The goalscorer ran towards the Stockgrove supporters flicking them the V-sign. The fancy dress brigade en masse responded with the Nescafé handshake and cries of 'Wanker!' So much for sportsmanship.

Stockgrove were down and almost out. They hadn't done themselves justice today. They had barely had a shot at goal and poor Sammy was looking lost up front by himself. Then the Thai youngster demonstrated why League clubs had shown an interest. An aimless punt upfield by Kev Hardaker was controlled on his chest by Sammy. He let the ball drop to his feet and in one sublime movement back-heeled the ball through the defender's legs. He span round and was away running on to the ball, closing down on goal with two home defenders forlornly chasing him. As the goalkeeper came out, Sammy dropped his right shoulder encouraging the keeper to go one way whilst he went the other, and he simply passed the ball into the empty net with his left foot. As so often that season, Sammy showed what a good prospect he was. The home supporters applauded the skilfulness of the goal. The Stockgrove supporters in the stand leapt to their feet and those on the touchline ran around in wild celebration. The Pope briefly ran on to the pitch, fell to his knees and kissed the floor before returning to hug Bashful. Postman Pat's head came off as he embraced Napoleon and Elvis was left all shook up by a nun jumping on top of him. Biggles started the chorus of 'Wonderwall' in homage to Sammy

Koonphool. This was swiftly followed by *'G-L-O-B-E'* and their trademark conga to the corner flag and back.

The goal came just four minutes after Bootle had scored their second and Stockgrove were back in the match courtesy of a moment of brilliance from Sammy. Game on. The home team were rocked by the goal and Stockgrove grew in confidence. Tommy instructed Gary Sweeney to push up front to rejoin Sammy. Stockgrove were starting to look the better side as they pressed for an equalizer. With just eight minutes left, their fight back was ended. Stan lost possession in midfield and the home team needed just two more passes before the ball reached their captain. He struck the ball low into the bottom corner beyond Woodsy's flailing reach. Gary Sweeney ran to retrieve the ball from the net.

'Come on lads, get your heads on, we can still do this!' he shouted, urging one last effort. Robbo sat despondently on his haunches. Butch gave his friend a consoling tap on the back of the head without saying anything. They both knew the game was lost. Tommy made a double substitution replacing Phil Whitaker with Rusky, and Leon Wilson with Lloydy. The home side dominated the closing stages hitting the post and forcing two good saves from Woodsy. Tommy knew his team were beaten and he was almost relieved when the final whistle blew. His team had nothing to be ashamed of. They hadn't played as well as they could but that happens. Tommy congratulated the opposition manager and wished Bootle good luck in the next round. He then walked on to the pitch and shook the hands of every one of his players. Gary was sat on the floor in the centre-circle watching the home team celebrate. Robbo had joined Tommy in walking round and shaking hands with each of the Stockgrove players. Tommy ordered all the players to gather round and they formed a huddle near the halfway line.

'I'm proud of you lads. Today we didn't play as well we can but what you've achieved in this competition has been fantastic. In the few years I've been with this club you've won every competition available for you to win. Today wasn't your day. You win as a team, you lose as a team. I'm proud of you lads, that's all I want to say.' It was a strange speech for Tommy to make. He wasn't prone to shows of emotion and some of the players felt awkward as they huddled together, arms linked round each others shoulders listening to Tommy speak. Now wasn't the time Robbo had intended to make the announcement, but Tommy had more or less been leading him into it.

'Look lads, Tommy's summed it up perfectly. I wasn't going to say anything for a few more weeks in case I changed my mind, but I'm finishing at the end of the season.' He quickly added, 'Not just the playing but the whole lot, the club secretary side of it as well. I suppose I've just had enough.' Nobody spoke. Butch and Phil shook hands again with Robbo and Tommy. They hadn't been as surprised as some of the others. The youngsters looked at each other not knowing what to say. Butch broke the silence.

'Well that's that then. Looks like it's your round Robbo.'

Nothing more was said as the players walked off, each with their own thoughts. Disappointment at losing the match was compounded by Robbo's unexpected announcement. The Stockgrove supporters had all waited to applaud the players off the pitch and the players returned the gesture.

By the time they had showered and changed, the Stockgrove players knew this season would probably be the last for the club. Neil Roberts had threatened retirement the season before, but Tommy talked him out of it. The players hoped and assumed Robbo would just keep on running the club. They didn't want to think it was going to end, although they knew it would sooner rather than later.

Tommy walked into the home dressing room whilst they were still getting changed. The noise and cheerful banter could be heard in the stony silence of the away dressing room. Tommy congratulated the opposition once more and wished them well. The Bootle manager enquired about the health of JC.

'Have you heard from your lad in the hospital?'

'Aye, they're still waiting in casualty, but your man's kindly offered to wait and drive them back once they're done.'

'You'll stay a while and have a drink then?' asked the Liverpudlian.

'Of course,' confirmed Tommy.

None of the Stockgrove lads wanted to have a drink at the ground. They'd rather have gone straight to the pub in St Helens owned by Emlyn's mate. It would have been rude though not to stay for at least one drink and besides, they would have to wait for Helen and JC to come back from the hospital. They had been happy to celebrate when they had won, now it was time to be magnanimous in defeat and share a drink with their hosts. The Bootle lads were no different to Stockgrove. They liked a drink and a laugh and they played Sunday football for the enjoyment. The centre-back who had injured JC was genuinely remorseful admitting it was a clumsy challenge. Gary Sweeney however, wasn't convinced. He gave the opposition centre-back and goalkeeper a wide berth in case he lost his temper, and in his own words, 'knocked one of the mugs out.' Gary's reticence aside, everybody was soon mixing well and talking about matches between rival teams. Leon Wilson was talking to the Bootle left-back, a season ticket holder at Goodison Park. Willo was reminiscing about the days of travelling on football specials up to Liverpool and the local scallies throwing bricks and stones at the train as it approached Edge Hill station. The Everton man was nodding in acknowledgement. He himself as a youngster would travel on football specials all over the country watching the great Everton side of the mid-Eighties; Reid, Ratcliffe, Sheedy. And now Everton were slumbering unable to compete with the financial muscle of Chelsea, Arsenal and Manchester United.

Helen rang Robbo to say she was on her way back with JC. They were fortunate that it had been a quiet Sunday afternoon in casualty and JC was only kept waiting for just over an hour before he was finally treated. The general bonhomie in the clubhouse had been helped by the fancy dress brigade who were mixing well with the locals. The trading of insults during the match had been forgotten. As ever, Frank started the singing and the Liverpudlians soon joined him in a chorus of 'You'll Never Walk Alone.' Kev cheered Gary up by pointing at the Bootle centre-back and stating, 'He'll always wank alone.' It was very puerile but it made Gary laugh all the same.

The Stockgrove supporters were singing '*Hey, hey, we're the Stockgrove*' as Helen, JC and the Bootle official entered the clubhouse. As they spotted the youngster limping in on crutches the song was changed to '*One James Connolly, there's only one James Connolly,*' to the embarrassment of the injured teenager. The man responsible for the tackle came over and shook JC's hand. The Stockgrove youngster confirming, 'No hard feelings, just one of those things.'

It was at this point that Gary Sweeney took the opportunity to relieve the bar of a small signed photograph of Neil Ruddock. Once he had done that he felt a lot better. They took liberties on the pitch; he liberated Ruddock off the pitch. They had taken the piss; he had taken the photo.

With JC back in the fold, the coach could make the short

134

journey along the East Lancs Road to St Helens. Players and supporters bade their farewells and boarded the coach. Sammy told JC about the match and Robbo's announcement. JC was sad to hear this would possibly mean the end of the club. The two lads had only played for one season and next year JC would be at university and Sammy — well who knows — but either way he would have moved on. The teenagers had enjoyed playing for the club and making new friends. It had been particularly educational for Sammy, learning ever more creative ways to swear. His rhyming slang was coming on a treat and he had a full repertoire of football clichés. As the players sat on the coach, Gary spoke to Robbo.

'No changing your mind then Robbo?'

'No, not this time mate. This is definitely Goodnight Vienna.'

'You know some of the other lads will go as well.'

'I know Gary. Time to move on mate, we're none of us getting any younger. What will you do?'

'I don't know mate.'

Gary's initial thoughts had been to take over as club secretary and keep the side going, but he knew how much time and effort Robbo spent running the club and organizing everything. The truth was, Gary didn't have the time or the inclination to do it. Besides, the heart of the club would be gone. Willo, Stan and Kev wanted to carry on playing, but Macca, Woodsy, Butch and Phil had already indicated that the end of the season would be as good a time as any for them to hang up their boots. Out of the youngsters, only Rusky would be available next season. The club could continue by signing on a host of new players and finding a new club secretary, but what was the point in that. It would be like playing for a new team and that wasn't what motivated Gary Sweeney to turn up every week. He wanted to play football with the same mates he had played with for over a decade. There would be no shortage of clubs wanting to sign Gary on and he would think about it more at the end of the season. Now he just wanted to get to the pub and have a drink with his mates.

Harry Thompson had been a publican for nearly thirty years. He knew Emlyn from the days when they worked in the same pub in Aberystwyth. Harry was always pleased to see his friend and if Emlyn was bringing a coach-load of thirsty people to his pub, then so much the better. Emlyn had pre-warned Harry two weeks before the match, 'The lads may be a bit boisterous but they're never any bother. They just like a bit of a sing-song and a drink.'

Harry assured Emlyn they would be more than welcome.

'We're used to crowds of rugby league fans in here Emlyn, so nothing your lads do will surprise me.'

Within ten minutes of the group entering the pub, Harry Thompson admitted to Emlyn he had been wrong and he was surprised. Emlyn hadn't told his friend about the fancy dress brigade, deciding it would be funnier just to see the look on his face when they walked in. Harry Thompson was upstairs when the Stockgrove players and supporters arrived. The pub had a snug bar and a saloon and the latter had been reserved for the coach party. Harry had put on a full buffet spread of sandwiches, sausage rolls, chicken and so on. In the snug, four elderly men were playing dominoes and a lone middle-aged drinker was sat on a bar stool flirting with the barmaid. Whilst the pub had two separate areas and two separate entrances, a common bar served them both. The barmaid had already explained to the lone drinker the reasons for the extra staff on duty and the food in the other bar. She wasn't too surprised when a steady stream of people began filing into the saloon bar. The barmaid did however, raise an eyebrow when she saw Bugs Bunny and Julius Caesar waiting to be served.

'I think they've arrived!' she shouted up to Harry. Emlyn was there to greet his old friend when he came down the stairs. Harry Thompson was already chuckling when he reached the bar area.

'Man alive, I've seen some things in my time but I've never had a Roman Emperor and a six foot rabbit drink in my pub!' The friends exchanged pleasantries as they caught up over old times. Harry removed the cellophane wrappings covering the plates of food and invited everybody to tuck in. The nun was the first to the food exclaiming, 'I'm starving!'

Kev was lightning quick. 'I'm not surprised living at a convent in Nuneaton.'

It was vintage Kev Hardaker and it set the tone for the rest of the evening. By now even the dominoes players knew this would be no ordinary Sunday night, as they finished their game and stood up to investigate what was happening next door. It was only five-fifteen in the afternoon and Harry was in for bumper takings this evening. Robbo invited the coach driver inside for some food and he became the subject of some predictable banter.

'Great fancy dress outfit mate, you look just like a coach driver,' was Big Frank's contribution.

Robbo was explaining his decision to retire to Leon Wilson and John Woods.

'I hadn't intended to announce it the way I did, but I suppose I was just putting off the decision to tell everybody. I don't want to feel like I've let anybody down. I said last season that would be my lot, but as it turned out Tommy was right to talk me out of it. I would have regretted not having a crack at the National Cup. But now it's different. Now I know the timing is right. I'm sorry lads.'

'Leave it out Robbo, don't be sorry,' said Willo. 'All the boys appreciate what you've done for the club; fuck me you *are* the club.'

Woodsy agreed, 'That's right mate. I know some of us have been a pain in the arse at times, what with the kit and paying our subs every week, but you shouldn't take it to heart Robbo.'

Woodsy's comments were intended to make Robbo laugh and they achieved their objective.

'Yeah, I'll really miss chasing you boys up for money every week and washing those dirty kits!'

All the supporters knew by now that Robbo had announced his retirement, and with it the likelihood of the club folding at the end of the season. Tommy decided that now was an opportune moment to say a few words of thanks. As he called for a bit of quiet, he was greeted with good-natured shouts and whistles of derision. Emlyn tapped a pint glass with a fork from the buffet to no effect. Harry Thompson rang the bell and boomed, 'QUIET GENTLEMEN PLEEEASE!' Everybody stopped talking, and on hearing the bell the elderly dominoes players glanced at their watches in confusion.

'Thank you mister landlord,' said Tommy. Harry nodded as Tommy began, 'I'd just like to say a few words while you're all sober.'

'Speak for yourself Tommy,' said the Pope.

Tommy smiled. 'Firstly, thank you to Harry and all his staff for the wonderful spread and the hospitality.' There was a pause as people applauded and a few shouts of 'cheers Harry,' filled the air. 'Secondly, thank you to all the players.' More cheers and whistles briefly interrupted Tommy. 'OK settle down. Thank you to all the players who have played, not just today, but over the years that I've been involved with the club. Every player in the squad today can be proud of what you've achieved in this competition. You've made me proud to be associated with you.' The supporters were all applauding respectfully, Tommy's serious tone and demeanour sufficient to deter anybody from frivolous comments. The players, some looking at Tommy, others shuffling uncomfortably and looking at their feet, waited for their manager to continue. 'Many years ago two men set this football team up; Neil Roberts and Paul Butcher.' People turned to look at the two men who were maintaining eye contact with Tommy. 'Both men have played for the club ever since and I know that Butch will be the first to agree with me, when I say that Neil Roberts — Robbo — is the reason we're all here today.' Butch led the round of applause that briefly interrupted Tommy once more. The Scotsman would normally call his friend 'Neil' but today, like everybody else, he would refer him by his nickname. 'Robbo has done all the paperwork for the National Cup, organized the coaches, the hotel . . . everything. And not just for the National Cup, but for the past Lord knows how many seasons. As you all know by now, Robbo is retiring as player and club secretary at the end of the season. I don't know at this stage whether the club will continue in one form or another next year, but I do know that each and every one of you owes a big thank you to Neil Roberts.' A big cheer was accompanied by applause and then people were singing, *'One Neil Roberts, there's only one Neil Roberts.'* Then shouts of 'Speech! Speech!' urging Robbo to say a few words. Embarrassed, Robbo was pushed gently towards the bar where Tommy stood. The two men shook hands.

'I don't really know what to say,' began Robbo.

'Well don't say anything then, just get the beers in!' shouted Gary Sweeney to another large cheer.

Robbo was smiling now. Gary's comments had broken the moment of awkwardness he had felt when he first stood next to Tommy.

'Thank you Tommy for your kind words about me and Butch. On behalf of the players I'd like to thank *you* Tom, for all the effort you've put in since you've been with us, and on a personal note, thanks for being a good friend.' There was more applause and wolf-whistles. 'Blimey this is beginning to sound like the Oscars, so I'll shut up now, but I can't finish without saying thank you to the supporters, every daft one of you . . . right, let's get pissed!' This produced the loudest cheer of the evening.

'Hey, hey we're the Stockgrove,' reverberated round the pub. Then a few minutes later *'G-L-O-B-E.'* The players were joining the supporters in the singing and everybody was shaking Robbo's hand. Then, courtesy of Big Frank's creative talents, Ottowan's remix *'D-I-S-C-O/G-L-O-B-E'* became:

He is R, he's retiring
He is O, he's out of 'ere
He is B, he is bye bye
He is B, he's bon voyage
He is O, oh ohhhh!
R-O-B-B-O
R-O-B-B-O . . .'

It wasn't McCartney and Lennon, but it was off the cuff and instantaneous and consequently all the funnier. Frank even tried one for Tommy but it came up sadly short.

He is T, he is tartan
He is O . . . oh fuck it, I'm pissed.'

Big Frank's creative juices weren't flowing as readily as the lager. As the night wore on and with the food in the saloon bar all gone, everybody began to move freely between the two bars. As the locals came in they soon got in the party atmosphere — it was difficult not to when Postman Pat insists you join him for a dance.

Some of the group decided to pop out for something to eat. The buffet was good, but all that drinking sharpens the appetite. Stan, Rusky and Butch were joined by Grumpy, Elvis and Bugs Bunny as they walked into McDonald's. Bugs had borrowed JC's crutches and was affecting a limp. The sight of poor Bugs Bunny on crutches intrigued one young lad. He held his mother's hand whilst his mum asked, 'What happened to you Bugs?'

Crouching down to the boy's level, Bugs replied, 'Well it's a bit of a long story, but basically I'm in the pub across the road, minding my own business and enjoying a pint of carrot juice. All of a sudden, Elmer Fudd and Yosemite Sam walk in and start putting the boot in for no reason. Bang out of order if you ask me.'

The mum laughed but the boy was not impressed. The real Bugs Bunny did not have a Cockney accent and the little lad tried to pull the impostor's head off. Bugs hastily joined the others waiting to be served. Elvis ordered his food king-size and Grumpy confused everyone by asking for a happy meal.

The pub meanwhile, was rocking. The Blues Brothers had appointed themselves as unofficial doormen and had a stint waiting outside greeting customers. The Harry Enfield Scousers had their wigs stolen by a group of local women who were getting into the spirit of things. A not so Bashful was chatting up one of the barmaids and the Roman Emperor was hosting a round of drinking games. Ale was drunk. Ale was spilt. Ale Caesar.

Just after nine o'clock, Robbo had to tell everybody the party was over. Another fifteen minutes and the coach had to leave. Harry Thompson was almost as disappointed as everybody else was. He had enjoyed bumper takings and his regulars had joined in with the festivities. The coach party had been no bother and were welcome back anytime.

The singing and jokes continued for another half an hour on the coach, but on the motorway the voices gradually quietened down as people began to nod off to sleep. It had been a long and eventful weekend.

CHAPTER THIRTEEN

The following Sunday, Stockgrove returned to league action. Nobody at the club had expected to win the National Cup and the team's progress in the tournament exceeded expectations. However, the defeat in Liverpool now meant that they had been knocked out of all three cup competitions they had entered that season. In the County Cup, they had surprisingly been eliminated in the first round. They had won the competition the season before and it was the first time in five years that they hadn't reached at least the quarter-final stage. In the League Cup, they had been defeated by an extra-time goal by Linford Old Boys. But victory today for Stockgrove against the same opponents would clinch the league title. Defeat for second-placed Linford would leave them seven points adrift with just two games remaining. Stockgrove still had four matches left and even if they dropped points today, they were still well placed to win the league.

The Stockgrove players had a point to prove to their opponents. Linford Old Boys was a misnomer; they were a young side full of teenagers and players in their early twenties. They had taunted the Stockgrove team during their League Cup victory earlier in the season; 'Old men', 'You're getting slow grandad'. There was some truth in the jibes, but today Stockgrove played their younger opponents off the park, winning 4-0. 'And they were lucky to get nil,' Kev said after the match. During the game, the Stockgrove players didn't miss any opportunity to hand out little digs to the Linford players; 'Not bad for a bunch of old men,' 'Men against boys,' 'Can we play you every week.' The disappointment of the previous week's defeat in Liverpool was forgotten. *'Hey, hey we're the Stockgrove'* and 'Wonderwall' were sung loudly in the showers as the team celebrated winning the league.

Woodsy carefully checked all his clothing for signs of itching powder or Ralgex, but there was no trace. His boots and gloves were where he had left them and hadn't been superglued to the wall or ceiling. Hardaker and Sweeney must be losing their touch; no practical jokes to celebrate the victory. Woodsy finished getting changed and checked his kit bag once more for signs of foul play or fowl play. There was no sign of Dave Pheasant, but Woodsy was still wary. Gary and Kev must be planning something. Was it a double bluff? He wouldn't want to play cards with the two men and he was sure they were trying to lull him into a false sense of security. This was psychological warfare and Woodsy couldn't take it any longer.

'All right you two, what is it? What have you done?'

'What are you talking about?' replied Gary, innocently.

'You two must have done something,' said Woodsy.

'Ah, come on Woodsy, would we do anything?' said Kev.

'Yeah, come on,' said Gary.

'Come on, come on,' said Kev.

The other players, who had maintained straight faces up until now, were laughing. Woodsy — the unflappable Woodsy — knew something was definitely going on.

'OK, I give up Kev . . . what is it?'

'Why do you keep asking me? Do you think I'm the leader? Do you think I'm the leader of the gang?' said Kev.

'Oh yeah,' added Gary.

Woodsy shook his head as everybody else laughed.

'I'll see you all down the Globe then boys,' said Robbo, 'and Woodsy, keep away from the kiddies' playground.'

There was more laughter and it was making Woodsy paranoid. Everybody was in on the joke except for him.

It was often the case after matches that most of the team would go back to the Globe for at least one drink. Some of the single lads like Butch, Kev, Stan and Rusky would make an afternoon of it — a super Sunday — settling in for the televised match. Rusky had been getting a lot of ribbing recently, particularly from Kev Hardaker whose company he was working for as a plumber's mate. Rusky had met his new girlfriend, Claire, on a night out in Milton Keynes a few weeks before Stockgrove won the league. Claire was sixteen and although Rusky wasn't much older, Kev couldn't resist teasing the lad. 'You coming into work tomorrow or have you got to help Claire with her homework?' was the standard sort of line Kev would come out with. Rusky didn't mind. Kevin Hardaker had been good to him, supplying him with work and paying for his driving lessons. Rusky hadn't been in the Globe since he started seeing his girlfriend. The day the league was clinched, everybody except for Danny and Lloydy went back to the Globe. Rusky was the last player to arrive, holding hands with Claire as he walked in.

'Heads up! Here they are, love's young dream!' bellowed Kev, whilst Butch, Phil and Willo gave out wolf-whistles. It was precisely the kind of reception Rusky had warned Claire to expect. The next few minutes however, Rusky had not anticipated. Kevin Hardaker walked over to Rusky and shook his hand. 'Glad to see you here mate. And you must be Claire. Very pleased to meet you,' he said, shaking the girl's hand gently. Every player from the team followed suit, shaking the hands of the young couple. Even Sammy and JC, who had already met Claire, were prompted by Kev Hardaker to go over and shake hands. For a moment, Rusky and Claire felt like royalty. Only for a moment though. In a finely tuned pincer movement, Kev, Gary and Butch upended the startled Rusky. He was carried outside, as the other players and the Globe regulars followed, scattering the resident geese as they did so. On the count of three, he was thrown into the canal. Sammy and JC were still laughing when the other players grabbed hold of them and repeated the feat. The three bedraggled youngsters emerged from the canal looking at each other in disbelief. Fortunately, nobody had lost their wallet or keys, just a bit of dignity.

'What do you look like boys?' said Emlyn. 'Come on lads, follow me,' continued the landlord. They were led upstairs to shower and then change into some of Emlyn's ill-fitting clothes. The youngsters stood for a moment looking at each other and shaking their heads. Sammy was the first to laugh followed by Rusky and JC. It was their coming of age as players for Stockgrove. If the young men harboured any lingering doubts about being accepted, they were dispelled when they plunged into the murky water of the Grand Union Canal.

'Sorry Claire,' said Kev, 'we were just showing our appreciation to the three lads.'

Claire smiled back without saying anything. She knew the players were all a bunch of overgrown children from Rusky's description of their antics. Now she had seen it with her own eyes. After her initial shock at seeing her boyfriend in the canal, she had to admit it was quite funny, especially with the other two being thrown in as well.

More wolf-whistles went up when the trio returned downstairs to the bar. Sammy and JC were wearing tracksuit bottoms and Welsh rugby shirts that swamped them. Rusky stood in a pair of shorts, football socks and a Cardiff City shirt that bellowed over his skinny frame.

'Oh my word, boyos! God help Welsh rugby and the Bluebirds if you three are the future!' said Emlyn.

Rusky walked over to Claire and shrugged his shoulders, 'I told you.' Claire held his hand and kissed him on the cheek. The rest of the afternoon and as it turned out, the rest of the season, Rusky, Claire, Sammy and JC were not allowed to spend any money in the Globe. The other players and Emlyn insisted on that. It was a simple generous gesture that showed the trio of young men belonged. And Claire was Rusky's girlfriend, which meant that she belonged too. Claire liked that.

Kimberley Woods arrived with Helen and Melissa. Kimberley noticed as soon as she saw her husband.

'Oh John, why is it always you they get?'

Woodsy was still unaware what had happened until his wife ran her fingers through his hair and showed him the glitter on her hand. There was uproar in the pub as Woodsy finally twigged what Gary and Kev had done. It had been over an hour since he put the hair gel on his head. Through the steamed-up mirror in the changing room he hadn't noticed, and when he had washed his hands afterwards, he still hadn't noticed. Woodsy went to the pub toilet to check in the mirror the results of Hardaker and Sweeney's handiwork. The pranksters had been subtle. They only doctored Woodsy's tub of hair gel slightly, but every time his hair caught the light it shimmered and he could see traces of glitter on his shoulders. He walked back into the main bar and was greeted by singing.

'*Come on, come on, come on, come on, come on . . . do you wanna be in my gang . . .*'

Now that he was aware, Woodsy could see traces of the glitter everywhere: on his trousers, his pint-glass and on some of the other people he had come into contact with.

The Globe would normally be quiet at five o'clock on a Sunday afternoon. The busy lunchtime period in the bar and restaurant would be over and the pub would usually be preparing for the evening trade. The restaurant was always busy from seven o'clock onwards and the main bar would also do good business on a Sunday evening. Today there had been no respite for the Globe employees. The Stockgrove players had been there since one o'clock and the regulars at the Globe, like Tony Smith and the others, were enjoying the day and talking to each other about the Liverpool trip. Matt Baker wasn't there; he was in Wigan visiting Caroline as he would regularly over the coming months. The Pope, Julius Caesar and the rest of the boys were all present in their civilian clothing and laughing about the weekend up north. The only ones in fancy dress today though were Rusky, Sammy and JC in their Welsh rugby shirts and Cardiff City top. Danny and Lloydy had been unable to come back to the pub after the match but they would hear all about their friends being thrown in the canal. The next time they went to the Globe, they would be prepared.

Emlyn had been kept busy serving behind the bar with Big Frank, and many of the drinkers were beginning to order bar meals. They still had a whole evening's drinking ahead of them and they had to keep their strength up. By mid-evening, some of the players had reluctantly gone home. Helen gently reminded Robbo he had work in the morning and Kimberley Woods informed her husband he could stay if he wanted to, but she had the car keys and it was a long five-mile walk home if he didn't leave now. JC and Sammy left shortly after with Rusky and Claire and gradually more players began to leave.

The pub was still busy as it filled up with its regular Sunday evening customers. Kev, Butch and Stan were the last players to leave the Globe that night. Between them, they had played a part in clinching the league title, terrorised their own goalkeeper and brought about a temporary revival in glam-rock. They had handed out involuntary swimming lessons and seen Emlyn and his wife laugh at the three teenagers in Welsh attire — happy Dais. They had just one more issue to resolve.

'Indian or Chinese?' said Butch.

CHAPTER FOURTEEN

Three weeks had passed since Stockgrove won the title and it was now confirmed that the club would not be continuing next season. Robbo was pleased their last ever league match would be on a Sunday, and not in midweek as it so often was at the end of a season. Not only that, it was May Day Bank Holiday weekend and everybody could have a drink at the Globe after the match without having to worry about work the following day. The day after Stockgrove won the league, Robbo was suffering more than the second year boys he took cross-country running. He didn't think he'd had that much to drink in the Globe, but he obviously had. It had been a good day, like so many in the past when the team had celebrated at the Globe and in the early days at the Stockgrove Arms.

Today would be the last day Robbo would have to collect the players' subs and wash the kit. The end of an era. He had no regrets. He was sure in his own mind his personal decision to retire was the right one. He had mixed feelings about the club folding. In some ways, it would be nice if the club continued even though it wouldn't be the same. Years of happy memories were tied up with Stockgrove Football Club, but it was no good hanging on to the past. Robbo didn't want to see the club continue if it meant it was going to be like some punch-drunk boxer trying to recapture former glories. The club he had co-founded had gone out at the top with dignity and that was the best way to go.

Before the players got changed, Kevin Hardaker was the first to pay his subs. It was the first time in all the years he had been playing that this had happened; paying his subs before a match and without being prompted. Robbo knew it was too good to be true as Kev pulled the coins from his kit bag. All in one and two penny pieces, he began counting the money into Robbo's hand.

'You horrible git!' said Robbo, laughing as he did so. 'Just throw it all in the pocket on the end of my bag and if it's so much as a penny short I'll be sending the boys round.'

Then Gary paid his subs and his too was all in pennies. Then Butch and the rest of the team all followed suit handing over their shrapnel, the highest denomination being a five pence piece.

'There you go Robbo, that should ensure you have a bit of Jimmy Floyd,' said Kev.

'Jimmy Floyd?' said Robbo.

'Hassle at the bank,' replied Kev.

'You bunch of strokers,' said Robbo, borrowing from Gary's vocabulary. The zipped pocket of Robbo's kit bag was bulging more than Butch's lunch-box. It was a home game for Stockgrove and Robbo would have to pay the ref his match fee, so he was relieved he had already been to the cashpoint that morning. Normally he'd pay at the end of the match but today he went to see the referee before the game. He handed over two notes and laughed when the match official said he didn't have any change.

'Don't worry, keep the change,' said Robbo.

When he returned to the changing room, Robbo was

bombarded with sachets of washing powder. They were all free samples from a supermarket and there were dozens and dozens bouncing off him and lining the changing room floor.

'Mr Sweeney and Mr Hardaker I presume,' said Robbo. It couldn't be anybody else responsible for supplying all the players with the sachets that were launched at the club secretary.

'I don't understand. It must be biological. Why does everybody automatically blame us?' said Gary.

'Come off it Gal, that innocent expression won't wash; it's time to come clean,' said Kev.

It looked like it could be another eventful day and Woodsy had treble-checked his boots and gloves for signs of sabotage before he took to the field. There was a large crowd for a league game, thirty-two to be precise, and most of the players' partners had come along to watch, together with a few of the boys from the Globe. Stockgrove won the match with two first-half goals from Macca. Danny and Lloydy replaced Sammy and JC at half-time and Leon Wilson made way for Rusky. The match was played in more light-hearted fashion than usual, but still seriously enough to win. The final whistle was the signal for Gary to sprint to the sidelines and collect the two cartons of eggs that Melissa had with her. Kev wasn't far behind in collecting the flour and both men ensured every Stockgrove player was soon covered. Despite his protestations, Tommy was covered too, but Kev had the good grace to remove the Scotsman's flat cap before he got him. One half of the pitch looked like a set from *Tiswas*, all that was missing was Sally James and Houdi Elbow. During a lull in the battle, the Stockgrove players found time to shake flour-covered hands with their opponents.

Washed and changed, Woodsy was relieved he hadn't been

singled out for special attention. Robbo had been the subject of the stitch-up before the game and nobody had escaped the post-match omelette. Better to be safe than sorry though, and Woodsy would leave his hair au naturel today. Danny and Lloydy were prepared for their inevitable dunking in the canal, wearing old jeans and T-shirts and carrying a spare set of clothes in the car.

The Globe was much busier than it was the day the league title was celebrated. It was a fine sunny day and there were lots of people sat outside making the most of the warm, holiday weekend weather. As soon as Danny and Lloydy arrived in the pub, they were upended, carried outside and launched into the canal to the amusement of everybody watching. With that bit of unfinished business taken care of, the serious drinking could begin.

The Globe was busy all afternoon and evening with people attracted by the good weather and all-day barbecue. The Stockgrove players and all the wives and girlfriends were there. Leon Wilson's little boy had been at the match that morning with his mum, arriving to watch the last twenty minutes. He couldn't understand why Daddy had his football kit on but wasn't playing football with the rest of his friends. His dad tried to explain about substitutes but it wasn't easy explaining to a three-year-old; it was easier explaining the offside rule to Denise. Not that Willo totally understood the law himself. At the end of the match, Benjamin Wilson wanted to join in with the flour and egg fight and cried when Mummy said he couldn't. 'The silly men and Daddy are just being childish,' Denise Wilson told her son. Then, back at the Globe eating his burger, Benjamin watched as his father helped throw two people into the canal. This being an adult lark wasn't as simple as it appeared; junior Willo would be having a serious chat with the other toddlers at the nursery to see if all dads behaved like this.

Fortunately, John Woods's two young children weren't present to see their dad becoming steadily drunker as the afternoon and evening wore on. After three or four pints, his guard had slipped. He thought the beer didn't seem right, but attributed the flavour to the burgers and onions he had been eating regularly throughout the afternoon. Gary and Kev had taken it in turns to engage Woodsy in conversation whilst the other man slipped the vodka into Woodsy's pint on the bar. He was such an easy target but it still amused Gary and Kev.

Later that evening, Joe Mortimer came in with his wife and the entire bar began singing 'Danny Boy'. Many days had passed since that night in the Spinners' Arms in Wigan, but Joe still didn't know why every time he walked in the pub there were people singing his favourite song. The arrival of Joe and the first singing of 'Danny Boy' led on to 'Wonderwall' and all the other songs that had been sung on the coach on the way to Liverpool.

Kimberley Woods decided it was time she and her drunken husband were leaving.

'Come on John, you've had enough for one night, let's go and pick the kids up from Mum's and go home.'

'One more drink sweetheart,' said Woodsy.

'Don't sweetheart me. Look at the state of you. Come on, we're going *now*.'

'Oh, come on babe, let's talk about it.'

'No, John, I don't want to talk about it.'

That was the cue for Woodsy to launch into song.

'I don't wanna talk about it, how you broke my heart . . .' He was sounding more Rodney Trotter than Rod Stewart and he couldn't remember any more words apart from those he had sung. It didn't matter though because Gary, Kev, Butch,

Stan, Emlyn, Big Frank — everybody — had picked up on the song and were serenading Kimberley, '. . . *And the stars in the sky don't mean nothing to me . . .*' Her frown was replaced by a slight smirk and then a big smile. The whole scene was so ridiculous she had to see the funny side as the men were linking arms and crooning to her. And in the middle of all his silly football mates was her husband, struggling to remember the words and drunkenly singing his own version one line behind. Out of sync, like Lee Van Cleef in a spaghetti western he was opening his mouth, '. . . *blue for my tears, black for the mirror, talk, talk about it . . . my har-aaaa-art. . .*'

At the end of the song there was a big cheer and Woodsy told Kimberley how much he loved her. Her husband's touchingly romantic gesture would probably have meant more to Kimberley if Woodsy didn't then go on to tell each of his remaining team-mates how much he loved them too.

Three hours after Kimberley dragged her husband from the pub, Emlyn rang the bell for last orders. Most of the team had drifted off home already, but Stan and Butch were still there as ever, and joined Emlyn and some of the regulars in having a late drink in the restaurant area. The next time everybody would be together was in a month's time for the end of season presentation and dinner.

CHAPTER FIFTEEN

The end of season awards were held at the Globe, as they were most years, with the entire restaurant being booked by the Stockgrove party and their guests. Compared to some of the celebrations at the end of the season, it was a low-key affair. There was a three-course meal and Tommy presented the awards. Sammy Koonphool was awarded Players' Player of the Year and Tommy nominated John Woods as Manager's Player of the Year. Robbo and Tommy both made speeches thanking all the players. Butch said a few words on behalf of everyone, thanking Robbo for all the effort he had put into running the club over the years. Butch had already confirmed his retirement along with Robbo and so too had Macca, Phil and Woodsy. The remaining players would all be joining new clubs next season. It was the end of an era and it meant that the tournament in Thailand would be the last matches played by Stockgrove FC.

The final award of the evening was presented by Gary Sweeney and it was given to his good friend, Robert 'Stan' Bowles for his over the top goal celebrations in the home match of the National Cup. Gary had made a special effort as it was the last time the award would be given. At Gary's request, Melissa had bought a vibrator at an Anne Summers party. Gary had sprayed it gold and mounted it on a wooden base with the engraving, 'Stroker of the Year'.

'There you go Stanley. It gives me a special buzz — but not as big a buzz as it gave Melissa — to present this to you.'

Inevitably, the evening was full of talk about the impending trip to Thailand. With the exception of Sammy, of all the people going only Gary Sweeney had visited the country before. He had spent time in Bangkok and Pattaya on the way to the World Cup in Japan. Gary had a bundle of tickets for all the England group matches and he was delivering them to a friend of a friend who lived in Pattaya.

The ticket-touting thing was more of a sideline for Gary. He knew plenty of people who acquired bona fide tickets, usually from sponsors, and he'd sell them on at a healthy profit. Gary's lifestyle meant that he had lots of contacts in the football world. Gary could sell stuff to his mates at Stockgrove, but that was just pin money. Like any businessman, networking was important to Gary and he had good contacts amongst the Spurs chaps, which made it easy to sell his wares. In the main, Gary sold clothes. There was always a ready market for designer clothing and had been for as long as Gary had been involved. From the Pringles and Fiorucci jeans of the early days to Stone Island, Prada and Paul Smith. He had contacts with lads in various parts of the country via his Spurs mates and more notably from following England abroad. The trips to watch England play abroad were self-financing for Gary. He could watch the match, have a holiday in a foreign country, enjoy the culture and enjoy the shoplifting. Gary found it easier to steal clothes abroad and he wouldn't have to steal too much; five jumpers and half a dozen shirts could easily rake in five hundred pounds. It wasn't just clothing and tickets for Gary. He would sell anything from paintbrushes to golf clubs. He even took orders and if he didn't have it in stock, he soon would.

When Gary travelled to England matches, he nearly always travelled alone and usually he'd take a circuitous route. He wasn't the subject of any banning orders, but he was known to the police and the least amount of attention he drew to himself the better. It was no good arriving on direct flights from England with all the other loons clutching their Head bags to their shoulders. He'd do his business on arrival and then meet up with people later. One of the few times Gary made an exception was the World Cup qualifier in Italy in October 1997, when he travelled together with Stan.

Gary had a wad of tickets for the match, all with sponsors' names on. He knew he'd be making a profit out of real fans who were going to matches, but it was business. Supporters who travelled thousands of miles to watch their national team play. Often they would travel without tickets prompting the anger of FIFA and UEFA. The governing bodies of football could not understand the mentality of a football fan travelling to watch a match without a ticket. They could never understand what drives people to go to these matches because they don't share the same passion as the supporters. Fans know they can travel to any match and get a ticket. Champions League matches, European Championship matches and World Cup matches; there were always tickets available if you were prepared to pay enough money. The flourishing black market existed partly because so many tickets were given to sponsors. Some of the tickets went to genuine football fans who were lucky enough to work for one of the big companies who provide huge financial backing to the major football tournaments. However, many more tickets went to people who had little or no interest in football and were keen to make a quick financial killing by selling on their tickets to agencies and touts. The tickets would be sold on the black market at inflated prices to the fans who had already spent a small fortune merely travelling to the country hosting the game. The poor football fan was being fleeced, not just by the cost of the tickets, but by airlines and hoteliers. Airlines and hotels would claim their inflated prices were a result of supply and demand at the time of tournaments and big matches, but it was usually blatant profiteering. And it was people from the British Isles who seemed to suffer the most. Not just England fans, but also those from Scotland, Wales and Ireland because they all travelled in such large numbers and followed their country's football teams in their thousands. There would never be enough tickets to meet the demand of all the supporters who travelled. Many fans just went to enjoy the carnival atmosphere and the ambience of the host towns and cities, and to be able to say they were there. Sometimes they'd find fellow supporters who had a spare ticket for the match and they'd be able to buy it at something close to face value. Other times they'd begrudgingly pay the inflated prices of the ticket tout or even directly from opposition fans. So often, you see English, Scots and Irish in the section officially designated for the other team. And for every fan that gained access to the ground, there would be another one watching in a local tavern or on a big screen in a piazza. The governing bodies of football would claim that without the financial backing from the sponsors there would be no tournament. This was nonsense as Gary and Stan well knew. The tournaments could exist without sponsors but not without supporters. The more supporters that filled the stadiums and watched on television, then the greater the market was for the advertisers and the more exposure that there would be for the sponsors' products. Half-empty stadiums with no atmosphere aren't sexy. Some of the money went back into the game helping develop grass-roots football worldwide and that was commendable, but how much more went into inflated salaries for football bureaucrats and mandarins?

Stan and Gary didn't know how many managers and players fully appreciated some of the sacrifices fans made to watch their teams. Players and managers would come and go; the fans were the only thing that remained constant. And the thing that wound Gary up the most was when players failed to acknowledge the supporters at the end of the game. Not so much at home matches, but at away matches watching Tottenham and England. It didn't matter what the score was, or how good or bad the team had been. How much effort did it take to walk thirty or forty yards to the pockets of away support and thank them for spending their hard-earned money? The players were privileged to be professional sportsmen. Stan would point out to Gary how much dedication and effort the players needed. Particularly in their teenage years, many footballers would have to make sacrifices whilst they saw their friends going to parties and nightclubs.

Stan was himself dedicated to his running. It was a passion for him that, like football, helped him forget his mundane job and unhappy personal life. He never thought as a teenager he'd be a professional sportsman, but he did expect to have more out of life than two failed marriages, a work-desk piled high with planning applications and an overdraft and credit card debt that would embarrass several small African countries. When he was clocking up the miles and training for his next marathon or half-marathon, he could temporarily forget the slings and arrows that life had thrown at him.

Gary Sweeney on the other hand was very happy with life

when the two men arrived in Rome in 1997, enjoying the warm autumn sunshine. Business was going well for Gary and the Italy trip would be a lucrative excursion. Stan had never been to Italy before, but Gary had been on a number of occasions and had travelled extensively throughout the country. He was far removed from the media stereotype of a hooligan. Well dressed and urbane he took the opportunity to see something of the countries he visited. He would spend the obligatory one evening of drinking in the Irish theme pub of whichever European city he was in. There was always a 'Murphy's' an 'O'Neill's' or a 'Flanagan's' wherever you were: Rome, Stockholm, Munich or Vienna. And on England trips, wherever there was an Irish bar there were large groups of Englishmen, without any hint of irony, singing anti Irish Republican songs. Gary would usually see faces from past England matches and it was a good opportunity to do a bit of business, buying or selling tickets and finding out the best places to go 'shopping.' Principally he was there to watch football, but he was still a businessman and a few items pilfered from Signor Armani or Signor Osti would finance his trip.

Gary liked Italy. The food and climate were most agreeable and the country was oozing with history and culture. Rome in particular was one of Gary's favourite cities. He enjoyed taking Stan to see the Coliseum, Vatican and other sights. On the day of the Italy match, they had lunch near the Trevi fountain.

'No offence Stan,' said Gary, 'but I'm in one of the most beautiful cities in Europe, enjoying a nice lunch in a romantic location, and the only thing spoiling it is your ugly boat on the other side of the table.'

'None taken,' laughed Stan.

The small restaurant was full with mainly English football

supporters. There were a few women in there with their husbands or boyfriends, but mainly it was men sitting in groups and discussing the prospects for the match that night, and joking with the Italian waiters about how many goals England would score.

Over the coming years, Gary would notice more women and children at England matches, home and away. As a result of Euro '96, it suddenly became trendy to watch football and there was positive discrimination by the FA in the ticket allocations to families. Gary didn't see that as a bad thing. He knew that whatever happened in the future, the core support at England matches would always be young men like him. He also knew it was almost inevitable that there would be trouble at some stage in the lead up to, or after the match. The reputation of England football fans went before them. Whichever country they were in, the local hooligan population would come out to taunt and provoke the English. Not that the English needed any provocation. There was enough inter-club rivalry that always surfaced at England matches, home and away. That afternoon Gary and Stan had been talking to an Oxford United supporter who had been glassed the night before, not by an Italian, but by a Swindon Town fan. All England fans drinking together and the poor lad had drunkenly said something that his attacker had taken offence to. Next thing he knows, his mates are leading him away to hospital for stitches. Gary had seen this rivalry at virtually every England match he had been to and this was to prove no different. It had surprised Stan. He couldn't understand how this could happen between fellow countrymen all there supposedly to support England. He could only assume it was the same thing that made young men fight in towns and cities the length and breadth of Britain on Friday and Saturday nights; too much drink. But at England matches, it wasn't always the drink that led to violence, although that was a large contributory factor. It was more about not letting people take liberties with you. People would lay out their flags and sing their songs all proclaiming their pride to be English. They had taken over a small part of a foreign land and they would protect it if attacked. It would antagonize the local hooligans as much as the Scots taking over Trafalgar Square in the days of the Home Internationals, had antagonized the English.

After lunch, Gary and Stan found a small bar near the Spanish Steps. The atmosphere was good with a mixture of tourists, locals and football supporters all mingling and chatting freely. It was just after two o'clock in the afternoon and the bar was lively but was far from being packed. The two men sat at a table next to three Italian women who were sharing a bottle of wine.

'You come to watch the football?' one of the women asked.

'That's right. Is it that obvious?' joked Gary.

'England are a good team but Italy will be too strong for you. The Azurri will win 2-1!'

Ever the pessimist, Stan agreed with the Italian woman.

'Bloody hell Stan, I'll get you a ticket in the Italian end and you can applaud Zola when he scores the winning goal!'

This had everybody laughing and the two men enjoyed a pleasant twenty-minute conversation about football and Italy in general, before the women said they had to go back to work. They were already half an hour late and they wished the men good luck for the match. During the twenty minutes they had been chatting, the bar had filled up considerably and there were a few Italian supporters wearing football shirts, who were chatting with the England fans. The men were enjoying the bottles of Nastro Azzurro and the first chants of *'Eng-er-land, Eng-er-land,'* were heard. It was the perfect place to enjoy a pre-match drink. The locals were friendly and both men were quite happy. They'd had a good lunch and they could spend a couple of hours in the bar before going back to the hotel and then on to the Olympic Stadium.

They were treated to a cabaret when a very small man of about forty stood up and started singing. He was wearing the red 1966 World Cup shirt and with his balding pate and missing teeth, reminded Stan of Nobby Stiles. He was about four foot ten and his mates encouraged him to stand on a chair. They called for quiet as he started singing his song. The other fans around him listened and then joined in when invited to. Gary and Stan both joined in too.

'I know a bear from Jellystone Park, Yogi, Yogi,
I know a bear from Jellystone Park, Yogi, Yogi Bear.
Yogi, Yogi Bear, Yogi, Yogi Bear . . .'

Within a few minutes the whole bar, Italians included, were watching and listening to Nobby singing, first about Yogi's friend BooBoo, and then BooBoo's girlfriend Suzy and her various sexual pecadilloes. Everybody was laughing and joining in the chorus, as ever more inventive ways to bring in 'bear' characters were introduced into the song. From Danni Behr, to Huggy Bear to the footballer Phillipe Al-*bear*, they were all included and the bar was rocking with laughter. The scene amused the Italian bar staff, who couldn't have understood half of the references and sexual innuendoes. But just as everybody was about to find out what Suzy did with 'cu-cum-bear', the sound of windows being smashed brought an abrupt end to proceedings.

A gang of twenty plus Italian football hooligans had driven up to the bar on scooters, thrown bricks and rocks through the windows and then sped away as quickly as possible. Hordes of angry Englishmen piled out of the bar to chase their attackers. By the time the last of the drinkers had left the bar the *carabinieri* were on the scene. There were some Italian men, wearing helmets with visors to disguise their faces, stood behind the police openly taunting the English fans. Gary had been one of the first out of the bar and by the time Stan got outside, he could just make out Gary away in the distance with five other England fans. It was a forlorn chase and the scooters were able to dodge the pedestrians and easily evaded their pursuers. When Gary and the others returned, the *carabinieri* were busy trying to arrest two English men who had been quietly minding their own business. Some Italian fans were pointing them out and accusing them of attacking one of them an hour earlier. It was a cowardly accusation to try to get two innocent people arrested. The owner of the bar told the police that both men had been in his bar at the time of the alleged attack. The Italians were making cut-throat gestures to the English fans and the police watched and did nothing, except for move on the large group of Englishmen who were congregated outside on the pavement.

'Fucking cowards,' said Gary when he came back. 'Did you see 'em Stan? Fucking cowards. Throw a few bricks, injure some innocent people and then have it on their toes. They never show up in England and if that's the best they can do at home . . . wankers.'

The five other men who had been chasing the Italians were all Doncaster Rovers fans and they were agreeing with Gary.

'You're right mate. They never show at Wembley; nobody does. We'll see what they've got tonight when everybody's together.'

Only two of the Yorkshiremen had tickets for the match and Gary took the opportunity to sell three of his remaining twenty tickets. He only charged the men ten pounds above the face value for the tickets. The men had briefly been comrades in arms and Gary appreciated that. He was already comfortably in profit from ticket sales and whatever he sold now was icing on the cake.

Gary knew that Stan wouldn't get involved in any fighting and he respected him for that. Stan was just one of the many thousands who went to enjoy the match and have a few days holiday. It had been a surreal scene outside the bar as lines of *carabinieri* and police cars had formed to separate and escort away the English supporters. People were walking up to the Nobby Stiles look-a-like and were shaking his hand and asking him about the remaining verses of the Yogi Bear song. Stan had been talking outside with an extremely attractive blonde English girl as he waited for Gary. She looked familiar but Stan had been scared to say he recognized her from somewhere. That would sound like a chat-up line with double helpings of mozzarella and gorgonzola.

'Did you see that Sophie what's-her-name?' asked Gary, as the two men walked back to the hotel.

'Who?' said Stan.

'That blonde bird from EastEnders. The one who plays Ricky Butcher's older sister . . . Diane, is it?'

Only then did the penny drop for Stan. Doh! In addition, there were even people shouting 'Ricky, Ricky!' Nobby Stiles had been doing Mike Reid impressions, 'G, g, g, gooooo . . . run around now!' and still Stan hadn't made the connection with the girl he had been talking to.

'Shit! That's who it was. Of course!' said Stan.

Stan told Gary about his conversation with the actress he had failed to recognize.

'You stroker, Stan!'

The match was Stan's first time watching England away. They had gone through three different police cordons and were relieved of any coins and lighters. They weren't even allowed to take in bottles of water. Gary had given him a free ticket and both men sat in the Olympic Stadium waiting for the teams to come out. They sat in the official section of England supporters and watched as a previously closed off part of the ground began filling up with ticketless England fans. Better to have them inside was the sensible approach taken by the home authorities. They herded the fans into a penned area inside the stadium and they were allowed to watch the game for free.

Stan was amazed by the vitriol shown towards the England fans by both the Italian fans and the police. Coins and missiles were being thrown at the two separate sets of England supporters. With the police failing to take any action against the home fans, the England supporters who were in the pen began picking up the coins and throwing them back at the Italians. This led to repeated baton charges against them. Stan watched in amazement as after three or four baton charges, the English fans, using nothing more than their fists, ran at the Italian police forcing them back. The police were wearing full riot gear: chest plates, knee protectors, helmets and carrying large sticks. Nevertheless, they were still forced back by a group of a few hundred Englishmen. It was an incredible display of bravado. If Stan had been watching at home on television he would have called it an act of stupidity. But not here in the ground. Actually being here and experiencing the hostility towards the English supporters, he felt proud. He didn't advocate violence in any shape or form, but here was a group of people standing up for themselves and refusing to be bullied. They were fellow supporters who were showing they would take no shit and he admired that.

Just before kick-off, the Italian section to Gary and Stan's left unfurled two huge banners that infuriated the English spectators. Both written in English, one was proclaiming support for the IRA and the other had an obscene message about Princess Diana who had died a few weeks before the match. The Italians threw more coins and missiles and then two flares were fired by the home supporters into the English section. And still there was no police activity in the home end to root out those responsible.

'Is it always like this?' asked Stan.

'More or less. Places like Poland are usually much worse. This is pretty much par for the course. Tomorrow there'll be the usual bollocks in the papers about the English fans causing havoc and that's what it will look like on TV as well. Honestly Stan, all I want to do when I come away with England is have a drink, watch the match, do a bit of business and have a few days holiday. If I want to have a tear-up I can do that at home with much less chance of getting nicked. But you've seen what it's like today. If somebody has a go at me, I'm going to have a go back. You can't let people take liberties.'

Stan listened silently to his friend. They were two very different people with contrasting outlooks on life, but Stan understood exactly what Gary was saying. After the bar was attacked earlier in the day, Stan was aware of a 'them and us' mentality. The police were almost complicit in most of the violence that Stan had witnessed and he had seen the insularity of the English as they had stuck together in large groups. He wasn't naïve enough to think that the English fans were completely innocent. Of course there were some fans intent on violence, he only had to think back to one England fan disfiguring another with a broken glass because of a club rivalry. And then he had seen Gary and the Donny Rovers lads form instant friendships because of their pursuit of the Italian hooligans. It was a strange loyalty, but it was loyalty nevertheless. The self-preservation society.

The singing and support from the England fans was relentless throughout the match. It was a tremendous tactical performance by Glenn Hoddle's men, nullifying the Azurri and deservedly earning the draw that saw them top the group and automatically qualify for the World Cup in France.

After the game, they were herded away from their seats and downstairs towards the exits, but they weren't allowed to leave. For nearly four hours and without refreshment, the English were kept sitting on the concrete floor by the police, claiming it was for their own protection as they cleared the outside area of all Italian fans. The English fans sat quietly and for the most part, patiently. Stan reasoned that the English fans had shown a quiet dignity. There was no singing or antagonism, just a morbid acceptance of the sort of treatment they had become accustomed to. There were a few wisecracks and the black humour that all football fans seem to specialize in. And amongst it all, three men dressed in boiler suits and carrying cardboard cut-out Mini Coopers: one red, one white and one blue. The English had come to Italy and done the job. The self-preservation society indeed, mused Stan.

The day after the match, Gary and Stan enjoyed another leisurely stroll around the city before catching their flight back home that evening. It was the perfect way to end. A beautiful city, glorious sunshine and groups of Englishmen smiling smugly as they mingled with the Romans.

They bought copies of the Italian sports paper *Corriere dello Sport* and sipped cappuccinos at a pavement café, wearing their Ray-Bans. They could easily have been mistaken for Italians were it not for their self-satisfied grins and the fact they couldn't understand what the newspaper was saying. The Italian papers were as fulsome in their praise of the English team as they were scathing on the performance of the home side. Gary and Stan may not have understood what had been written, but it was clear the Italians were 'guttedo' and England's performance was 'topo drawero'. Happyo dayso.

CHAPTER SIXTEEN

As Neil drove home from school with Helen, the local radio station played 'Eton Rifles'. The track had appeared on Kev Hardaker's National Cup compilation tape.

'What does this remind you of love?' he asked his fiancée.

'What?'

'This song. Does it remind you of anything?'

'Not really. Why?'

Robbo had so many things in common with his future wife but sadly, music was not one of them. He'd sing along to a Madness CD at home, serenading Helen with his version of 'It Must Be Love', but he had never managed to convert her to Paul Weller and the band. That was one step beyond. Helen's musical tastes were more Celine Dion, Michael Bolton and Robbie Williams. The latter Robbo could tolerate but the former two he could not; Celine Dion Dublin and Michael Bolton Wanderers was how Robbo referred to them.

"Eton Rifles'...The Jam...Kev's tape on the coach trips...'

'Oh that,' said Helen, indifferently.

It had been the best part of four months since the Stockgrove trip to Liverpool, but the lads would still talk about it when they saw each other. In the Globe over a few jars, it was amazing how often the conversation would come round to the National Cup days. 'Happy days,' Gary called them. 'Happy fucking days'. And every time people spoke about the games and days out there was laughter. Happy days indeed, thought Neil Roberts as he drove home with Helen. It was the last day of the school term and the trip to Thailand was just five days away.

As soon as the trip was announced, many of the players were asking Sammy questions about his homeland.

'How hot is it in July?'

'Is it monsoon season?'

'What about mosquitoes?'

'Is there any English food over there?'

The Thai youngster had answered them all in his usual, quiet, polite manner. Sammy could have flown out three days before the others, but he told his father he wanted to wait and travel out with his friends from Stockgrove. After the trip to Thailand, Sammy would be returning to England to study for his business degree at the University of London. He was still considering whether to sign for Chesham United. Sammy still had hopes of becoming a professional footballer, but he was sensible enough to know it would be a lot of hard work if he was to fulfil his personal dream and at the same time keep the promise he had made to his father about obtaining his degree.

Neil and Helen were in holiday mood as they drove home from their last day of work. Joe Koonphool and the people at the Nok brewery had taken care of everything. All Neil had to do was fax a list to Nok head office in Bangkok of the names of all the people travelling. The Nok head office arranged all the flight tickets via an agency in London and Robbo had received them the week before. Similarly, all the hotels, transfers and internal flights had been taken care of.

It was a welcome change for Robbo not having to organize anything. When he had received the flight tickets, he called people to let them know and they came round in person to collect them. That way, if anybody lost the ticket or missed the flight it was their problem. Too often in the past he had mollycoddled the players, and even with this trip some of the lads were relying on Robbo for everything, asking him about visas and inoculations. Helen couldn't believe that these men were unable to find out the answers themselves, but Robbo just accepted it.

'Honestly Neil, some of them are worse than bloody kids.'

Robbo hadn't thought of it like that, but Helen was right, the lads had come to rely on him too much over the years. For Robbo that didn't matter now. He just wanted for the trip to go smoothly and for everybody to enjoy their free holiday courtesy of Joe and Nok brewery. All together, including wives and girlfriends, there were twenty-two people flying to Thailand. At least, that's what everybody thought.

CHAPTER SEVENTEEN

Steve and Vicky Bennett were the first to arrive at Heathrow and they sat near the Qantas check-in desk waiting for the others. Steve knew how lucky he had been to have his name drawn out of the hat. He may not have played for the club this season, but he had played plenty of games for Stockgrove in the past and as far as he was concerned, he was as deserving as anybody of a place on the trip.

The desk wasn't due to open for another thirty minutes and the couple sat patiently as gradually more of the party arrived. Within forty-five minutes of Steve and Vicky arriving, everybody was present except for Butch. Neil rang his friend's mobile but it was diverted to voicemail. Robbo left a brief message. The check-in desk hadn't been open long, there was no rush they'd wait for Butch and all check-in together. As the group waited, some standing and others sat, they were chatting excitedly about the trip. Robbo began to think again about the amount of time he had actually spent playing football and socializing with these people. Some he had known since school and they had watched each other grow up, get married, have kids, get divorced and get drunk. There'd been many good times on and off the pitch in the fifteen years he had been involved with Stockgrove Football Club and it was a little odd to think they would be playing their last match six thousand miles away from where they had played their first. Robbo's phone rang.

'Shit! You're joking . . . OK, mate . . . You'll try and get on the flight tomorrow . . . Yeah, I'll tell them. OK, Butch . . .'

The assembled group were now looking with concern at Robbo, but he couldn't keep up the pretence, his smile giving the game away. 'Butch is just parking-up, he'll be here soon.'

'You had me going for a minute,' said Helen.

'You donut Robbo,' said Willo.

When Butch appeared, Robbo was the only one not surprised to see Kevin Hardaker with him. Kev had obviously given Butch a lift down, some of the group began to think as they caught sight of the two men. Now he was coming in to wave them off and wish them well; a nice touch on Kev's part. Then as they got nearer, Stan commented, 'How long does Butch think he's going for? Look, he's even got Kev carrying one of his bags for him.'

When the two men reached the others, it was Kev who spoke first before anybody else had the chance. 'Right, what are we waiting for, let's check-in.'

'Well done mate, it's good to see you,' said Neil Roberts as he shook his friend's hand.

'Cheers Robbo. I wouldn't have done it without you and I'm not quite there yet. This is the easy bit. I've still got to get on the bloody thing yet!'

Helen, confused, looked at her fiancé. As Robbo explained to Helen, then so Kev began to tell the others as they approached the check-in area.

When Kev announced in the Globe that his fear would prevent him from going to Thailand, Robbo was as surprised and shocked as anybody. The day after Kev had told everybody, Robbo drove over to visit him to see if there really was no chance. His friend spoke frankly about what actually happened on that flight to France, how he had panicked and cried. Kev was becoming distressed just retelling the story and Robbo for the first time appreciated just how deep Kev's phobia was. It shocked Robbo to see his friend like that. Kevin Hardaker was a wisecracking individual who it seemed had won life's lottery. Lots of money, a successful business, no shortage of female company and a bundle of charm that made him instantly likeable. The more Robbo thought about it, the more he couldn't believe that somebody as positive and as happy-go-lucky as Kev couldn't get over his phobia. Robbo had spoken to Helen about it, but hadn't gone into detail about Kev's story. His friend had asked him not to say anything such was his sense of shame and failure.

Robbo began to research phobias on the Internet. He was surprised to see just how common the fear of flying was. He read about the various successful cases where people had managed to overcome their fear through hypnotherapy. Over the following weeks, Robbo contacted practitioners explaining the situation. The feedback that he got convinced him that if Kev could make that first step and go and see somebody, then he could be helped. That first step Kev would have to make for himself, nobody could do that for him. When Robbo went to see Kev again, he told him about his research and handed him the printouts about the successful cases. Kev thanked his friend, but he had already done his own research over the years and convinced himself that his case was different and was beyond help. But Robbo persisted, telling Kev he was one of the most positive people he knew. Even if he couldn't fly to Thailand, what was the harm in seeing a hypnotherapist who may be able to help him overcome his phobia in the long-term. Kev knew Robbo was right. He had missed out on enough holidays over the years and would continue to miss out unless he could conquer his phobia. The persistence of Robbo began to change Kev's opinions, but mostly it was the thought of letting the other lads down. When Phil had told Robbo he wouldn't be able to go to Thailand because Michelle was pregnant, Phil apologized. Kev had the same feeling of letting his friends down; letting the rest of the team down. Of course neither man was letting anybody down, but it was their own sense of loyalty and camaraderie that dictated their feelings. Since the trip had first been announced, Kev had grappled with his phobia again. It was something he didn't have to confront very often, but now here it was resurfacing. Robbo had told him it was a brave thing to talk about it in the pub in front of the other lads. Kev agreed that he had surprised himself that night and now Robbo was telling him he had taken the first step in conquering the phobia. He had told his friends and nobody had ridiculed him. Everybody agreed the trip wouldn't be the same without him and now Robbo was going out of his way to help him. Even if it didn't work, Kev owed it to Robbo and his team-mates to at least try.

'Fuck me, Robbo, you're like an old woman the way you go on! All right mate, I'll give it a go.' He stipulated a couple of conditions that Robbo agreed to. Firstly, it was to be kept completely secret that he was seeing a hypnotherapist. Secondly, Kev wanted Robbo to go with him to the initial appointment, 'Not to hold my hand, but if you come with me Robbo then I can't bottle out at the last minute.'

In the meantime, the list of names had been given to Nok in Thailand and Steve Bennett had already been drawn out of the hat as Kev's replacement. This didn't concern Kev or Robbo at that stage, the first hurdle was to attend that initial

177

meeting with the hypnotherapist.

Kev's first appointment with Dr Robinson had been in mid-April and now just over three months later Kev couldn't believe the progress he had made in such a short space of time. After the third meeting, he was feeling positive enough to book his own flight ticket to Bangkok ensuring he was on the same flight as the others. That gave him a double incentive. His friends would be there and once he made it to the airport and told them he was going his own pride wouldn't let him back out. Not only that, but he had also spent nearly six hundred quid of his own money, plus the money for treatment sessions.

In June, he flew to Paris for the weekend. He did it on the spur of the moment as a last minute booking. He was feeling positive and only had three days from the time he booked it to the time he flew, so he didn't have too much time to talk himself out of it. He was apprehensive as he approached the airport and had to remember his breathing exercises. Kev had reasoned that if he could fly to Paris, the monkey would be off his back. He was scared when he boarded the plane, but he did it. He was still scared, but he controlled his fear. The weekend was a personal triumph for Kev and as soon as he got back, he rang Robbo from the airport. Nobody else knew — not even Helen — it was just Robbo and Kev. Then a week before the Thailand flight, Kev told Butch he'd be on the plane to Bangkok. Butch was sure it was some kind of a wind-up until he spoke to Robbo who confirmed everything.

And now here they all were, checking-in for the flight to Thailand, and Kevin Hardaker talking about his achievement and the part played by Neil Roberts. Helen was holding her boyfriend's hand, she was so proud of him and not in the least bit angry that she had been kept in the dark as Kev had requested.

'I'm going to have to watch you Neil Roberts if you're so good at keeping secrets. When we're married you could be up to all sorts of mischief.'

'How do you know I'm not already?' said her boyfriend.

Helen playfully punched Neil on the arm.

As the plane picked up speed on the runway, Kev was apprehensive about take-off. He knew that feeling would probably remain with him whenever he flew in the future. Take-off and landing would be the most stressful, where different noises could be heard and it would be easy to convince himself the aircraft had some sort of fault.

He remembered what he had been taught by the hypnotherapist and once the aircraft was flying level he could relax with the others. Before long, he was enjoying a drink and the in-flight movie. He was soon flirting with the forty-something stewardess, a formidable looking woman who even Kev was struggling to charm.

Neil Roberts thought how great it was that everybody could make the trip. Only Phil Whitaker and Michelle were missing. Michelle's pregnancy had been a difficult one. The baby would be their first and Robbo thought about his friend Phil as he watched the movie. He thought about the days gone by when Butch would go clubbing with Kev Hardaker. Robbo and Phil tagged along occasionally, watching Butch and Kev who were irrepressible. Kev was the one with the chat, the gift of the gab, and Butch was his wing-man with the big reputation. The man who all the ladies wanted to see if he really was that well-hung. Kev hadn't changed too much over the years, he was still a tart, but Phil was a family man and the happiest he had ever been in his life, and so was

Robbo with Helen.

The twelve-hour flight was nowhere near as bad as Kev had imagined. He had plenty to keep his mind occupied. For the first few hours of the flight, there was plenty of banter with the other members of the group. Nobody had actually asked the question they all were thinking, 'How are you Kev, are you OK mate?' The man had managed to deal with his phobia and he was respected for that, there was no need to be insensitive and draw attention to it just when he seemed to have conquered his demons. There was a time and a place for mickey-taking and this wasn't it. If Kev suddenly started getting a panic attack when they were thousands of feet in the air, then nobody would know how to react. After watching a couple of films and having something to eat, some of the group were able to sleep. Kimberley Woods had to nudge her husband when he began to snore. Robbo was reading the Tom Clancy book he had bought the year before but had never got round to reading. The long flight gave him the opportunity to get into it at last, but he still found himself regularly checking his watch and the screen in front of him detailing the route and current location of the plane.

As the aircraft made its descent into Bangkok airport, the people on the left hand side were amused to see a golf course next to the runway.

'You wouldn't be able to play there Tom, not with your slice, you'd be a danger to incoming flights,' said Robbo to his golf partner sat behind him. Robbo was suddenly aware that Kev may have heard and it may have got him thinking about his phobia again. He shouldn't have worried. Kev didn't hear him and neither did Tommy. The Scotsman's ears hadn't cleared properly from the altitude descent and he just smiled and nodded at Robbo's comment, assuming that he had been talking about the golf course because that's where he had been pointing.

After a short delay at passport control, the group collected their baggage and walked through to the arrivals hall. Sammy led the way and he soon spotted his father in the waiting crowd. Joe Koonphool was there with a colleague and two female members of staff from Nok brewery who were placing garlands of flowers around their guests' necks, *waiing* in traditional Thai fashion as they did so. Similarly, Joe and his colleagues *waied* and then shook hands with every one of the visiting group, as they were welcomed to Thailand. The first dozen people in the Stockgrove group had managed to avoid the taxi touts, but the remainder were not so fortunate as a barrage of men in suits with official looking passes and clipboards bombarded them.

'Hello, sir, where you go?'

'You want taxi?'

'Hello, sir, this way please, taxi . . .'

Sammy rounded up the stragglers and dismissed the unwelcome taxi touts as he escorted everybody towards the people from Nok. Even as the group were making their way to the coach that would take them to the hotel, those at the back were being subjected to a fresh group of taxi touts. The Stockgrove party walked outside to wait for the coach to drive round and collect them. As they did so, they encountered the heat for the first time since they had left the air-conditioned comfort of the terminal building. It was hot, but not as hot or as humid as Robbo or Helen thought it would be. The sky was grey and there were spots of rain in the air. As they got on the coach and drove along the expressway, the view of Bangkok wasn't as they had imagined either. They had seen plenty of books and brochures on Thailand, but none of them showed pictures of the airport expressway. The number of modern high-rise buildings surprised them, as did the absence of any major traffic. The M25 was far worse than the infamous Bangkok traffic. Then as the coach exited the expressway and headed towards downtown Bangkok, they changed their opinion about the traffic. It was gridlocked, and the last couple of miles took over an hour and a half as the coach finally crawled its way down Silom Road to their hotel, the Holiday Inn.

'Oi, oi, Robbo! Bit different to Haydock. There's no space for any racecourse around here,' commented Gary who, like everyone else in the group, had been amused to find out they were staying at the Holiday Inn.

'Let's hope this one brings us better luck mate,' replied Robbo.

Joe left the group to check-in and said he would be back at six o'clock to escort the group to dinner. It was three o'clock now so it gave everyone time to shower, unpack and have a catnap. Joe, Sammy and the Nok delegates said their farewells and headed off to the Nok headquarters in nearby Siam Square. Dinner that evening would be the last time for three days that Joe Koonphool would see the group until they flew to Chiang Mai on Tuesday. He had arranged for a tour guide to take care of the Stockgrove party in his absence.

The Koonphools lived in a five-bedroom house with its own grounds in a smart residential area in the Bangkok suburbs. They also owned a luxury condominium in town and this is where Sammy and his mother would be staying for the next three days. Joe Koonphool had business to attend to and would be driving down to Rayong the next day before flying up to Chiang Mai ahead of the others.

The Stockgrove party were all enjoying a drink in the wonderfully named 'Cheers Bar' at the hotel when Joe,

Ladawan and Sammy Koonphool arrived on time at six o'clock. In his dealings in Europe, Joe was accustomed to arriving at meetings on time. However, it was not the same in Thailand. In Thailand, scheduled meetings would often take place hours after the original time and in some cases, the following day. Sammy was also very punctual in England, but after a few weeks in Thailand he would revert to 'Thai time'.

The Koonphools led the group to the Skytrain station where they took the elevated electric train to Sukhumvit. When they arrived, Joe led the group down a dark side road.

'Bloody hell, where's he taking us,' whispered Woodsy to his wife. Then they saw a bright display of lights ahead and the restaurant where Joe had made the reservation, 'Cabbages and Condoms.'

'Have a word!' said Gary Sweeney when he saw the name of the restaurant. Tommy and Sylvia looked at Sammy who smiled and assured them that the food was excellent. They walked through the outside dining area, which was dotted with trees and foliage festooned with brilliant white fairy lights. It was a beautiful garden setting that they walked through on their way to the 'Condom Room,' where they would be dining. Joe explained that there were other similar restaurants in Thailand set up by a group promoting the use of contraception for family planning and AIDS prevention. The proceeds went to the charity and there was a shop on site where you could buy souvenirs. The restaurant was beautifully set out and the food was superb. At the end of the meal, each diner was presented with a side plate containing two items: a mint and a condom. Tommy and Sylvia were chuckling as they received theirs.

'What am I meant to do with this?!' laughed Tommy.

'Put it in your mouth and suck it Tom, but I'm not sure what you do with the mint,' responded Kev, making everybody laugh.

As Joe spent more time with the group over the coming seventeen days, he would get to know the characters that Sammy had talked about in his phone calls home. He had already met the players when he attended the National Cup game against Erdington Casuals. Joe had also met Big Frank and the supporters from the Globe who had dubbed him 'top man.' The Thai man would learn a few more expressions over the coming weeks, but tonight he wanted to try out the phrase he had already learnt.

'Ah yes, good joke Kevin, you are top man.'

This nearly brought the house down. The way Joe had said it was hysterical. A highly amused Kevin Hardaker could only say, 'No Joe, not me, *you* are top man. Absolute quality.'

Sammy had told his father about Kev, the man with the phobia for flying who had used hypnotherapy to control his fear, and who had paid for his own flight and accommodation in order to join his friends from football. Friendship and loyalty had motivated Kev to seek help for his phobia. Joe was hugely impressed by the story when his son had told him earlier that evening. At the end of the holiday, Joe would discreetly present Kevin Hardaker with a cheque, courtesy of Nok, that more than covered his expense. Kev was right — Joe really was top man.

Amidst the laughter, Joe quietly called for the bill paying with his personal credit card. He didn't want anybody to know he was paying for the meal out of his own pocket. This was a private thank-you gesture to the group from Stockgrove. They had all helped to make his son's stay in England an enjoyable one. The other diners protested when Joe was paying, insisting on paying their share.

'No problem. Don't worry, I pay with company credit card; business lunch,' fibbed Joe Koonphool.

CHAPTER EIGHTEEN

The following morning, Sammy and his mother arrived at the hotel with the tour guide. The guide introduced herself as 'Bunma, but you call me Ma, no problem.' Everything was 'no problem' in Thailand. Joe and Sammy said it frequently and it was a phrase the Stockgrove group were to hear many more times. Sammy explained that it was about keeping your cool. *Jai yen yen, mai pen rai,'* the Thais would say.

The group had enjoyed a good night's sleep, which helped them to shake off some of the effects of the long flight. It was a beautiful morning in Bangkok with clear blue skies and the temperature was already over eighty degrees as they walked to the Skytrain station. From there it was a short journey to the river pier. This was how Neil and Helen imagined Bangkok as they made their way upriver in the tour boat. There was an English commentary from Ma as she pointed out landmarks and places of interest. As they motored their way along, the Chao Phraya River was alive with activity. Longtail boats were ferrying tourists towards the canals, known as khlongs, and there were ferries full of commuters and schoolchildren with Buddhist monks stood at the back in their saffron robes. Improbably small tugboats were pulling huge waterborne cargo trains hundreds of feet long. The congested Bangkok roads seemed a world away as the tour group took pictures capturing the colourful riverside scenes. Luxury hotels and condominiums jostled for space amongst the shacks and wooden buildings housing restaurants and markets. On their left, they saw Wat Arun a large five-pronged temple and then on their right, the shimmering rooftops of Wat Phra Kaeo and the Grand Palace, looking majestic as the sunlight glimmered. A myriad of colours: gold, white, green and azure were caught in the click of the cameras as the tour party snapped away. Ma handed out bottles of ice-cold water that were gratefully accepted.

They disembarked and walked towards the entrance of the Grand Palace where children selling postcards, and women selling parasols and souvenirs were encouraging people to buy their wares.

'Only one hundred baht, good price. You like, how much you pay?'

The group weren't hassled though when purchases were gently declined.

'No problem madam, good holiday for you.'

'You buy later, sir, I give discount for England man.'

The tour group had been asked to dress respectfully and the men wore long trousers and the women made sure their shoulders and knees were covered. Sammy had advised everybody the night before they had to wear a shoe that covered their heel and they watched as two backpackers wearing flip-flops were declined entry. The temple at Wat Phra Kaeo was one of the most important sites in Thailand housing the revered Emerald Buddha. The players, wives and girlfriends were surprised at how small the figure was sitting atop its high pedestal. They wandered around the sprawling complex with Ma the tour guide describing the various buildings. Then next door, they visited Wat Po and the massive gilded figure of the Reclining Buddha, its sheer size contrasting with the diminutive Emerald Buddha. There were monks in saffron robes mingling with the tourists from all corners of the globe. Local people were making offerings to Buddha images and there was a school within the temple grounds, which had children outside playing basketball. And everywhere the group went, there was the smell of jasmine and incense. This was the Bangkok Neil and Helen had seen in the holiday brochures, but the pictures only told half the story. For the young couple it was the smells and sounds that made the whole scene so memorable.

By now, it was lunchtime and the group were tired and hungry. They left the temple complex and were taken by Ma to an unlikely looking restaurant.

'Is this where we're eating?' asked Stan, looking worried. 'It doesn't look very clean.'

Sammy assured him there was no problem. 'Don't be fooled by appearances Stan. It might not look much, but judging by the number of local people eating here, it must be good.'

The restaurant was in a wooden building, which was open-sided and located in a small side road away from most of the noise and pollution. Ladawan Koonphool and Ma both spoke with the proprietor. Tables were soon being pulled together and more plastic chairs hastily brought out to accommodate the large group. It was a tight squeeze, but they were all seated as the menus appeared and Sammy, Ladawan and Ma were bombarded with questions.

'What's this one like?'

'How hot is this one?'

'Which one isn't too spicy?'

All the questions were politely answered and the group

ordered their meals opting for safe combinations of rice and vegetables, or rice with chicken or pork. Butch and Kev ordered a beer but everybody else had water or a fruit shake. The meal was good and even Stan, a confirmed meat and two veg man, said he quite liked it. Robbo asked for one bill and insisted that the tour guide, Sammy and his mother would not be allowed to pay for their meal. Instead, Robbo divided the bill up evenly between the other diners leaving a generous tip. The parsimonious Kevin Hardaker was the only one to query the amount, not because it was too high, but rather the opposite.

'Is that right Robbo? Surely, it's got to be more than that. Have they included the drinks?'

The bill was correct and the three Thai people *waied* to the rest of the group in respect for their meals being paid for. After lunch, they all walked back to the pier and took the boat back downriver towards their hotel. It had been a tiring day with the effects of the heat taking its toll on some of the group. Ma advised them it was best not to try to cram too much sightseeing into one day. Today was only Sunday and they still had all day tomorrow and most of Tuesday before they caught their flight to Chiang Mai. When they arrived back at the hotel, Ma asked them if there was anywhere in particular they would like to go whilst they were in Bangkok. Helen automatically said the floating market and virtually the entire group agreed.

'No problem, we can go tomorrow morning but must leave 7 a.m. Not too early for you?' said Ma

'Too early for me love, I'm on holiday,' joked Butch.

'OK, you can sleep, everybody else go, but you must take care your health and have sleep for beauty,' replied the tour guide.

Her turn of phrase endeared her to everybody and

Butch was the first to agree he did need his beauty sleep. The women in the group unanimously agreed they wanted to go shopping that evening. Even on holiday, Robbo was organizing and he suggested that everybody do their own thing for the remainder of the day. They had all been given maps of the city and had an idea of how to get around. The Skytrain was easy enough and there was no shortage of taxis and tuk-tuks, the noisy little three wheel vehicles that will take you anywhere if the price is right. By splitting up into smaller groups, nobody could complain they were doing something they didn't want to do. They could ask the tour guide, Sammy or his mother for recommended places to visit.

'This good IQ,' agreed Ma to Robbo's suggestion, 'maybe you take my job and I play football Chiang Mai.'

Everybody had warmed to the young guide and her sense of fun.

'That's right Ma, you come and play football with us, but you have to shower with us after the match,' teased Kev.

'No problem for me, but I think you not like, I fat too much,' responded the guide, despite the fact that she had a figure that most Western women would kill for.

As the women chatted to Ma about the best places to go shopping, the men began to discuss their own plans. Those with wives and girlfriends reluctantly agreed they had best keep on the right side of their better halves. They had only been in Thailand for twenty-four hours and there'd be plenty of time for having a beer, but that evening if the girls went shopping then they would be going too. That left the single men to make their own entertainment. Sammy would be staying at home with his mother, so it left the four youngsters; Rusky, JC, Danny and Lloydy, and the three veterans; Stan, Butch and Kev.

'Everybody will think they're our kids,' commented Kev.

'Grandkids more like,' replied Rusky.

'Cheeky git.'

Kev was pleased with Rusky's backchat. The young lad had toughened up a lot mentally in the past year and wasn't as introverted as he had once been. This was no doubt due to the youngster's working environment. The other plumbers would take the mickey out of each other in the same way as the Stockgrove players did. The lad was becoming accustomed to working on building sites and if he didn't want to become the butt of all the jokes then he'd have to learn to dish it out instead of taking it all the time. Kev and Butch had taught him that and it was good advice for the young Rusky. When he socialized with the Stockgrove lads, it paid to be quick witted and he was learning fast. He was still seeing Claire and the young couple were as disappointed as each other that Claire couldn't join her boyfriend in Thailand. She was in Florida with her parents on a holiday that had already been booked and paid for by the time the Thailand trip was announced. 'Never mind Claire,' Butch had told her, 'you can always go to Thailand for your honeymoon. Isn't that right Rusky?'

Unlike Rusky, the other three young men — JC, Danny and Lloydy — were still at school. When the students first started playing for Stockgrove, some of the senior players were wary because they had preconceived ideas about public schoolboys. Neil Roberts had told the older players that the youngsters were all talented footballers and that was all that mattered. When Robbo said this, he knew it wasn't all that mattered. He knew better than anybody that the youngsters would have to fit in and be accepted and that wouldn't happen on the basis of football ability alone. They'd have to endure the mickey-taking and get on with lads from different social backgrounds. There was never any problem. The youngsters were all very good players and in Sammy's case, exceptional. They were well-spoken, polite and exuded confidence that belied their years. The contrast between the public schoolboys and Rusky was stark. The apprentice plumber wasn't as self-assured and lacked the social skills that the public schooling had given the others. Perhaps Rusky's lack of self-confidence emanated from an alcoholic father who regularly beat him and his mother until he left them three years ago. Kev had been like a father to Rusky in the short period they had known each other, and at first it didn't seem fair to Kev that the three public schoolboys enjoyed all the advantages and benefits that Rusky didn't. Despite the apparent differences, Rusky had many things in common with his peers. They were all the same age and liked the same things. They shared a common love for football, computer games and girls. Danny was into the same music as Rusky, 'that bloody hip-hop techno dance shit,' Kev called it, showing his age as he did so. Kev was pleased that Rusky got on so well with the other youngsters and they had all gradually become bolder and cheekier towards the senior players. They'd take the piss out of Butch's beer belly and Robbo's receding hairline and then, on Monday morning at school, it would always be 'sir' or 'Mr Roberts', when they spoke to their sports teacher.

Butch suggested to the other single men that they should hit the town later on and investigate the infamous Bangkok nightlife.

'Have a few beers and check out a go-go bar, eh lads?' he suggested.

'Don't you lead them astray,' said Helen.

'Don't worry I won't,' replied Butch.

'I'm not talking to you Butch, I'm talking to the four youngsters.'

Ma confirmed the details for the following morning's trip

to the floating market and, bowing to peer pressure, Butch agreed to forego his lie-in the following morning and join the others.

It had been a tiring few hours walking around the temples and Grand Palace, and everybody was ready for a siesta in the air-conditioned comfort of their rooms. Ma said goodbye in her own inimitable way, 'Good sleep for you, see you in morning. *Sawat dii kha.*'

That evening, the single men were the first to emerge from their rooms and meet in the hotel bar. They had one beer in there before heading off on the Skytrain towards Sukhumvit. Ma had circled on Butch's map, areas of nightlife and beer-bars where they'd be able to enjoy themselves. There were a lot of circles.

Shortly after the seven single men had left, the other players and their partners began to congregate in the foyer, sitting in the large comfortable sofas as they waited for one another. Leon and Denise Wilson were the last to arrive and the group of fourteen headed for something to eat in the indoor shopping plaza a few minutes walk from the hotel. Once they'd had their fill of various orders of Thai food and pizzas, the women hit the shops with the men tagging dutifully along. The women had already reasoned that the money they weren't spending on flights and hotels meant they could indulge in spending in the shops. Leon and Gary began talking to each other about finding Butch and the others, but Tommy advised them that if they stuck with the women at least they could curb their spending.

'Leave them to their own devices and they'll buy up all of Bangkok,' said the Scotsman.

'Years of experience Tom?' asked Gary.

'Aye, and years of credit card bills,' replied Tommy.

In the first shop they went into, Sylvia Boyle bought a handbag and a pair of shoes and Tommy was already reviewing his previous opinion about being able to curb the women's spending. 'I should have gone with Butch and the others. I think I might be in need of a stiff drink by the end of the night!'

'Don't worry, just how much shopping can you do in a few hours?' said Robbo.

A lot, was the answer. The women were in retail heaven. There were shops selling leather handbags, shoes and clothes all at a fraction of the price in England. Every other shop seemed to be selling shoes, and within an hour all the women had bought at least one pair and Sylvia and Kimberley had bought two. John Woods calculated the women hadn't spent much in real terms compared to back home, but Macca pointed out, 'That's right Woodsy, but we're here for over two weeks. We only came in here for something to eat. The girls said they wanted to look at the street market up the road. At this rate we'll all need to buy new suitcases!'

They made their way out on to Silom Road, which was as usual lined with traffic. It didn't matter what time of day they headed on to Bangkok's streets, the traffic congestion was a permanent fixture. Joe Koonphool said it wasn't unusual for people to live ten miles from their workplace, but still face a three-hour commute each way. The congestion free Skytrain had a very limited range in the city centre and most people either drove or relied on the bus network. The Stockgrove party walked slowly along the street, taking care to avoid tripping over the uneven pavements. Bangkok was not a city designed for pedestrians. The pavements were narrow, uneven, and crowded with vendors selling lottery tickets, fruit and all manner of weird and wonderful food. It seemed you could buy any food you want in Bangkok: smoked fish on sticks, barbecue chicken, grilled grasshoppers, noodles, whole ducks hanging roasted and glazed on bits of string. The group couldn't help but notice that Thai people loved to eat at all hours of the day. Just as the roads were full of traffic at all times, then so they would see people sitting at roadside tables, eating and chatting away on their ever present mobile phones. For the first time since they had arrived, they were really observing Bangkok at night. As they walked, the smells were constantly changing; a waft of durian fruit, a blast of fried chillies, the fragrance of cut flowers. But the noise of the traffic was constant. The ubiquitous tuk-tuk, phut-phutting its way along with its noisy engine, the blue and red buses, the yellow and green taxis and the motorbikes. Hundreds of motorbikes. Sylvia Boyle was shocked when she saw how many people were sat on one motorbike. Often they would see whole families on one bike; a boy of five sitting at the front holding on to the handlebars, then his father sat close behind and driving the bike and behind him the mother carrying an infant in her arms. Some riders were wearing crash helmets to comply with the law but most were not bothering. Children not even in their teens could be seen in their school uniforms giving a lift to two or three of their friends, and everywhere in the traffic there were drivers with their mobile phones held to their ears.

The Stockgrove group reached the side roads of Patpong which were lined either side with bars, their neon lights flashing, *'Pussy-a-go-go'*, *'Kiss-a-go-go'*, enticing passers-by to watch the shows inside. And in the middle of the street were stalls selling counterfeit designer goods: handbags, watches, hats, sunglasses and more bloody shoes! A maelstrom of humanity was jostling for the limited space as people of all shapes, sizes and nationalities perused the goods on sale. There were backpackers, single men, married couples, and amongst them all were the Stockgrove posse. Gary Sweeney began looking at the Burberry handbags and purses.

'Something you want to tell us Gal?' asked Willo, as he saw his friend inspecting two purses.

'I could make fifteen to twenty quid profit on each of these.' There was no need for Gary to steal these purses, the price was low anyway and the lady vendor would always come down in price.

'You like mister? You buy for your wife? Very good copy, make in Thailand.'

'How much,' asked Gary.

'One thousand baht.'

'Too much,' said Gary walking away.

'OK, OK, I give good price for you . . . five hundred baht.'

Gary smiled and turned again as if to walk away.

'OK, sir, how much you give me?'

'I buy ten, I give you one thousand baht,' replied Gary, knowing his opening gambit was far too low and expecting to be haggled to something over two thousand baht.

'Ooooweeee! One thousand baht! Oooh you want me die?' replied the vendor, melodramatically clasping her hand to her forehead and laughing as she did so.

Gary was enjoying the charade with the woman who was basically in the same line as business as he was.

'I'll tell you what I'll do love, and I'm cutting my own throat 'ere, but a grand and a half . . . one thousand five hundred.'

The vendor probably didn't understand anything except for, 'one thousand five hundred.'

'You very tough man, I have young baby. Two thousand baht.'

'One thousand eight hundred,' countered Gary.

'OK, OK,' said the Thai woman.

195

'Job done,' said Gary, pulling out two, one thousand baht notes and handing them over.

The vendor handed him back his change.

'You keep for your baby,' said Gary, as he smiled and gave the two hundred baht back to the woman. Whether her young baby existed or not, the extra money meant more to the Thai lady than it did to Gary. He'd still obtained a bargain and had enjoyed the bartering.

Whilst this scenario was being acted out, Steve and Vicky Bennett were at a stall a little further up. Vicky was delighted with her Burberry purse as she walked back to see the others.

'Look Melissa, only eight hundred baht, I haggled him down from one thousand,' she said, excited by her bargaining prowess. Melissa didn't have the heart to tell her about Gary's bulk buying discount.

'Ooh, that's lovely Vicky.'

Butch, Stan, Kev and their four young protégés had finished their meal at McDonald's and were sat in a beer-bar off Sukhumvit Road. In a land renowned for its magnificent cuisine, they had been unable to resist the lure of the golden arches.

'You need a bit of stodge inside you if you're going out on a session,' Stan had said.

They liked the bar the moment they entered. Like many others, it was open-sided and they sat in bamboo chairs cooled by the ceiling fans above. There was a dance area and a live band who played a mixture of Thai and Western songs. As they had walked in, a young waitress had escorted them to a table and asked what they would like. This had happened in the hotel bar too, but they didn't think it would be the norm, expecting as they did to stand at the bar and wait. This was far more relaxed as the young lady took their order.

'Seven Pavarottis please,' said Kev.

The waitress smiled but clearly didn't understand. 'Seven . . . ?'

'Sorry sweetheart, seven large Singha's,' confirmed Kev.

The waitress wrote on her pad, smiled and went away. Kev had already decided that a large bottle of the local beer — a large Singha — would be a Pavarotti, and with the same logic, a small Singha would be a Kylie. The young JC knew the beer was correctly referred to as 'beer Sing' but this was no time for pedantry. If you said Singha beer Thai people understood what the *farang* meant.

Sammy had spoken about the farangs in Thailand, which was a term referring to all foreigners, but specifically Westerners. The Thai teenager explained it was a word in common use and they would hear it a lot. It was not normally used in a negative way or as a term of abuse, but in the football tournament they would be referred to as the 'farang team'.

A few minutes later seven bottles of Singha were on the table.

'Moment please, I get condom for you.'

The group looked at each other. 'Did she say what I thought she said?' asked Kev.

'Christ, I know you're good with the ladies Kev, but that's ridiculous!' said Stan.

The waitress reappeared with seven multi-coloured polystyrene drinks coolers and eased the bottles into each one simply saying, 'Condom,' as she did so. She then placed the drinks chitty into the holder on the table and looked around to see if anybody else was waiting for a drink. It was all very civilized. Every time drinks were ordered, a new chitty was added to the others and the bill would be settled in one go when they had finished. What a great system they all agreed. No arguing about who's going to the bar or whose round it is. Just call the waitress over from the comfort of your chair, place your order and divvy up the bill at the end of the night.

'What a fantastic country, can you imagine this in England?' commented Butch, as he sank back in his chair listening to the band playing 'Hotel California.' Despite the heat, humidity and traffic, or perhaps because of it, the Thais seemed to be very service oriented.

The waitress reappeared with seven ice-cold face cloths, which served to reiterate Butch's point.

The four teenagers were smiling at a table of three Thai girls behind them. The girls would make eye contact, smile and then look coyly down at their drinks.

'All right boys, I hope we're not cramping your style,' said Stan, as he noticed what was happening. Butch and Kev were looking, now that Stan had drawn attention to the lads' behaviour.

'You behave yourself Rusky, you're practically a married man,' said Butch.

'She won't know, she's in Florida.'

'That's right,' said Lloydy, agreeing with Rusky, 'while the cat's away . . .'

'Well that's a shocking attitude I must say,' joked Kev. 'I can't believe you youngsters today; all you want to do is drink and shag . . . fair play!' he concluded, clinking bottles with each of the teenagers.

Butch agreed. 'Some things never change, eh Kev? Think what we were like twenty years ago.'

'Speak for yourself Butch, I was still at primary school reading *Janet and John* books. Stan'll tell you . . . he was the teacher!'

Stan added dryly, 'Yeah, that's right. And Kev was the only student in a class full of five-year-olds to have passed his driving test.'

Kev clinked bottles again, this time with Stan for his witty riposte.

The seven men were joking and laughing as more beer was ordered. As the night progressed, they got talking to three men from Newcastle who were on holiday. They told the Stockgrove lads they were having an easy night as they were flying to Ko Samui in the morning, but the night before they had been on a bar crawl all along Sukhumvit Road and were now recommending places to visit. Just after eleven o'clock, the Stockgrove group left and wished the Geordies a good holiday. The teenagers were now waving at the girls they had been smiling at for most of the night and Danny blew them a kiss.

'It's a bit late for all that boys, now that you're leaving,' stated Kev. 'Looks like you might have to watch and pick up a few tips from the old master.'

'Yeah, very old master,' replied Danny cheekily.

As the men stood outside, a girl in her early twenties carrying a clipboard approached Stan.

'Excuse me, sir, you speak English?'

'I should hope so, I *am* English!' said Stan.

'Oh, you work in Thailand?'

'No, I'm on holiday here.'

'Welcome Thailand, good holiday for you.'

The girl had an official looking pass clipped to the pocket of her white polo shirt. 'I work for tourist company, we make survey of holidaymaker in Thailand. Take only two minutes. You can help me please?'

'Of course,' agreed Stan. How could he refuse this charming young lady? The girl handed Stan the clipboard and he began writing out the appropriate answers: Robert Bowles; local government planning officer; 27–40 age group; holiday; first visit; my favourite thing about Thailand is the friendly people.

As Stan was filling out the form, the girl was engaging in polite conversation. Stan was telling her about the football tournament in Chiang Mai, and she in turn was wishing Stan's team good luck and telling him how much she loved Michael Owen and David Beckham.

'My team Manchester United,' Stan told her.

'Same same me!' replied the young girl excitedly.

When Stan had finished writing, the girl pointed out the detachable slip at the bottom of the form, which gave details of a prize draw. The first prize was a two-week expense paid holiday in Thailand. The second prize was the equivalent of five hundred pounds worth of shopping vouchers and the third prize was a guided tour of Bangkok. There were one hundred first prizes to give away and five hundred each of second and third prizes.

'Thank you very much, sir. You write for me hotel name and room number and if you win somebody call you.'

As Stan was writing his hotel details he said, 'I only stay Bangkok until Tuesday then go Chiang Mai,' speaking in the same manner as the Thai girl, dropping words but still conveying the meaning.

'No problem, tomorrow they make draw for prize, good luck for you, good luck in Chiang Mai. England football number one!'

Stan was charmed again by the young Thai woman. The other six were looking at their maps whilst Stan was filling out the questionnaire.

'No, that's the direction we came in. What were those places the Geordies were talking about?' asked Butch.

'Soi Cowboy and Nana Plaza,' replied Rusky.

'Trust you to remember,' said Butch. 'Well I can't see Soi Cowboy, mind you it sounds like a bit of a gay area if you ask me, loads of blokes in stetsons, checked shirts and moustaches.'

'No, it sounds more like Kev's building company, they're a load of cowboys!' said Rusky. The other three youngsters exchanged high-fives with Rusky as they all laughed. Butch was laughing too.

'Nice one Rusky.'

'Fuck me Butch, don't you encourage him, that's all I need …plum and plumber!'

The group were in good spirits and eventually Butch found Nana Plaza on his map.

'Ah, look, there it is, Nana Plaza, it's one that Ma has circled already,' said Butch.

'Well if it was already highlighted, why have you just spent five minutes looking for it? You should get your eyes tested mate,' advised Kev.

Rusky, fortified by the Thai beer, agreed. 'You're getting old Butch, either that or too much wanking!'

'Sadly, you're right on both counts young 'un,' conceded Butch, clipping the teenager round the back of the head as he did so.

JC was talking to Stan about the lady with the clipboard.

'You're a dark horse Stan. She was lovely.'

'Yeah not bad. Plenty of life in the old dog yet.'

'OK boys,' announced Kev. 'Let's jump in one of those fuck-fucks or whatever they're called and see what this Nana Plaza is all about. We'll probably get there and it'll be a poxy shopping centre.'

Butch hailed a tuk-tuk and as he was negotiating a price, Lloydy flagged down a yellow and green 'taxi-meter'. The three veterans clambered into the back of the tuk-tuk and sped away. The four youngsters got in the taxi and followed for the short journey to Nana Plaza. A price of fifty baht had been agreed for the taxi ride, which was twenty baht cheaper than Butch's negotiating skills had managed with the tuk-tuk driver. The traffic was still heavy, but aided by some nifty driving and unusual and unique interpretation of traffic signs, the tuk-tuk driver arrived fully five minutes before the taxi.

Nana Plaza was not the shopping centre Kev had feared. It was a three-storey complex of bars and go-go joints. The men's eyes lit up as a gaggle of attractive Thai women greeted them, each one trying to entice the group to drink and spend money in their particular bar. One girl took Danny by the hand and led him to the bar where she worked. She sat Danny in a chair, gave him a cold flannel to cool his brow and proceeded to gently massage his shoulders. The other men watched on.

'Looks like we're going in this bar then,' said Kev. They walked across to the open-fronted bar and joined Danny. More women came to greet them, and they were soon comfortable as they sat back in their rattan chairs and ordered a round of Pavarottis. They were all being pampered by different women now, but the women's attention was diverted when a group of eight middle-aged Japanese men walked in. The Japanese men were immaculately turned out in shoes, smart trousers and crisply ironed long-sleeve shirts. By contrast, the Stockgrove lads were wearing trainers, shorts and T-shirts. It was a no contest. The Japanese looked like they had more money and the girls weren't stupid. If they could keep the Japanese men happy and tempt them into a few 'extras' then the girls would reap the financial benefits.

'What's that all about then?' asked Rusky. 'How come

they're all over us and then they do the off?'

'Ah, Rusky. So young and so much to learn,' said Kev. 'You didn't think they were interested in us for our boyish good looks and witty conversation did you Rusk?'

'Well . . . I thought . . . you know . . . we might have been in.'

'Give them enough money and you could have been in — and out — and in and out all night, if you get my drift,' said Kev.

Butch sniggered at Kev's comment. 'Kev's right, you youngsters really have got a lot to learn. Once we've finished these beers we'll try one of the go-go bars upstairs, all right?'

The teenagers couldn't drink up quickly enough as Butch and Kev described what was likely to be going on in the go-go bars.

'How come you two are such experts?' asked Lloydy. 'I thought you'd never been to Thailand before.'

'I've never been to the North Pole either, but I know it's bloody cold!' said Kev.

As they were finishing their drinks, the Japanese men left the bar and the girls rushed eagerly back to the Stockgrove lads.

'Too late for that now girls, you should have thought about that before you disappeared with the Japs,' said Butch. 'Mind you, if any of you want to inspect my Jap's eye at close range you're more than welcome.'

The girls were all over the Stockgrove players now, sitting on their laps and putting their arms round the men's shoulders.

'I'm not an easy pull,' quipped Kev.

The men were all laughing at the fickleness of their admirers. Butch and Kev were half tempted to stay, but the teenagers were practically salivating at the prospect of the go-go show. They settled their bill, left a large tip and left the bar. The girls were imploring them to stay.

'Where you go darling? Stay, I show you good time.'

'You forget me already.'

'I love you handsome man.'

At every bar the men passed, the scene was the same. One or two girls would come out and try to persuade the group to go inside. They could see Western men playing Connect Four with Thai ladies whilst others were having their shoulders and egos massaged by exquisitely beautiful young women. It was *Fantasy Island*, but it still didn't prepare them for what they were about to see in the go-go bar, as they walked up a small flight of stairs to the second floor of the entertainment complex.

Kev was the first to enter the go-go bar and was soon struck on the head by a ping-pong ball. It didn't take long to find out where the errant ball had come from. The youngsters were open-mouthed as they looked across at the stage. The three older men looked at each other with big grins on their faces.

'That's why the Orientals are so good at table tennis. I never saw Desmond Douglas do that!' exclaimed Kev.

A willowy Thai woman in her mid-twenties, with long silky black hair was sat on a small stage area. She was wearing nothing more than a pair of black high-heels as she sat, legs akimbo, performing a display of such dexterity, that nobody who witnessed it would be able to watch table tennis again without a smile on their face. The teenagers watched in amazement as ping-pong balls were fired into baskets placed strategically around the stage. Every now and then, as somebody walked into the club, a ball would be fired at the newcomer to the approval and laughter of the assembled crowd. There were nearly as many women in the audience as men. It was far removed from the dirty raincoat clientele the teenagers had been expecting. The woman finished her act to great applause.

'Joking apart lads, that must take years of practice to achieve that level of vaginal control,' said Stan.

'You're right mate, I wonder how many days a week she trains. Must play havoc with the neighbours, ping-pong balls bouncing off the walls at all hours,' said Butch.

They could have been Hansen and Lawrenson talking about how Beckham spends hours on the training ground perfecting his free kicks.

'I reckon I could do that,' said Kev, pausing briefly to set up the gag, before adding, '. . . everybody reckons I'm a tight twat.'

It was exactly the sort of self-deprecation that everybody liked about Kev. He never took himself too seriously.

The next performer on stage surpassed her colleague. Lighted candles disappeared and then reappeared, still burning. Then, as the Stockgrove players collectively grimaced and scrunched their noses up, razor blades were inserted into the woman. The teenagers sat, transfixed. They were drinking small Singhas now — Kylies — whilst Butch, Kev and Stan ordered a bottle of local whisky. In between the individual displays of vaginal acrobatics, topless beauties danced seductively round poles. 'Lucky bastards. I'm moving to Gdansk,' cracked Kev.

There were definitely worse places to spend the evening. 'What are those numbers on their knickers?' asked Rusky, as he noticed a small white disc on the girls' bikini bottoms with a number written in black.

'It's how they do the Thai lottery. And to think we get Dale bloody Winton!' said Kev.

Stan revealed the real reason to the youngsters.

'Do you mean if we want to shag one of them, we just call one of the staff over, she tells the girl and —'

Butch interrupted Danny. 'All right son, don't get over-excited, but yeah, basically that's how it works . . . apparently.'

The youngsters couldn't believe it and the older men were also tempted to have a go on the Thai lottery, but their bottle went. If they had lost their bottle they only had to look at the next performer on stage, as the lights were dimmed and the theme music from *Star Wars* was played. She positioned herself over an empty bottle of whisky and slowly lowered herself until the whole thing disappeared. She stood up to the applause of the crowd with the bottle still hidden from view. The woman then walked — a feat in itself — to the edge of the stage where a bald, heavily perspiring man eagerly caught the bottle as it was released from its temporary internment. And then the climax, so to speak, of the show. A glass container with a live frog was placed on the centre of the stage. No, surely not thought the incredulous Stockgrove players. Christ, they'd like to hear David Attenborough narrating this; *Wildlife Up One*. The amphibian went the same way as the bottle, but this time there were no eager volunteers to catch the thing. The woman lay on the floor, arched her back and lifted her pelvis before projecting the frog back into its container.

'Un-be-fucking-lievable,' said a stunned Butch. 'And to think I only popped out for a newspaper and a pint of milk.'

'I'll tell you what,' said Kev, 'they should prescribe this place for anybody suffering with conjunctivitis. It's a real eye-opener. Let's give it five minutes boys. After watching that bird with the bottle, I've got to see how they collect the empties in this place.'

CHAPTER NINETEEN

Butch was woken up by the phone ringing in his room.

'Wakey, wakey, Mr Butcher. Good night last night?'

'Robbo? Shit, what time is it?'

'Half-six. The coach goes in about half an hour. So, heavy night was it?'

'You could say that. Listen mate, you'd better call the others to make sure they're up as well.'

'I'm just about to. See you downstairs.'

The tour party congregated downstairs and were waiting for the last three to show up. The four youngsters: Danny, Lloydy, JC and Rusky were talking with Sammy and his mother about the nightlife in Bangkok, when Butch, Kev and Stan emerged from the lift, looking and feeling terrible.

'Here they are, the oldest swingers in town,' said Helen. 'God, you look awful.'

'Cheers Hels,' was all Kev could manage in response.

'I don't understand,' teased Helen, 'the young lads over there look fine.'

'Yeah, but they weren't drinking what we were,' said Butch.

The three men had started drinking the local whisky, *Mekhong*, and had got through one bottle and were halfway through another when they left. They were amazed when the waitress gave them a ticket as they were leaving. It looked like a raffle ticket and the waitress explained that next time they came in, they just had to hand over the ticket and the half-full bottle they had left would be served to them. Thailand really was geared up to customer satisfaction.

'Never mind chaps, you can have a sleep on the coach,' said Robbo.

Ma laughed when she saw Butch, unshaven and bleary-eyed. 'Now I think you need sleep two weeks for have beauty,' she said.

'I think you're right love,' said Butch.

The coach took just under two hours to arrive at Damnoen Saduak with a brief refreshment stop on the way. When the coach arrived at the car park, they were the first tour group to arrive. They made their way on to the 'James Bond boats,' as Ma referred to the longtail boats, which slowly ferried the group along the canal to the floating market area. They passed houses on stilts with children playing in the water and adults washing. Ma had told them the water here was clean unlike the canals in Bangkok seventy miles away. As some of the group took photos, the children smiled and waved. Then the boats veered on to another canal and soon they could see the thriving activity of the market. They disembarked the longtail boats and stood on the wooden platforms on the side of the canal surveying the busy scene. It was a kaleidoscope of colour with boats laden with fruit and vegetables: red and green chillies, bananas, rose-apples, pineapples, rambuttan, papaya, mangoes and many more they had never seen in their local Sainsbury's.

Ma led them to another boat and the first eight of the group carefully got in and were paddled gently along the labyrinth of canals. They were followed by two more boats carrying the remainder of the tour party. The waterways were clogged with vessels bumping into one another. Thai women in traditional blue jackets and bamboo hats were pulling alongside in their boats and inviting the Stockgrove group to buy their wares. The men who had been averse to shopping in Bangkok agreed this was a far more convivial way of doing it. There were boats selling handicrafts, clothing, nuts and spices and many could not resist the temptation.

'You can't come to the floating market and not buy something,' stated Denise Wilson, as she handed over twenty baht for some watermelon and pineapple. There were plenty of local people enjoying the shopping and sitting by the canalside eating noodle soup. There hadn't been too many Westerners when they first arrived, but after about half an hour it became noticeably more crowded with other tour groups. Once out of the boat they walked along the canalside walkways and over the wooden bridges to take more photos and soak up the atmosphere. Despite the fragile nature of their health, Butch, Kev and Stan were delighted they had made the effort to get out of bed. It had been very tempting to sleep in, but now they were here they were snapping away with their cameras the same as everybody else. Ma suggested the three men should try some *som tam*, a spicy papaya salad, as a cure for their hangovers.

'No way. I'm sticking to bottles of water,' said Stan. Butch and Kev were more adventurous and said they would give it a go. The tour guide and the food vendor both laughed as Kev tried his first mouthful. His eyes watered and then he grimaced as he forced himself to swallow it. Then he rapidly reached for some water, which only helped to spread the heat to the rest of his palate.

'Jeeeez that's hot! I mean proper spicy.'

Butch didn't know what all the fuss was about until he tried his, almost choking as he did so.

'Stone me, you're not wrong!'

Both men were partial to Indian food and they liked their curries and their vindaloos, but this was spicier and yet more subtle. Kev gamely tried another few mouthfuls but had to admit defeat. Butch managed to eat his, telling Kev it was an acquired taste.

'I'll tell you what Kev, once you get over the initial assault on the old taste buds, it's actually quite moreish. Go on Stan, try some.'

'I'll pass on that one. I can still taste that whisky from last night and the smell of that stuff isn't doing me any favours either.' Stan was feeling bad enough without his bodily systems being further attacked by more unfamiliar substances. All he wanted was a bacon roll with loads of brown sauce and a mug of tea. The spicy food gave Butch and Kev something to think about other than their hangovers so the tour guide had been right.

From the floating market, the coach stopped briefly at the town of Nakhon Pathom and they visited the Buddhist temple there with its enormous golden coloured chedi. Sammy and his mother talked to the others about Buddhism and how it influenced the way most Thai people led their lives. Stan would chat to Sammy in England about Buddhism. By no means a religious man, Stan was intrigued by the Buddhist belief and had read a few books on the subject. He wasn't about to don orange robes, a pair of sandals and shave his head, but the teachings in the books made a lot of sense to him. He sometimes wondered to himself what he had done in a previous life to deserve the bad karma he was getting this time round.

From Nakhon Pathom, the coach headed for the Rose Garden Country Resort where they had dinner. The resort was in a beautiful setting of landscaped gardens and lakes. After lunch they were treated to a Thai cultural show. There was a display of Thai dancing — no frogs involved this time — and Thai boxing. Outside, a troop of elephants performed a few tricks to the applause of the crowd. Then as they left, Helen and Kimberley couldn't resist the opportunity to have their picture taken with a baby elephant. It sat on its rear legs before turning to each woman and kissing them on the forehead with its trunk.

The tour party arrived back at their Bangkok hotel in the late afternoon and everybody thanked Ma for being so helpful. In turn, she thanked them and wished them well with the football tournament.

'Good luck for you in Chiang Mai. I hope England can win but I think you drink beer too much and Thailand win!'

They would fly to Chiang Mai the following day and they had no more excursions planned in Bangkok. That night nobody felt like doing too much. It had been another exhausting day and most people were going to have something to eat, watch television in the room and go to sleep. A few arranged to do some more shopping and Kev, Butch and Stan ridiculed the four youngsters who said they were going to have an early night. The older men had a meal at the hotel before adjourning to the bar, finally calling it a night just after midnight.

The next morning, Stan was woken by a phone call to his room.

'Hello Mr Bowles, I'm Alan Johnson from Siam Holidays and I'm delighted to tell you that you're one of the lucky winners in our prize draw.'

'What prize draw?' asked Stan, momentarily confused.

'You filled out a survey on Monday evening and —'

'Ah, yes! Sorry. I do remember, I'm just a bit sleepy.'

Alan Johnson apologized for his early call, and Stan explained he was going to Chiang Mai that afternoon. The man from Siam Holidays said that it wasn't a problem as they had an office there, and he gave Stan a telephone number and a contact name to ring. When Stan visited the Chiang Mai office, they would explain in full the holiday he had won. Stan thanked the man and looked forward to telling everybody about his good fortune.

When Stan saw the others in the foyer, he proudly announced, 'I've won a holiday!'

As they asked what he was talking about, he began to explain about the meeting with the girl with the clipboard. Gary Sweeney was the first to blow the wind out of Stan's sails. 'You pilchard Stan!'

'What do you mean?' queried Stan.

'It's a timeshare scam.'

Gary explained how they had all been approached in Patpong by young men and women with clipboards conducting tourist surveys.

'I sussed it straight away,' said Gary, 'so I asked the girl straight off — timeshare? She says yes, and explains that she has to hand in at least ten completed surveys every day to get paid. So we all filled in forms for the girl and her friends giving moody names. I've been Harold Roberts police inspector, James Carruthers barrister, Mickey Hazzard accountant and Brian Law bus driver.'

As Gary was talking, Stan realized how gullible he had been. He wouldn't have fallen for it in England so why did he fall for it last night? That didn't take too much working out on his part. He had been charmed by the young attractive Thai girl and within minutes of meeting her — a total stranger — she had his name, occupation, hotel name and room number.

'Don't worry about it Stan, it's all part of the learning curve in Bangkok. There's so many scams and con-artists over here and the thing is, most of them are so plausible. You're not the first to get caught out and you won't be the last . . . mind you, you're still a stroker!'

CHAPTER TWENTY

Kevin Hardaker's newfound confidence was tested on the approach to Chiang Mai as the aircraft was buffeted by turbulence. His nerve held, but he freely admitted he was relieved when the plane touched down safely. Joe Koonphool was there to meet his wife and son and the Stockgrove group. As in Bangkok, there were representatives from Nok with garlands of flowers, but unlike Bangkok airport, there were no taxi touts as they boarded the coach that would take them to their hotel.

Robbo and Helen were both struck by the difference between Chiang Mai and Bangkok. There was still a lot of traffic in Chiang Mai, but it had only taken them a quarter of an hour to get from the airport to the hotel. They had already passed dozens of temples and seen the remains of the old city walls and the moats that defined the area of the old town. There were no sky-scraping office buildings and despite the traffic, the city seemed more relaxed than its bigger, brasher brother, further south.

The hotel would be their home for the next fourteen nights and a very comfortable one it was too. The women were delighted when Joe pointed out the proximity of the night market. Kev couldn't resist a dig at Gary's shopping expedition in Bangkok.

'I suppose you're happy with that as well, Gal. I hear they do a nice line in handbags.'

'You won't be laughing when I've got two hundred quid in my sky rockets,' replied Gary.

Gary rarely missed an opportunity to make some money. Buying and selling came naturally to him, and in other circumstances he could easily have ended up on the trading floors in the City of London, like some of the Essex chaps he knew at Spurs. Gary knew three men that sat in the East Stand at Tottenham who had made their money in the City during the Eighties. Unlike many of their counterparts, they knew the good times wouldn't last forever and invested in property in England and France, with other money ploughed into high interest accounts and gilt-edged bonds. When their peers were crying into their filofaxes and selling their Porsches, the three friends were still very comfortably off. Although they had enjoyed holidays in the Caribbean and membership at exclusive golf clubs, they hadn't lived beyond their means. They had managed to avoid the temptation to snort their money away, unlike some of their friends who spent fortunes on the Devil's Dandruff and Columbian Marching Powder. In their forties now, they were semi-retired living off income from their property rentals and keeping their hand in with the stock market. They knew Gary well and if they needed any golf equipment they'd place an order with him. They often told him he should be working in the City and he would joke that he already did, but it was just when the banks and exchanges were closing that he started his working day. His business dealings enabled Gary to enjoy a comfortable lifestyle. He had been going out with his girlfriend, Melissa, for six years, but they had actually known each other since they were eighteen. Melissa had always known what Gary did for a living and accepted it. She worked at a telephone call centre and Gary often joked that his 'job' was safer than hers was: 'At least I won't be relocated to New Delhi.'

Melissa's company had always said they had no intention of closing down the call centre in Stevenage, but that's what the other companies had said before they moved their operations to the sub-continent and found new premises and employees at a fraction of the cost. Give your employees an atlas of Great Britain and a few video tapes of *Coronation Street* and they were ready to deal with the British public. Although Gary joked with Melissa, it was a subject that made him angry, believing that the Government should not be allowing British companies to relocate abroad in this way. However, he knew as well as anybody it was a global economy, and he had made plenty of money via his own trading links with Europe and Asia. Gary had always lived on his wits and he liked the fact that Melissa didn't try to change him. She knew he was a thief and he had been involved in football violence, but she accepted it because he had been ever since she had known him. Melissa tolerated Gary's lifestyle, but it didn't stop her worrying about him being arrested. As he got older, Gary knew he would have to diversify his business. He didn't want to be breaking into golf shops or pilfering from department stores when he was fifty. Similarly, he didn't want to be chasing opposition fans up and down Tottenham High Road and attacking them with his Zimmer frame. He had spoken with the three chaps at Tottenham about the stock market and he was looking at setting up a portfolio of shares. In addition to that, the ticket touting, which had always been a lucrative sideline, had the potential to be a legitimate business and Gary had the acumen to make it work. Melissa

216

agreed she would be much happier if Gary set up a bona fide business and kept away from football violence. She wasn't naïve enough to think that he wouldn't still have some shady dealings going on here and there, and he'd always go to Spurs. Gary loved his football, that would never change, and Melissa didn't want it to. If it wasn't for football, then Melissa and all the other wives and girlfriends wouldn't be in Thailand now and about to hit the shops again.

Sammy Koonphool was staying with his parents at the apartment block owned by Nok. The brewery used the apartments to house visiting overseas businessmen and employees on short term contracts. They were beautifully appointed with three bedrooms and a large balcony affording splendid views of the surrounding mountains. There was a gym and a swimming pool as well as a business centre where people could work. It was perfect for Joe, and on his frequent visits to Chiang Mai he enjoyed his stay. The average length of Joe's trips abroad would be ten days, but when he had to visit the brewery's operations in Thailand, it was usually only two or three days that he'd be away from the head office in Bangkok. Initially he didn't like being away from home and his family, but he gradually got used to it. With his son at school in England, his wife would often stay with her sister when Joe was away. Ladawan Koonphool had never liked her husband or son being away from home and looked forward to Joe's promised semi-retirement. He told his wife he was going to cut back on his workload in the next couple of years and eliminate all the foreign business trips. At the moment though, he was very much the public face of Nok. Once Lanna Beer had been established in Europe, then his younger deputy would fulfil Joe's public relations role. Sammy Koonphool had been at school in England for over three years and there wasn't a day gone by when his mother didn't miss him. Whenever Sammy flew back to Thailand his mother doted on him. She couldn't be prouder that her son was a talented footballer with dreams of playing professionally and representing his country.

After Joe's interview about Nok brewery appeared in the Bangkok Post, other newspapers picked up on it. The coverage given to the Nok football tournament had been beyond Joe's expectations, and Thai television had featured on their news programmes some of the matches played in the regional stages of the competition. Further coverage would be given to the grand finals in Chiang Mai, which had been promoted as a festival weekend with all age groups playing their final matches. The in-house tournament had not escaped attention, principally because of Joe Koonphool's son playing for the team from England. Some of the group matches were being played in the capital, but Stockgrove would play all of their matches in Chiang Mai. They had been drawn in the same group as the American investment company and that would be their first match in two days' time. They'd also face the two teams from Nok's Bangkok operations; one from head office and one from logistics. The other group featured the visiting teams from Singapore and Hong Kong, and the Thai teams from Surat Thani and Chiang Mai. The top two teams from each group would play off in the final, which would be the last match played at the festival weekend in twelve days' time.

The overseas teams were all being flown and accommodated at Nok's expense for the duration of their stay. The brewery's generosity didn't extend quite that far to their own teams from Thailand. They were being flown in on the morning of the matches and straight back afterwards. The Nok players had the prestige of representing the company plus the bonus of a day off work for which they would receive double pay.

For the days that Stockgrove didn't have a game, Nok brewery had again laid on tours and sightseeing trips as well as the services of a dedicated tour guide. As in Bangkok, Joe Koonphool would have very little free time to spend with the group. The Koonphools would be spending most of their time in the apartment in the west of the city, some distance from the Stockgrove hotel.

The interest in football in Thailand, like much of South-East Asia, was huge, and the interest in the English Premiership was immense. As the group from Stockgrove had been out and about in Bangkok the Thai people, men and women, would more or less ask the same questions:

'How long you stay in Thailand?'

'Where you come from?'

'You like football?'

'What team you like?'

Everybody met in the foyer at six o'clock to eat at the hotel restaurant. After dinner the entire party, with the exception of Stan and Butch, headed on foot to the night bazaar. The two men had decided that a few cold beers at the hotel bar was more appealing than walking around the shops.

The Chiang Mai night market was a sprawling affair of shops and street stalls selling clothes, shoes, jewellery, luggage, food and handicrafts. It was possible to buy anything and everything, from American DVDs to Chinese herbal medicine. The stalls were full of many of the fake designer goods they had seen in Bangkok, but here there were more of them over a wider area. Inside a covered market area there were more shops selling better quality goods, and a dining area in front of a large stage where the diners were being entertained by a display of traditional Thai dancing.

As the group were wandering along the narrow crowded pavements stopping to look at stalls, it was immediately evident that they would not be able to stick together as one and they decided to all break off into couples and do their own thing.

Kev and the four teenage lads were looking at the sports shops and stalls selling counterfeit branded goods. The youngsters bought Diesel trainers and Lacoste polo shirts and Kev bought a Rolex watch for five quid. Pleased with their purchases, but soon bored after half an hour walking around, they sat and watched the Thai dancing display with a couple of Pavarottis, and when the dancing finished, they people-watched. Kev was guessing the nationalities of the tourists walking past and was soon becoming expert.

'Swedish . . . Japanese . . . British . . . Not sure, maybe Korean . . . Italian, eight o'clock at night and wearing sunglasses; yellow card for that, almost a straight red . . . German without a doubt —

'How can you tell, Kev?' asked Lloydy.

'Got to be German. No fashion sense, beer belly, mullet hairstyle, blonde moustache; all dead giveaways . . . and her husband's just as bad.'

The youngsters joined in the game of national stereotypes and the middle-aged Brits were just as easy to spot with their khaki shorts, sandals and white socks. The hardest to differentiate were the younger backpackers who had all adopted the same look. The women with plaited hair, multi-coloured tops and ethnic skirts, and the men with goatee beards, scruffy T-shirts, combat pants and flip-flops.

'D'you lads ever fancy doing that? Backpacking, I mean,' asked Kev, as he pointed at a young couple consulting their *Lonely Planet* guide book.

'I've thought about doing it in my gap year,' revealed

Lloydy.

'Doesn't really appeal to me,' said Danny.

'No, nor me,' concurred JC.

'What about you Rusky? Does the thought of living out of a rucksack for twelve months appeal to you?'

'Can't say it does,' responded Rusky, sipping his beer.

Kev surprised the youngsters with his next statement.

'I must admit, it's something I've always wanted to do. Not backpacking as such . . . no, fuck all that; living in hostels, no toilet paper, cold showers, cockroaches. No, I mean travelling round the world, seeing different places, different cultures.'

Rusky looked at Kev and said, 'Seriously mate, yeah?'

'Yeah, I'm serious,' replied Kev.

'Well what stopped you?' asked Rusky. The words were barely out of his mouth before he added, 'Shit, sorry mate, I forgot, I wasn't taking the piss.'

'No that's all right Rusk. I tell you what though; I wish I'd have been able to get on a plane when I was your age. When I think of some of the lads' holidays I've missed out on. Even made me split up with one bird 'cos I wouldn't fly to Cyprus with her to see her sister get married. I didn't tell her about the phobia thing and she just thought I was being anti-social. Mind you, she was a bit of a bunny-boiler, so I was well out of it.'

'So what about now Kev? Now that you've flown here there's nothing to stop you,' said JC.

'You're right son, and to be honest I've thought about nothing else since we've got here. If it hadn't of been for Robbo I'd still be in England. He pushed me into getting myself sorted out with the Paul McKenna bod. I don't mind telling you lads, I was still shitting myself at Heathrow when we were checking in, but I didn't want to let Robbo down, let the team down. I know it sounds daft.'

The four youngsters were listening intently to Kevin Hardaker as he paused and sipped his beer. It didn't sound daft to them, but this was the first time anybody had heard Kev speak so seriously. Usually it was just a couple of one-liners or a funny story, never anything like this.

'And when I got on the plane,' continued Kev, 'I knew I was going to be all right. Once I'd set foot on the plane and sat down I mean. I was still nervous, but I remembered my breathing exercises and what I'd been taught and I looked round and I saw all the lads from Stockgrove . . . fucking hell boys, listen to me babbling on.' Kev was quite emotional. The lads had never seen Kev like this and they weren't sure what to say. Danny broke the awkward silence.

'Everybody's pleased you made it Kev, it wouldn't have been the same without you.'

'Cheers son.'

The others nodded to agree with Danny. Kev looked down at his drink, partly in embarrassment and partly in thought. None of the youngsters spoke. It didn't seem an appropriate time to talk, so they listened. The man was clearly getting something off his chest and after a few moments, Kev spoke again.

'I mean it lads . . . about the travelling. I mean you're all what — seventeen, eighteen? It's easy to take things for granted, but if you get the opportunity to travel . . . I tell you, I'm already thinking about places I want to go to. Look at this country. I mean, how many days have we been here and just look at some of the things we've seen and done already, and I could have missed all that. Boys, I'm telling you, see as many countries as you can and try new experiences. Take the opportunities while they're there, they might never come round again.'

The boys had listened quietly as he spoke. At times, Kev

had sounded like their parents, but Kev's talk had more resonance and meaning. Perhaps because he was more like a big brother than a parent. A worldly-wise big brother who they played football with and who made everybody laugh. When Kev spoke, he displayed a vulnerability they had never seen before. Maybe it had always been there, but he camouflaged it with his humour and now there was no humour to disguise his feelings. Kev spoke again, 'Bloody hell boys, I sound like a born again Alan Whicker. Let's have another beer somewhere.'

Kev settled the bill and led the lads towards the Red Lion pub he had spotted earlier. The youngsters followed behind whispering to each other, 'Alan who?'

CHAPTER TWENTY-ONE

John Woods didn't appear for breakfast on Wednesday morning. His wife explained to the rest of the group that he had been up most of the night with a stomach upset, and he'd be spending the day in bed trying to recover.

'Typical, the day before our first match as well,' said Robbo. 'I'll give him a shout when we get back and see how he is.'

'He can be a bit of a drama queen, but I must admit he does look rough,' said Kimberley.

After breakfast, the Stockgrove group met their Chiang Mai tour guide for the first time.

'My name is Serin. Welcome everyone to Chiang Mai, "Rose of the North" and I hope you have very pleasant stay.' The young guide was twenty-six and had a degree in tourism. He had read and studied all about America, Australia and Europe, but he had never been outside of Thailand. Even in his own country he had never been anywhere further south than Bangkok. He loved to speak with foreign visitors and hear about their countries, hoping one day to have enough money to visit America and England. When Serin had been given the job of escorting the Stockgrove group, he had been particularly pleased. His employers had explained the group were in Chiang Mai for two weeks as guests of Nok brewery and were playing in the football tournament.

'My team is Chelsea. Before I like Liverpool, but now no good so I like Chelsea more,' Serin said.

'Chelsea no good, Queens Park Rangers number one team,' said Willo unconvincingly.

'Ah, Queens Park Rangers play Premier League before,' and then he paused, thinking for a moment, before declaring triumphantly, 'Gerry Francis.'

Willo was stunned at the Thai man's knowledge of his beloved Rangers.

'That's quality, Serin. We'll have you singing "Captain Jack" before the end of the week.'

The obscure reference to the QPR song was as lost on Serin as it was on everybody else. The tour guide outlined the plan for the day. The Stockgrove party would be taken on a tour of the city and enjoy a leisurely cruise along the river. It was an overcast day but still very humid and the players didn't want to exert themselves too much. Tomorrow they would play their first match in the tournament.

As the Stockgrove party were driven around in three minibuses, Robbo and Helen were struck once again by the contrast between Chiang Mai and Bangkok. The old city they were seeing today had a plethora of temples and there was lots of greenery, which the sprawling Bangkok streets lacked. Chiang Mai had a provincial feel that Robbo and Helen liked. After a tour of the city, they were driven to the temple of Doi Suthep, sitting high on a mountain overlooking Chiang Mai. They climbed the many steps that led to the beautiful temple complex. The air was clean and fresh as they looked down on the hazy city below. They watched as local people left orchids and lilies and lit candles at the feet of Buddha images. None of the players were particularly religious, but it was an enjoyable spectacle lacking the stuffiness and formality of churches in their home country.

The minibuses zigzagged their way down the mountain and back to the city and the river. A lazy, two-hour cruise along the river was the perfect way to end the day. They stopped off at a farmer's fruit farm before returning to a riverside restaurant for a late lunch. It was still humid but rain was beginning to fall and a cooling wind had picked up. The players hoped the weather would remain the same for the following day and their opening match against the American team. The weather was the one factor they could do nothing about and the hotter it was, the more it would favour the local teams in the tournament. Despite being driven around in air-conditioned minibuses and then cruising along the river, many of the players felt tired. Just being outside in the heat was energy sapping and that was without doing any running around. Ninety minutes of football was going to be hard work.

Driving back to the hotel they passed a building site.

'There you go Butch,' said Kev, 'we'll get a job for you here. I'll go and have a word with the site manager in the morning.'

The two men were looking at the workers toiling in the heat.

'Forget that,' said Butch, 'look at the state of that scaffolding!'

The scaffold was a precarious looking bamboo affair strung together with rope. The workers were split evenly between men and women and the equality in the workforce surprised Butch and Kev. Nobody on site wore hard hats; they all wore baseball caps or the traditional Thai straw hats. Many of the workers wore scarves around their heads and faces to protect them from the sun. But there was no protection for the feet with the workers wearing sandals or flimsy trainers.

'Health and Safety would have a field day here Butch,' said Kev. They were astounded later when Sammy told them just how little the building site workers earned each month; Butch and Kev would easily spend that in a night out back home.

They got back to the hotel half an hour before the heavens opened. The lightning storm was spectacular and the rain and thunder the most violent anybody had experienced. The storm lasted an hour before finally abating. The streets outside were flooded and some were impassable to motorists, the storm drains unable to cope with the ferocity of the downpour.

The following morning there was barely a cloud in the sky as everybody, with the exception of Woodsy, ate breakfast. The Stockgrove goalkeeper was still laid low and had ruled himself out of the match. The players were going to have a day lazing round the hotel, conserving their energy for the four o'clock kick-off. The wives and girlfriends took the first opportunity they'd had to do some serious sunbathing. Some of the players played snooker in the games room, whilst others went for a gentle swim.

Later that afternoon, the coach arrived to take the Stockgrove party on the short journey across the city to the university campus where the matches were being played. The team from America were yet to arrive at the ground. They had flown from Bangkok the day before the match and were staying in a hotel in the old centre of Chiang Mai. The weather was still very warm, but the sky had clouded over and the heat from the earlier part of the day had relented slightly. The small stadium had floodlights in each corner and the pitch was framed by an oval running track. Concrete terracing going back fifteen rows encircled the running track and there was just one small stand, which offered shade and provided seating for over six hundred people. The pitch was lush green apart from well-worn patches in the penalty areas and in the centre-circle. Had the pitch been a racecourse, then Phil Whitaker would have described the going as good to firm. The previous day's deluge had drained quickly and the majority of the Stockgrove players elected to wear moulded studs.

Stockgrove changed into their red, white and blue Nok sponsored kit. The American team had arrived and were in the other dressing room changing into the all yellow kit that Nok had provided especially for the tournament. Inter Continental Finance (ICF) Limited were Nok brewery's financial investors. Gary Sweeney in particular found this amusing. 'So if we win, we can say we done the ICF!'

The Americans had never played together as a team before although they had all played 'soccer' at various standards in high school and college. The team featured three expats, two from Ireland and one from England, who had been living and working in the States for a number of years. When the investment company had received the invitation from Nok in Thailand, there was no shortage of volunteers for the team. Much like Stockgrove, the offer of a free holiday had great appeal, but the Americans had their own way of dealing with the issue of who would go. A series of selection trials were held to find the best players from the company. They may not have played together as a team before, but on an individual basis they were all reasonably good players.

There were a number of bigwigs from the brewery, including Joe Koonphool, sat in the stand along with the wives and girlfriends of both sets of players. The teams lined up for pre-match photos and two photographers from the local newspapers were on hand to take pictures of the match itself. Water bottles had been placed at numerous points around the pitch and at any break in play, both teams could avail themselves of the opportunity to replace lost fluid.

Butch replaced the unfortunate Woodsy in goal. Kev moved into the centre of defence to partner Robbo, and Rusky and Danny were at fullback. Lloydy and Steve Bennett started on the bench. With under a minute gone, Kev played a back pass to Butch who completely missed his kick, his studs catching in the turf. He turned round in horror to see the ball roll into the net. The American side were as amazed as Stockgrove; surely the game can't be this easy. But they were soon exchanging high-fives and their partners in the stand watching, were on their feet cheering. Butch looked accusingly at his studs and then at the turf beyond the six-yard box. He stood with his hands on his hips, staring out as Stockgrove restarted the match. There were no recriminations from the Stockgrove players. Butch had dropped a bollock, simple as that. He had a shocker; a mare; a stinker — a Reggie Blinker; he'd naused up. Butch knew it better than anybody and didn't need to be reminded. It was a shock for Stockgrove, but at least it had come in the first minute and they had the whole match left to sort themselves out. Four minutes later and parity was restored. Macca latched on to a loose ball inside the penalty area and fired his shot high into the roof of the net. Both sides were finding it hard going in the heat and humidity, but Stockgrove were comfortably the better side and further goals from Sammy Koonphool and Gary Sweeney gave them a 3-1 lead at half-time. The American side weren't lacking in spirit, but the English side were too strong for them. In the second half, Sammy completed his hat-trick and Leon Wilson scored to complete a 6-1 thrashing. The match had been played at walking pace in the second forty-five minutes as both sets of players tired in the conditions. The teams exchanged handshakes and were thankful for the shade of the changing room and the cooling showers. With the match won, it was safe to give Butch some stick for his howler.

'You stroker Butch! We'll have to get Woodsy a commode for the next match and wheel him out,' said Gary.

'Never mind getting Woodsy back, we'll get our feathered friend from Suffolk back . . . Dave Pheasant! Fucking hell Butch, what were you doing?' said Kev.

Butch had a rueful smile as he sat shaking his head. He tried desperately to think of a witty response but he couldn't. He would just have to take the good-natured abuse and the mickey-taking. This is what he would miss above all else when he hung his boots up at the end of the tournament. It was hard to believe that Stockgrove had another two or, hopefully, three matches left to play and that would be it, the club would be finished. He was on the receiving end today, but at other games it had been somebody else, with Butch amongst those doing the piss-taking. Apart from his mistake, he'd had very little to do, dealing with one shot at goal and a couple of crosses. The next two matches against Thai opponents were likely to be a much sterner test, and Butch hoped that Woodsy could shake off his stomach upset and be fit to play.

CHAPTER TWENTY-TWO

It was eleven o'clock and Neil Roberts was just getting ready to go to bed. The match earlier in the day had left him exhausted. Despite the ease of the victory and the slow pace of the game, he was very tired and looking forward to some shut-eye. The phone on the bedside table rang, briefly startling Helen who was just getting into bed.

'Probably one of your players wanting you to read them a bedtime story,' she joked.

Robbo picked up the receiver and heard a lady from reception say, 'We have a call for you, sir.' There were a couple of clicks and a faint buzzing noise before he heard, 'Neil? It's Andy. Haven't woke you up have I? We weren't sure what time it was over there.'

'No, it's all right bruv. What's the matter, what's happened?'

Robbo was concerned that his brother was calling. Something serious must have happened back home. His brother immediately eased his concerns.

'No, nothing's wrong. Phil and Michelle asked us to call you, they had a little baby girl this morning. Nine weeks premature, so they're keeping her in hospital for a few days to keep an eye on her.'

'Everything's all right then?' asked Robbo, seeking reassurance.

Helen was sitting up now, worried that something was wrong. Looking at her boyfriend, she mouthed the words, 'What's happened?' Still listening to his brother, Robbo placed his hand over the mouthpiece and told Helen that Michelle had given birth to a baby girl. Andy was confirming everything was fine as Helen moved closer to the phone to hear what Neil's brother was saying.

'Michelle's just rung from the hospital and spoken to Pauline.'

Robbo's sister-in-law, Pauline, was Michelle's best friend.

'Phil and Michelle asked us to call you so you could let everybody know. Deborah Louise they've called her. I tried to ring you earlier, I left a message on your mobile.'

'I leave it switched off, I just check for messages each morning,' explained Robbo. 'Send them our love, but we'll give them a call in a few days when they've had a chance to get themselves sorted out a bit.'

Andy asked his brother how the Stockgrove trip was going. 'Yeah fantastic,' said Robbo. 'Food's great, weather's hot, people are friendly . . . that's right, just like Milton Keynes! We won our first match 6-1 and that was with Butch in goal . . . yeah Butch. Long story, don't ask! Listen mate, this must be costing you a fortune . . . OK, and you bruv . . . Yeah I will . . . OK Andy, see you soon. Bye.'

Helen was eager to hear the bits of conversation she had missed.

'How much does she weigh?'

'I don't know, Andy didn't say.'

Helen tutted, 'Honestly . . . men.'

'He just said she was nine weeks premature and they're

keeping her in for a few days to keep an eye on her, but everything's OK.'

'And Michelle?'

'I don't know, I mean Andy didn't —'

'Oh Neil!' interrupted an exasperated Helen.

'Michelle must be all right,' said Robbo defensively. 'Andy didn't say she was being kept in as well . . . Oh, I don't know, we'll ring them in a couple of days.'

'Men! Bloody useless!' She gave Neil a playful punch in the ribs. Robbo responded by taking his pillow and hitting Helen gently on the head.

'So, you wanna fight, mister,' said Helen as she manoeuvred herself on top of her boyfriend. 'I'm broody, let's practice making babies,' she said with a glint in her eye. Robbo was forgetting about how tired he was, but then Helen added, 'Oooh, I must ring Kimberley and the other girls.'

'What, now? This minute?'

'Yes Neil, now, this minute.'

Robbo was left briefly frustrated, his ardour softer, as Helen rang the other rooms.

At breakfast the next morning, the players all agreed to go out that night to wet the baby's head. Robbo rang Sammy at the apartment he was staying at and invited the Koonphool family to come for a drink that evening. It was another new phrase for Sammy, 'wetting the baby's head,' but basically, the British mentality was the same as Thailand; any excuse for a get together and a drink with friends. Sammy looked forward to meeting up with everybody later, but his parents were dining out with some people from the brewery and wouldn't be able to attend.

Woodsy was still feeling a bit fragile, but he was sufficiently well to join the others for the excursion to the elephant training camp.

'The bowels are OK this morning,' he proudly announced at the breakfast table.

'Thank you, John,' said Kimberley. 'We don't need to know about your bowels when we're about to eat breakfast.'

'No you're wrong Kimberley. After Butch's performance in goal we're all concerned about the state of your husband's bowels. So Woodsy, how was it on the crapperteria this morning? On a scale of one to ten — one being a real pan splatterer and ten being proper laying cable — how did you score?' asked Kev.

The women shook their heads, but Willo picked up Kev's theme.

'Yeah, come on Woodsy, out of ten and don't give us any crap.'

'Probably about a six,' replied an earnest Woodsy, earning the wrath of his wife for joining in with the conversation. The men laughed. They didn't expect the women to understand the delicate relationship between a man and the bathroom. It was something ingrained in men as they moved through adolescence into adulthood before peaking in later years. That morning routine, doing your ablutions. Wake up and then shit, shower, shave, although the order wasn't set in stone, that was left to individual preference. It was very much a British male thing; reading the sports pages of the paper and spending at least ten minutes having an Eartha Kitt. Picking out the winner of the three-thirty at Kempton Park or doing the *Sun* crossword. And with business taken care of, the routine wouldn't be complete without proudly announcing to the next occupant of the toilet, 'I'd give it ten minutes before you go in there.' Makes you proud to be British.

* * *

When the bus arrived at Chiang Dao, Serin the tour guide took them across the rickety looking wooden bridge that spanned the river and led to the elephant training camp. The smell of dung was heavy in the hot, humid air and grew stronger the closer they got to the first elephants they saw, a mother and baby. Robbo, Helen and most of the others, bought bunches of bananas and fed them to the elephants. It was a daily routine for the animals. They knew the arrival of the tourists signalled food, and the more playful they were the more food they would get from the tour groups.

The Stockgrove party sat on wooden benches near the river's edge and watched a group of six elephants, including the mother and baby, being washed and scrubbed by their handlers, the mahouts. The elephants rolled around in the water and used their trunks to shower themselves. Then as a finale, they sprayed water in the direction of the watching tourists, the spray just reaching the front row of the wooden benches to everybody's amusement. Once the bath time display was over, the crowd were taken to the main area where the elephants would perform their tricks. The spectators sat in a wooden grandstand, cameras poised, as the elephants went through their paces. Moving huge logs with ease, each elephant used its legs and trunk in unison with remarkable dexterity. Then a display of acrobatics from these huge, lumbering creatures as they balanced on their hind legs and then sat down, legs crossed, before their mahouts gave them the instruction to play dead. The assembled crowd were soon laughing as the elephants played football. One of the handlers approached the crowd looking for a volunteer and Butch was chosen from the many who put their hand up. He took his position in front of a small goal and a football was placed on an imaginary penalty spot ten yards in front of him. The elephant, with the mahout sat on top, began its long run-up. It was more of a 'walk-up' than a run-up, but it made the whole scene funnier for that. The power and precision of the elephant's spot-kick caught Butch by surprise and he didn't even get a hand to the ball as it shot past him and nestled in the net. Danny Cartwright had the whole event on video camera and Butch was laughing and shaking his head when he returned to his friends in the stand. The other tourists gave Butch a round of applause, but the Stockgrove players jeered him.

'So Butch, talk us through it mate. First the goal against the septic tanks and now this. Is there no beginning to your goalkeeping talents?' quipped Kev.

'Looks like my position's safe then,' said Woodsy.

'Aye, your position in goals is safe, but Gary and Sammy had better watch out. If I can find a shirt big enough I'll be signing on the elephant!' said Tommy.

The elephants went on to perform more tricks; one played a harmonica and another used a paintbrush and easel to complete a colourful abstract painting. It was a thoroughly entertaining display and the group rounded off the morning by trekking on elephant-back through the jungle to a local hill-tribe village. The long line of elephants in single file was a fantastic sight. Kimberley Woods laughed as the elephant in front of them carrying Colin and Wendy McSwiggen, emptied its bladder, producing a torrent of foaming urine followed by a large turd. The elephant hadn't broken its stride as it did its business.

'There you are love, that's what you can do on the football pitch if you've still got the runs!' said Kimberley to her husband.

'Must you talk about things like that,' replied Woodsy in mock indignation.

They had lunch back at the training camp before drifting

236

gently downriver on a series of bamboo rafts. They passed through lush green countryside and waving villagers. Thai youngsters were swimming and catching fish using a snorkel mask and a small harpoon device. And at one village, an enterprising teenager waded out to meet the rafts. He was holding on to an inner tube that housed an icebox containing soft drinks and beer. Such resourcefulness had to be rewarded and several of the group bought drinks from the floating bar. They saw more elephants and water buffalo bathing in the river as they glided along. The coach had driven on ahead and was waiting to take the group to their final stop of the day, a small craft village, where they watched the process that turned elephant dung into paper. There was a shop selling photo albums, address books and greetings cards all made from recycled elephant dung. All of the women bought something, the novelty proving too much to resist. It had been another enjoyable day.

Back at the hotel, Robbo suggested everybody meet in the foyer at eight o'clock and they'd go and celebrate Phil and Michelle's good news.

Stan and Woodsy had both said they wanted to have a suit made up by a tailor recommended by the tour guide. Within thirty minutes of returning from the elephant trip, they were showered, changed, and standing in the shop of the Indian tailor in downtown Chiang Mai. They picked out the cloth and thumbed through old catalogues to show the shop owner the type of design they liked. They were measured and told to come back in two days for a fitting. The owner would send a car to collect them from the hotel. This was an unbelievable personal service. Free transport and a made-to-measure suit within forty-eight hours. The cost was a fraction over one hundred pounds each and that included two made-to-measure cotton shirts and two silk ties each. Stan and Woodsy thanked the Indian man and walked along the street to catch a tuk-tuk back to the hotel. In a side street, they could hear two dogs barking but paid no real attention at first. From the corner of his eye, Woodsy saw the two dogs running towards him. He carried on walking, ignoring the dogs and chatting to Stan about their bargain in the suit shop. The larger of the two dogs stopped short of Woodsy and continued to bark, but the smaller one didn't seem able to stop, or perhaps it hadn't wanted to, and collided with Woodsy's left leg. That's all it felt like, a collision. Both dogs continued barking, but now Woodsy could feel the heat in his calf.

'Little bastard! He's bitten me!'

The two dogs were still barking, the little one following close to Woodsy's heels as they continued to walk. He was tempted to turn round and give it a swift boot up the jacksie but thought better of it. There was blood beginning to seep from the four puncture holes the dog's teeth had made.

'Bloody hell, Woodsy, how's your luck; first you get the raging abjabs and now this.'

They hailed a passing tuk-tuk and went back to the hotel.

'You're not having a good time of it at the moment are you dear?' said Kimberley Woods as she cleaned her husband's wound. 'I'll ring Wendy, she's bound to have some antiseptic.' Wendy McSwiggen had some antiseptic cream and some advice. Woodsy had a tetanus booster before he came out to Thailand, but he hadn't thought about rabies until Wendy mentioned it. 'He'd better get to the hospital in the next couple of days for a rabies injection,' said Wendy.

Woodsy didn't exactly panic, that wasn't in his nature, but he decided there was no time like the present.

'Right, I'm off now. I'll give Robbo a shout, he'll know what to do. Perhaps I can get Sammy to come along and help with the translation.'

Neil and Helen didn't see Woodsy before he went to the hospital; they were out buying postcards and souvenirs. They were looking forward to toasting Phil and Michelle's good news with the rest of the group. If they could just win the tournament, everything would be perfect. As the couple were contemplating how wonderful life was, Neil's brother was leaving a message with the hotel reception, asking Neil to phone home.

CHAPTER TWENTY-THREE

Woodsy was having a mare. Trouble in the toilet department and now a dog bite. This was bad karma. There had been no answer from Robbo's room and nobody else had Sammy's telephone number. If he was going to the hospital that afternoon, he'd be going alone. Kimberley had been unsympathetic. 'Stop making such a drama out of it. The hospital staff will all speak English, just take your insurance details.' She was used to her husband's ailments in England. Woodsy had never suffered from a cold in his life, only flu. He had never had a headache, only migraines. When he came back from football with an injury, he was a sudden expert on self-diagnosis, often checking on a medical website to confirm his condition. 'Definitely a broken rib, I'm displaying all the classic symptoms,' or, 'Looks like it could be a metatarsal, probably be out for a month.' He never was though. The broken ribs suffered on a Sunday were miraculously cured by the Tuesday, and the damaged metatarsals never needed medical attention. Kimberley Woods knew why God had made women the child-bearers; if it was up to the likes of her husband, the human race would have died out long ago.

Woodsy was spurred by his wife's lack of compassion. He

could be foaming at the mouth and delusional in the next twenty-four hours thanks to the rabies-infested dog. He had convinced himself by now that the dog was a diseased, mangy little git. He went down to reception and asked the lady there where the nearest hospital was. The attitude of the Thai woman couldn't have contrasted more with his wife's. She asked Woodsy what happened and he retold his story about the dog — by now a large savage beast — which he had to fight off to save himself from more serious injury.

'I don't really want to go to hospital, it's only a little scratch, but my wife's worried I might get rabies,' lied Woodsy.

'Yes, your wife correct. No good when dog in Thailand bite you. You must go hospital for vaccine.' The receptionist wrote down in Thai the name of the hospital. 'Give this to tuk-tuk driver. He can take you there, fifty baht.' She then took another piece of paper and wrote down a description of what had happened to the unfortunate Englishman. 'Take this and give to hospital. I think they speak English no problem, but I write that dog bite you and you need vaccine.'

Woodsy thanked the lady for her help and walked outside where a fleet of tuk-tuks were parked, the drivers relaxing, stretched out on the back seat. They sprung into life as a potential fare approached. 'Mister, mister, tuk-tuk?'

Woodsy walked over to the first driver and handed him the piece of paper.

'OK, eighty baht.'

'Fifty baht,' replied Woodsy, remembering what the receptionist had said. The driver agreed to the price without hesitation. This bartering lark was easy he thought, as they sped noisily away.

Woodsy found the main reception of the hospital without any trouble. He was helped by the large sign written in both Thai and English that said 'Main Reception'. Once there, he handed over the piece of paper to the lady at the desk. She said something to Woodsy in Thai. Woodsy's eyes widened and he furrowed his brow. The lady smiled.

'You speak English?' she asked.

'Yes,' replied Woodsy, blankly.

'Dog bite you, bad luck for you. Moment please.' She looked at her watch and then motioned for Woodsy to sit on one of the orange plastic chairs. Just as he was sitting down, a young Thai man in a white jacket appeared and said, 'Come with me please, sir.' The two men walked for about thirty yards down a corridor and then turned right.

'Where you come from?'

'England,' replied Woodsy.

'Ah England, you like football?'

'Yes, very much. I'm here in Thailand to play football.'

'You play football? Which team?' asked the Thai man, excited this was a former Premier League player now plying his trade in Thailand. Woodsy too realized the potential misunderstanding.

'I play with an English team called Stockgrove. We're here to play friendlies,' said Woodsy, hoping he had made the situation clear.

'Yes, Thailand very friendly. My team Liverpool, you play them before?'

'No, not yet,' said Woodsy who was pleased to arrive at another desk before the conversation got any more confusing. The Thai man said something to the nurse sat behind the desk. She looked at her watch and then the clock on the wall behind. The Thai man wished Woodsy good luck and the Englishman thanked him. The nurse made a telephone call and then escorted Woodsy to the emergency room. Bloody hell, thought Woodsy, this could be more serious than he first thought. The nurses keep checking their watches and now he was being personally escorted to the emergency room. Time must be of the essence when a rabid dog has bitten you. If he had listened to Wendy or Kimberley and gone the following day, he could be dead by then.

The man outside the emergency room gave Woodsy a card to fill out. It was written in Thai and English and asked for his full name, address, next of kin — shit, next of kin! The completed card was handed back to the man and he registered the details on the computer and then looked at his watch. What is this thing with the watches? It was beginning to unnerve Woodsy. Sammy had said Thai people don't worry about time and that time keeping was very informal.

'Injection room close five o'clock,' said the man at the computer. 'Now you come here we have to give you injection in emergency room.'

Woodsy felt a little bit stupid; so that's why everybody had been looking at the time. He was given a prescription sheet and shown to a counter where he paid for the medicine. Once he had collected the tablets and vaccine he was taken back to have the injection. A nurse came outside and led him into the emergency ward. There were people with breathing apparatus and others who looked like they had been in serious motor accidents, and here was the silly farang with a minor dog bite. His awkwardness was compounded when the nurse called a doctor over. The doctor then called his colleague over. There were now two doctors and one nurse all talking in Thai, smiling and looking at the Englishman in his shorts and T-shirt. One of the doctors called a group of people across and now there were nine people looking at Woodsy's hairy white leg with the small abrasion caused by the dog.

'These are medical students,' the doctor said by way of explanation, 'I tell them we must give you vaccine for rabies.'

'You come from England?' said the doctor.

'Yes that's right,' confirmed Woodsy, anticipating the next question would be football related. But it didn't come.

'Yes . . . yes,' the doctor replied.

The group dispersed, Woodsy's temporary VIP status over. One nurse cleaned his wound and another nurse gave his injection. There didn't appear to be any staff shortages here. Woodsy had lost count of the number of different people he had spoken to or who had looked at his leg since he entered the hospital.

'Dog bite you. He OK?' asked the nurse as she injected Woodsy in the arm.

'Sorry, is who OK?'

'The dog. I think maybe he die,' she replied, smiling.

Woodsy burst out laughing and played along with the joke. 'Yes, I think so too. Maybe tomorrow I come back with dog and you give him injection.'

The nurse smiled again, 'Yes I think so. You like football?'

'The Land of Smiles' thought Woodsy; even in the hospital the service was first class and they want to smile, joke and talk about football. From the time of entering the hospital to the time of leaving, it had taken less than thirty-five minutes. Bit different to back home. He looked at the medical card, which gave the dates of the next four injections. He would be able to have one more in Thailand but the other three to complete the course would be in England. Nobody in the hospital there would want to talk to him about football.

Ten minutes after Woodsy had gone to the hospital, Neil and Helen had returned to the hotel and were reading the message at reception to ring home. They both thought the same thing, but couldn't bring themselves to say it. Not Phil and Michelle's baby. Please God, not that. They rushed to

244

their room. Neil found his mobile and switched it on. There were two messages on his voicemail and a text message, all from his brother, asking him to ring home as soon as he could.

'Hello, Pauline? It's Neil . . .' Robbo could hear his words echoing back in the satellite delay.

'Oh Neil . . . I . . .' His sister-in-law was crying at the sound of his voice. He could hear her tearfully calling her husband to the phone.

'What's happened Andy?'

'It's Dad, he's had a heart attack. He's all right, he's in the hospital now. We've just come back, but Mum's still with him.'

Brian Roberts was fifty-eight. He didn't smoke, only drank on social occasions and played golf twice a week. He was a tall man and had a physique that would put many men his junior to shame. Like his sons, he had been an active sportsman in his younger days. The news shocked Robbo. He knew something had to be wrong for his brother to call, but Robbo thought it was little Deborah Louise. He never thought for one moment that it would be his father.

Helen was listening to Neil speak as he sat on the edge of the bed. He leant forward and looked at the floor, elbows resting on his knees, his mobile phone in his left hand and the palm of his right hand pushed against the middle of his forehead, his fingers pushing into his scalp. From the one side of the conversation she could hear, Helen deduced something had happened to Neil's father. She stood helplessly, wanting to sit next to her fiancé and hold his hand, but somehow it didn't feel right.

'I'll leave my mobile on all the time from now on, but I'll give you a ring in a couple of hours when I've got some things sorted out here. Get some rest Andy and tell Mum I'll be home as soon as I can. Take care.'

Helen sat next to her boyfriend and held him as he told her what had happened. Neil was calm, almost without emotion, as he spoke. Helen had tears in her eyes but Neil didn't see them. He was gazing at the wall, shell-shocked, as Helen hugged him. Robbo knew he had to get home as soon as he could, but he couldn't think straight. Helen offered to make a cup of tea. It was a moment straight out of the soap operas that Helen loved so much; any hint of crisis in Weatherfield or Walford and somebody's reaching for the kettle and the tea bags. It was an instinctive reaction by Helen and one that Robbo appreciated. He averted his gaze from the wall and watched his fiancée fill the small kettle with bottled water from the fridge. She plugged it in, flicked the switch and then took the two cups and saucers and placed a tea bag in each. The normality of the tea-making routine helped Robbo to think in a more orderly fashion. Organization was one of Robbo's key strengths, but when he had finished talking to his brother his thoughts had been all over the place. His father was seriously ill in hospital and he was on the other side of the world. He had felt helpless as he spoke to his brother, but now with the kettle slowly beginning to warm up he was starting to think more clearly.

'I'll have to sort out a flight home. Will you come with me Helen if I go into town and find a travel agent?'

'Of course I will. Look Neil, why don't we speak to Joe first. We'll have to tell him what's happened and besides, he'll know the best place to go to sort out the plane tickets.'

Neil knew Helen was talking sense, but it didn't seem fair to burden Joe. The Thai man had been so kind already. Helen knew her boyfriend well enough to know what he might have been thinking.

'Really sweetheart, if we speak to Joe, the brewery might

246

have some arrangements with the airlines which means we can get home quicker.'

Robbo paused briefly as he mulled over Helen's advice. 'You're right love, I'll give him a call, but there's no need for you to fly home as well.'

'Yes there is darling. I'm coming with you.'

Now more than ever, Robbo needed his best friend and soulmate and she hugged him tightly.

Joe made the arrangements personally. There was no trouble in sorting out the flight from Chiang Mai to Bangkok, but there was no availability on a flight from Bangkok to London until two days' time. Joe contacted Nok head office in Bangkok and asked them to ring every airline possible for availability on any flight that evening. Eventually they found two business class seats with EVA Airways and Joe authorized the payment for the tickets.

Robbo felt useless waiting around in his hotel room as Joe was busy making all the arrangements. He knew that once he was on the flight from Bangkok to London it would be more bearable. He didn't want to tell the other players and their partners that he was going home early, it would put a downer on the whole trip, but he would have to. Of course he would have to; he couldn't just go without saying anything.

Butch was the first man Robbo went to see. Butch didn't know what to say — what *could* he say? He just had to offer support for his friend.

'Look mate, anything I can do. If you want me to tell the rest of the boys . . .'

'Cheers Butch. I was about to knock on a few doors now, but to be honest mate I don't really feel like talking to anybody at the moment. I know I should tell everybody me and Helen are going home but —'

'Go back to your room, see Helen and sort your packing out. I'll speak to everybody else and if you want to see them before you go back that's up to you, but I'll make sure everybody leaves you in peace to get on with things.'

'Thanks Butch. I'll give you a knock in an hour or so.'

'No worries mate, I'm not going anywhere. I'm still trying to find the hard-core Frankie Vaughan on the TV.'

Robbo smiled. He appreciated his friend's levity. In a handful of words, Butch had spoken volumes about the two men's friendship. They weren't empty words from Butch when he had said, 'anything I can do'. Butch would never forget how Robbo had helped him cope with his marriage breakdown. It was the worse period of Butch's life, but Robbo and Kev came through for him. Proper mates.

Joe Koonphool drove to the hotel to meet Neil Roberts.

Sammy's father handed Neil a sheet of paper with all the flight details and reference numbers. There were contact names and numbers in Chiang Mai and Bangkok in case Joe himself was unavailable at any time. A car had been arranged to take Neil and Helen to the airport for the flight from Chiang Mai. Joe had also booked a day room at Bangkok airport, where the couple could stay in comfort for the few hours they'd have to wait before they could check-in for their flight to London. Neil and Helen both thanked Joe for everything he had done.

'Tell Sammy —' Robbo corrected his informality quickly. 'Tell Somsak I want him to score the winning goal in the final for the team of crazy farangs.'

'I'll tell him,' smiled Joe. 'The final's being filmed by the brewery, so I'll send you a copy of the match on DVD if your team get there.'

A few minutes after Joe left, there was a knock on Robbo's

door. Helen answered and gave Kevin Hardaker a hug. Kev shook Robbo's hand.

'Butch has just told me what's happened. I thought twice about disturbing you, but I had to see you Robbo before you went. I just want to say I hope everything works out for your dad. We'll all be thinking of you.'

'Nice one Kev. It sounds like the old man's going to be OK. Andy said the doctors were pleased with his progress. I think what makes matters seem worse is that I'm so far away.'

'That's right mate,' agreed Kev.

Neil Roberts spent the first few hours of the flight from Bangkok to London thinking about his father. It was easy to take your parents for granted and Robbo had been guilty of that. It was easy to assume they'd always be around; the two people who had always taken care of him. Even into adulthood, Robbo's parents had helped him out financially when he was at university in Loughborough. They had given him the deposit for his first house when he started teaching and they had always supported him in everything he had done.

Brian Roberts had worked on the railways for forty years. When Neil and Andy were younger, he'd often finish a night shift and come home to take his sons to their Saturday morning rugby or football matches. He had always made time for his two boys. His two sons would be the first to admit they didn't fully appreciate it at the time. Children tend to take things for granted and they never told their dad how much they loved him. All these thoughts were going through Robbo's head. Snapshots of a happy childhood playing in the local park and picnics by the river with Mum and Dad. Robbo was stirring up memories of childhood friends and places which had been undisturbed in the recess of his mind for over twenty years.

Neil Roberts was dozing in his seat, almost asleep, but still aware of the flight attendants wheeling the drinks trolley past. He was tired, emotionally and physically, but his mind wouldn't let him sleep properly, too many thoughts racing through. Opening his eyes and looking at his watch already adjusted to UK time, he thought about his mum and his brother. Would they be at the hospital now? Was his mother sleeping properly? Was Andy coping? He had never had to deal with anything like this before. His maternal grandparents were both sprightly octogenarians, but his father's parents had both died in a car accident when Neil was six years old. He couldn't remember too much about it, but now as he was trawling through his childhood, he conjured up images of living with his aunt for two weeks and Dad telling his two sons to be on their best behaviour. He couldn't remember asking about why Mummy was crying or where were Grandma and Grandad. Questions he must have asked, but he just couldn't remember. He had a flashback to a photo in his grandparents' house of Grandad Henry in his RAF uniform, and then, bizarrely, he was thinking about Frank Marinelli and his Biggles costume at the National Cup matches. What would Grandad have made of the boys from the Globe? He would have liked them, thought Robbo. His only memories of his grandad were pleasant ones. Memories of time spent in the small allotment where Neil and Andy would help their grandad dig up potatoes. Memories of the lingering smell of pipe tobacco that distinguished his grandparents' house. Happy memories.

Robbo was trying to banish any negative thoughts about the possibility of his father dying. The initial phone call from his brother was a shock. It was only later when he was speaking to Joe, Butch and Kevin about his father's heart attack that he began to pick up on the positive things Andy had told him: 'doctors satisfied', 'comfortable', 'good progress.'

Neil Roberts appreciated the extra comfort and privacy of business class. He looked across to his girlfriend and smiled at her asleep, her head tilted to face him, her mouth slightly open and her nose occasionally twitching. He reclined his seat level with Helen's and tried once more to get some sleep.

The flight was four hours away from Heathrow when Brian Roberts suffered the second cardiac arrest that was to prove fatal.

CHAPTER TWENTY-FOUR

The players and their partners still met in the foyer at eight o'clock as arranged. Butch and Kev hadn't been quite sure what to do, but everybody needed to be told about Neil and Helen going home. Butch had seen a few of the group and told them, but most of the others had been unaware. Tommy and Sylvia had been in town looking for souvenirs for their grandchildren. Robbo had really wanted to see Tommy before he caught the flight from Chiang Mai, but everything had happened so quickly. The coach had arrived back at the hotel from the elephant trip at four o'clock. Three hours later Neil and Helen were checking in at Chiang Mai airport for the flight to Bangkok.

Butch had relayed how positive Robbo had sounded, together with the encouraging comments from the doctors. Tommy told the group about his own father who had suffered a heart attack at the age of fifty-three, but survived and went on to live an active life until he was eighty. The heart attack had served as a warning and Tommy's father quit smoking, although he was never able to give up the drink completely. As the group listened to Tommy, they felt more positive. Many had family members or knew friends that had a similar story to tell. They all thought Brian Roberts would be OK. The whole thing was made worse from Robbo's point of view by the fact that he was so far away from home. Naturally, he would have felt helpless but once he got back to England and saw his family it would be all right.

The Stockgrove party had moved into the hotel bar and were feeling a lot brighter than they had been. Butch lightened the mood by proposing a toast to Phil, Michelle and little Deborah Louise. Nobody felt much like going out into town, they were all happy enough sat in the comfortable seats of the hotel bar. Everybody in the group knew Phil and Michelle and were obviously delighted for them both, but Robbo's situation was different. They all felt sorry for Robbo and the situation he was in, but only Butch and Kev had actually met Brian Roberts before. Robbo's parents still lived in the same house in Essex that had been their home for twenty-five years, only venturing to Milton Keynes for Sunday lunch with Neil and Helen every now and then.

The following day was a sunny one in Chiang Mai and the Stockgrove players and their partners spent most of the day sunbathing by the pool. It was a warm summer's day in England too, but Neil Roberts would be making the funeral arrangements for his father. There was no need to tell those in Thailand about the death of his father. There was nothing anybody could do and besides, nobody really knew Brian Roberts so there was no need to spoil anyone's holiday. There was a chance that one of the girls might ring or text Helen, but Robbo hoped they wouldn't. It would be better if they found out when they got back to England. Robbo knew none of the lads would ring him. Not because they weren't concerned, but they'd take the attitude that no news is good news. That's probably what they'd tell their other halves too

— 'He'll have enough on his plate, let's leave him in peace' — that's the attitude Robbo himself would take. Perhaps it was a macho thing; not wanting to be seen to be displaying too much compassion, or maybe they were doing the male thing of ignoring bad news in the hope it will go away.

Robbo knew he should ring Joe Koonphool to thank him again for everything he had done. He'd wait until everybody was back from Thailand.

On Saturday, Stockgrove beat the team from Bangkok head office 1-0. As the players had arrived at the university stadium, it had been a strange feeling not to have Robbo there. They had played matches without him before, but not many. It wasn't his playing ability they missed, they missed *him*; Neil Roberts, their mate. The man who above anybody else had deserved to be there when Stockgrove played their last ever matches. There was still the usual banter in the changing room. There had been no impassioned, 'let's do it for Robbo' speeches. They weren't Americans. Nevertheless, there was a collective feeling they should go on to win the tournament, partly for Robbo, but mainly for themselves. It would be a fitting way for Stockgrove FC to finish.

Kevin Hardaker had his best game of the season filling in at centre-back for Robbo. The whole team played well and Macca scored the crucial goal that set up their final group match with the other Bangkok team, with the winner of that match progressing to the final.

The days preceding the final group match were spent mainly topping up the tan. The weather had settled into a pattern of sunshine and showers. In the late afternoon, cloud would bubble up and a sudden strong wind would be the signal that rain was on its way. A short, violent downpour for thirty minutes or an hour would then blow away leaving a pleasant warm night. There was no need for John Ketley here, the Stockgrove group had begun to judge the weather quite well and make their plans accordingly.

There had still been no news from Robbo, and Kimberley wanted to contact Helen.

'No Kimberley, we agreed didn't we?' said John Woods.

'I know but they're my friends, I'm concerned about them.'

'We all are babe. I know it sounds hard, but there's nothing we can do here. We've all got to get on with the football tournament and enjoy our holiday.'

How could he talk about enjoying his holiday, thought Kimberley, as she frowned silently at her husband. Woodsy responded to his wife's frostiness. 'But we can't do anything about it Kimberley. They're my friends as well and I care about them too, but we've got to get on with things here.'

'As if nothing has happened you mean.'

'That's not what I'm saying and you know it,' replied Woodsy firmly. He didn't want to argue with his wife and he hadn't intended for his tone of voice to be confrontational. There was a moment of silence before Woodsy joined his wife sitting on the edge of the bed in their hotel room. He rested his hand on his wife's knee.

'Come on sweetheart, let's go for a walk,' he said softly.

Kimberley sighed slightly, squeezed her husband's hand and kissed him on the cheek.

It had been five days since Neil and Helen had gone back to England. If everything was OK, then Helen would have rung to say so, that's what Kimberley believed. It was also what her husband believed, but he wasn't going to admit it.

A crowd of nearly three hundred had gathered on Wednesday

afternoon to watch the final group match between Stockgrove and the Bangkok-based logistics team. The spectators were a mixture of university students and curious locals who had been reading about the farang team in the local newspaper.

Results in the other matches meant that whoever won would progress to the final to play the team from the Chiang Mai brewery. A draw would be good enough for the Thai side because of their superior goal difference. They scored eight goals without reply against the hapless Americans.

Stockgrove attacked from the first whistle. They dominated the game and it must have surprised their Thai opponents to see how good the team from England were. Macca, Stan, Willo and JC were winning every ball in midfield. They were playing their best football since the early rounds of the National Cup. Despite their dominance, Stockgrove had nothing to show for their efforts until ten minutes before half-time. A neat through ball from Macca released Sammy Koonphool. With a defender snapping at his heels he ran into the penalty area, and as the keeper advanced to close the angle, Sammy sent a deft chip that just eluded the keeper's fingertips and floated into the net. Two minutes later Macca and JC combined to give Gary Sweeney a chance. He was twelve yards out and he hammered his shot against the inside of the post and into the goal.

Tommy Boyle was delighted with his team's first-half performance. 'Just keep playing the way you are; let the ball do the work.' Stockgrove continued with their passing game in the second period as Tommy had requested. The Bangkok side had some good individual players, but too often they dribbled the ball into trouble and were easily dispossessed. The Stockgrove team did tire as the game went on and Macca and Willo made way for Danny and Lloydy with half an hour left. Woodsy was never seriously troubled; a couple of speculative long-range efforts were easily dealt with. Stockgrove saw out the game quite comfortably and were delighted to reach the final. It may have only been a friendly tournament but there was national pride at stake: English, Scottish and Thai.

Joe and Ladawan Koonphool were watching in the stand and the Nok VIPs were congratulating them on the performance of their son. Sammy had another excellent game and scored an exquisite goal. Some of his friends were at the match and there were more travelling up from Bangkok at the weekend when they finished work, so now they would be able to see him play in the final. It had been good for Sammy to see his friends and for them to see the football team he had spoken about in the phone calls and emails home. The crazy men who threw people in the canal, superglued football boots to ceilings and put dead pheasants in kit bags. When they asked which one was Sammy's schoolteacher, he had to explain about Neil returning home. Sammy was sad that Neil and Helen would miss the remainder of the trip in such circumstances. The couple had been good to him in England. They may have been his schoolteachers, but they had also become his friends. Next year would be strange for Sammy. Living at university and making new friends wouldn't be difficult for the sociable Thai youngster, but he wouldn't have much free time on his hands. He had decided he was going to sign with Chesham United when he returned, and combining the football training with his studying was going to be hard work. He wouldn't have as many opportunities to see his friends from school and mates from football.

CHAPTER TWENTY-FIVE

Stan was loving life in Thailand. In the short space of time he had been there, he had begun to fall in love with the country. It was seductive; the weather, the friendliness of the people, the grace and charm of the women and the whole laid-back attitude to life in general, all appealed to Stan. He was even taking to some of the food. He was bored in England. His job in the planning department was OK, but it wasn't exactly fulfilling. It paid the mortgage, but it wasn't paying all the bills and the mountain of credit card debt he had been trying to claw back ever since his second marriage break-up. Stan liked the people he worked with in the council office, but it wasn't where he wanted to be in five years' time. It wasn't where he wanted to be in five weeks' time.

In Chiang Mai, Stan hired a motorbike and would happily drive round the town by himself whilst the others lounged by the pool. He drove out to the surrounding mountains and countryside. Around the city he discovered numerous cafés and coffee shops where he'd park up for an hour, enjoying a drink and watching the world go by. And when he was in the coffee shops he'd feel at ease. There was one shop in particular he liked, or more accurately, there was one woman in one coffee shop that he particularly liked. She was in her mid-twenties with olive skin, shoulder length black hair, big chocolate-brown eyes and a cheeky smile. The first two occasions Stan went in, she had said nothing, only smiled and served Stan with his coffee. On the third occasion, she started a conversation.

'Excuse me, sir, you work in Chiang Mai?'

'No,' said Stan, 'I'm just here on holiday.'

'You not have wife, you come alone?'

Stan smiled, 'No not married, I come with friends. We play football Chiang Mai.' Once again without knowing it, Stan was slipping into the idiosyncratic way of speaking English that the Thais had, reducing the language to its simplest form by eradicating certain words.

'You play Thai team, yes? I see newspaper, farang team stay Chiang Mai. Excuse me, moment please.' The Thai woman disappeared into the kitchen area, resurfacing a minute later with a copy of a local newspaper. She opened it up to page five and there was a colour picture from Stockgrove's game against the American team. Stan could clearly make out Sammy and Gary and somebody else who he suspected was Macca.

'Yes, this my team!' he said, pointing at the players in blue shirts.

'Your country England or USA?'

'England my country.'

'Good country. Number one football,' she said, and then without hesitation or embarrassment she added, 'Why you not have wife?'

The sudden change of tact from football to his marital status threw Stan. If it had been a British woman asking the question he would probably have responded by saying 'mind your own business you nosey cow!' But the way in which the

Thai woman had asked was funny and didn't feel the least bit intrusive. Stan surprised himself by how much he opened up to the Thai woman, speaking about his two failed marriages as she pulled up a chair and sat opposite him.

'You good man I think, but have bad luck with lady. You have girlfriend now?'

'No have girlfriend,' said Stan.

'You stay Thailand you have girlfriend, sure, one million per cent,' she laughed.

'I think so too,' agreed Stan.

The Thai woman stood up and left Stan to drink his coffee while she cleaned the other tables. Stan couldn't make out whether the girl was being friendly, flirting with him or just having some fun. He decided it was probably a combination of all three. A combination he liked.

'My name Robert, but friends call me Stan.'

'My name Lek, friends call me Lek,' replied the Thai girl with an impish grin. The girl was feisty and she had a better command and understanding of English than Stan had given her credit for.

'You have husband, Lek?'

'No have,' laughed the Thai woman.

'Boyfriend?' asked Stan as a follow-up.

'No have. Thai man break my heart before.'

Stan was keen to find out more, but his English reserve prevented him from asking any more questions. He hardly knew the girl and although he had opened up and spoke about his failed relationships, it was because he wanted to. If Lek wanted to tell him about her Thai boyfriend that was up to her, he wasn't going to push the subject. There was a pause as Lek seemed to lose her sense of fun. Stan guessed this was a recent break up and the conversation had struck a raw nerve. Feeling awkward, Stan wasn't sure what he should say but he felt that he should say something. 'Another coffee please,' was the best he could do.

Two more customers came in the shop and Lek was busy attending to them as Stan sipped his coffee and thought about his holiday in Thailand. He had already decided he was going to come back. He fancied the idea of two weeks on a beach somewhere: Ko Samui, Phuket or Krabi. He had enough accrued leave at work and Stan was already thinking that Christmas and New Year would be a good time for a holiday. It was only five months away and it would be a great time to escape the cold and damp of England. When he was married, the festive period was usually spent arguing. Whose in-laws were they going to visit for Christmas lunch, who was coming to them on Boxing Day, how much should they spend on presents; all were cause for conflict. And since he had been single, Christmas and New Year were a drag. He'd go down the Globe on Christmas Eve and most of the Stockgrove lads and all the regulars would be there, and it was always a good night. But then on Christmas Day he'd wake up alone in his house with nobody to exchange presents with. He didn't bother with a Christmas tree; bah humbug. He'd pop down the pub for a couple of pints at lunchtime and then walk to his parents' house for Christmas dinner. He'd eat too much, drink too much and fall asleep watching the blockbuster movie. After the turkey sandwiches he'd walk back home, watch a bit of telly with a couple of cans of beer and then go to bed. On Boxing Day, he always woke up early and went for a run. He had a blow out on Christmas Day, but that was usually the only day of the year when he did. And then at New Year it was even worse; everybody seemed to be in couples. He'd have to contend with the not so subtle matchmaking attempts of Kimberley Woods or Helen. He knew they meant well, but if he was going to have another nightmare relationship, he was well capable of doing that by himself without outside interference.

Christmas and New Year were times when Stan would reflect too much on the past. By the time he had finished drinking his coffee he had made up his mind. He was definitely going to be spending this Christmas in Thailand. As Lek collected his empty cup and joked with him once more, he just had to decide whether it would be a beach or Chiang Mai that he'd be visiting.

'On Saturday my team play football at university. Four o'clock we play team from Chiang Mai. You come look?' Stan knew he must have had too much caffeine. What was he doing asking this girl if she wanted to come and watch him play football? Why would she want to? They hardly knew each other, Stan was at least ten years older and the girl was beautiful. Stunningly beautiful. She was out of Stan's league. She was Premiership and he was Vauxhall Conference. He regretted asking her at the point when he was holding up four fingers to indicate four o'clock. The Thai waitress said nothing. She just smiled serenely and moved her eyebrows up and down a couple of times. Bloody hell thought Stan, what does *that* mean? He had enough trouble deciphering signals from women back in England. Out of his league. She was Manchester United and had a great Arsenal, and he was Accrington (never mind plenty more fish in the sea) Stanley.

CHAPTER TWENTY-SIX

As the coach drove into the university campus, everybody on board was stunned by the number of people. The university grounds were thronged with men, women and children all enjoying the weekend festival. There were bouncy castles and small fairground rides for the kids. There were stalls where the adults could throw darts at balloons and fire air guns at targets to win prizes. There was a large market selling clothes, and a huge blue marquee packed full with Thai people eating. A covered boxing ring had been set up and was staging bouts of Thai boxing featuring local fighters. From the coach, the players could hear the whining piped music that accompanied each round, as the boxers kicked and punched each other to the approval of the large crowd watching.

The car park was full of coaches and minibuses that had been used to ferry the teams from all over Thailand to compete in the grand finals of the Nok tournament. The whole scene had amazed the Stockgrove group. They knew it was a big tournament, but the actual scale and the number of people in attendance shocked them. The finals of the junior matches had all been completed by the time Stockgrove got there. They could still see children walking around in football kit and carrying trophies almost as big as them. They'd be congratulated by the adults and bow and wai in return. There was bunting everywhere displaying the Thai national flag. At the pitch where the adult matches were taking place, flagpoles had been erected. There was one with the Thai flag and others with flags from Singapore, Hong Kong, America and Britain to respect Nok's guests from overseas. Joe Koonphool had been right when he said the tournament was good business sense from Nok brewery's perspective. The event had plenty of column inches in local and national newspapers and had been featured regularly on television news bulletins. Nok brewery had a merchandising stall that was handing out free T-shirts and baseball caps featuring the brewery's name and logo.

The players hadn't been nervous in the previous matches in the tournament, nor in most of their league matches throughout the season, but they were today. The last time most of the players had experienced butterflies in the stomach was the National Cup match in Liverpool. The importance of the match on Merseyside, the new surroundings and unfamiliar opponents had all contributed to the pre-match nerves on that occasion. The nerves weren't a bad thing; they helped to sharpen performance. The lads had all been playing long enough to know that. When they were playing in league matches there was rarely any pre-match tension. Without being arrogant, they expected to win every league match they played because they were the best team in the league and they had proved it over a number of seasons. They knew the individual players on some of the opposite sides and were friends with many of them. In County Cup and National Cup matches, that familiarity wasn't there. And in Chiang Mai as they got changed for the game, the familiarity most definitely wasn't there. They may have played three matches already at the university stadium, but today they could hardly recognize the place. It had been transformed by the stalls, fairground rides and swarms of people enjoying their day out. The whole day had a sense of occasion about it much in the same way as the match in Liverpool. There were no supporters from the Globe to cheer them on, but this was the final of a tournament. It was also the last ever game for Stockgrove FC and the players were determined to win.

Tommy Boyle gave his last team talk. His Harris Tweed flat cap was at home in Milton Keynes having a well-deserved rest. He had a new titfer more suited to the tropical climate; a cheeky little tan-coloured cotton number from Marks and Sparks. The Scotsman was keen to win but if his team lost, he wouldn't be too disappointed. He didn't tell his team that. He told them they hadn't travelled thousands of miles to come and lose. However, they were here as guests of Nok brewery and they had thoroughly enjoyed the hospitality accorded to them by their Thai hosts. If the lads played well, then Tommy would be pleased, irrespective of the outcome. The conditions were in favour of the home side and Tommy knew his team had done remarkably well in the group games to cope with the heat and humidity. He read out the team and added, 'It's the last game for the club, so enjoy it . . . and you'll enjoy it more by winning it.'

Tommy had probably underestimated how much the players wanted to win. They had been their usual jovial selves in the dressing room as they changed. There was no sign of the nerves or excitement that the players all felt. Even Colin McSwiggen, the ex-professional footballer, was nervous.

The players came out of the changing rooms and were surprised to see the team from Chiang Mai waiting in the small tunnel that led up to the pitch. Two officials from Nok brewery were on hand and instructed both teams to line up in single file. One of them told Tommy that both teams would also line up on the pitch for the anthems. Bloody hell, anthems! Nobody said anything about that. Surely, they're not going to play the National Anthem. The Stockgrove players couldn't believe it when they were told. The referee and the two linesmen led the teams out into the dappled sunlight of the stadium. The single stand was almost full and the terraces were well populated without being anywhere near full. Nevertheless, a crowd of over one thousand had been tempted away from the activities outside. There were a large number of supporters for the home town side as well as people curious to see the team from England with the Thai centre forward; the team they had been reading about in their newspapers. There was polite applause as the players came on to the pitch and lined up in front of the main stand. The Stockgrove players were waving to their wives and girlfriends. Nothing too extravagant, just a smile and a wave of acknowledgement, after all they still had a football match to win. Two sets of cheerleaders lined up on the touchline about ten yards from the players. They were all female students at the university and one group were wearing full England football kits whilst the other group were wearing the kit of Thailand. The Stockgrove players had no inkling all this was going to happen. Joe Koonphool had said nothing about this, even Sammy didn't know. An extremely strange, tortuous rendition of 'God Save The Queen' was played over the tannoy. Colin McSwiggen would never be able to show his face again at Parkhead; dressed in red, white and blue and stood respectfully listening to the National Anthem. The shame of it. Only Gary Sweeney made any attempt to sing, as the whole crowd stood in silence and applauded at the end of the music. The Thai anthem came on and the Stockgrove players were taken aback by the volume of the crowd as they sang along, and nobody sang more proudly than Sammy Koonphool. At the end of the anthems, the cheerleaders began to dance and the players exchanged greetings. A line of Nok officials were introduced to the teams. Joe Koonphool had a special word of encouragement for his son as newspaper snappers and a television camera crew captured the moment. If the club was going to be playing its last ever game, then this was a memorable way to finish. Joe Koonphool hadn't been joking with Neil Roberts when he said he would send him a copy of the match on DVD.

The pitch had been well watered and was in much better condition than the ones they were used to at the start or end of an English summer. The weather was hot, but there was a breeze and dark clouds obscured the mountain tops that fringed the city. The Stockgrove players wouldn't be using the conditions as an excuse if they lost.

In the early stages, the two teams were well matched. Stockgrove weren't playing as well as they had in the previous matches. The team from Chiang Mai were quick to close their opponents down and disrupt their passing game. The home side came closest to scoring after twenty-five minutes, but Woodsy made a good save pushing the shot around the post. Shortly after that, Gary Sweeney had Stockgrove's best chance, but he directed his header straight at the goalkeeper. The first half was by no means a feast of football, but it was evenly contested and intriguing enough with the contrast in styles. The Chiang Mai team were relying on individual performances, running at Stockgrove and taking players on. The English side passed the ball more and played more of a team game.

The second half was similar to the first, but Stockgrove were playing better. Gradually, they began to take control and enjoy more possession. Sammy was a threat every time he got the ball and the midfield were looking strong. It was very much against the run of play when Chiang Mai scored. Willo had conceded the foul when he obstructed a Thai forward just outside the box. The referee indicated an indirect free kick. The player taking the kick struck it into the right hand side of the net. Woodsy would have struggled to save it, but he made no effort to do so because the ball had gone directly into the goal from the kick. The Stockgrove keeper couldn't believe it when the Thai referee signalled towards the centre-spot. How could he award a goal? Woodsy stood open-mouthed with his hands on his hips as the other Stockgrove players looked round. Willo scratched his head and Woodsy felt like protesting but wasn't sure how to go about it. He didn't want to shout at the referee or cause a scene.

'Butch, have a word with the ref, he can't allow that to stand.'

Paul Butcher was as amazed as his goalkeeper was. The referee had definitely signalled an indirect free kick. The Chiang Mai side were already back in their own half and waiting for the resumption when Butch approached the ref. Aware of the need for tact and diplomacy, Butch said to the official, 'You give obstruction, yes? Indirect free kick, nobody else touch, no goal.'

'Yes,' replied the referee and he smiled; the Thai smile that the Stockgrove party had seen so often in the two weeks they had been in Thailand. It completely disarmed Butch. He didn't know whether the ref had understood the point he was trying to make or not. Either way, Butch wasn't going to argue. This wasn't like dealing with a referee back in England. Butch gave a wry smile that seemed to meet with the approval of the man in black who smiled again, but even more broadly this time, and motioned for Stockgrove to kick-off.

'You start again please.'

Butch walked back towards Woodsy and shrugged his shoulders. He wasn't angry or annoyed, just perplexed. If it had been in England, he would have been fuming and so would players like Gary Sweeney and Colin McSwiggen. But they weren't in England and as much as they wanted to win the game, this was no time to cause embarrassment for their hosts by protesting about the legitimacy of the goal.

There was still over twenty minutes left to play and Stockgrove had been looking the most likely side to score up until the free kick. The cheerleaders had all celebrated the goal, even the ones in England kit, by dancing and doing cartwheels on the running track. Five minutes from time, they were doing cartwheels again when Sammy equalized for Stockgrove. It was a simple tap-in from inside the six-yard box following good work by JC and then Gary. The same people who had cheered the Chiang Mai goal were now cheering for Stockgrove. The players weren't sure whether this was a particularly Thai brand of impartiality, or whether it was for the Thai youngster who had scored the goal. Whichever it was, it had been good to hear.

The final whistle blew with the score level at 1-1. Tommy walked on to the pitch to prepare his team for the period of extra-time that would follow. Before the match, Tommy had asked one of the Nok officials what would happen in the event of a draw. 'You play extra-time, twenty minute. Ten minute each half, hot too much. If no win, penalty shoot-out,' he was told. That was clear enough for Tommy, so why was the referee now walking towards one goal and placing the ball on the penalty spot. Butch and the others laughed when they were told extra-time had been disregarded. It seemed that in all matters, even football, there was a distinctly Thai way of doing things. None of the players were complaining. They were all hot and tired and foregoing extra-time was quite a sensible decision.

Sammy, Gary, Macca and Butch all scored their penalties and they were matched by their opponents. Willo took the fifth kick and fired it over the crossbar. If the Thai team scored the next penalty, they would win the trophy. The Chiang Mai player hadn't looked confident as he walked up to take it and Woodsy guessed the right way. The Thai player may not have looked confident, but he couldn't have struck the ball any better and it gave Woodsy no chance, eluding his outstretched glove. There were a few moments of celebration by the Thai side before they came and shook hands and *waied* to their opponents.

There was disappointment from the Stockgrove team. Everybody had been keen to win and losing on penalties was a horrible way to lose any football match. They consoled themselves with the fact that they had played well during the tournament and they'd had a fantastic time in Thailand.

'Christ Almighty, what's the world coming to,' said Macca. 'The English lose on penalties yet again, and I'm not jumping up and down celebrating.'

The Chiang Mai players insisted that the Stockgrove team joined them on a lap of honour. It was a bit over the top and the players were reluctant to go, but they didn't want to cause any offence. Most of the crowd had already dispersed, but there were still plenty of people present to applaud both sets of players. Stan spotted Lek in the crowd waving at him as he jogged past. He stopped to take off his boots, letting his team-mates pass him, before returning the greeting. He didn't want to endure a load of mickey-taking from the lads, and so far he hadn't told anybody about the young woman who worked in the coffee shop. He was delighted to see her and would visit her the following morning at work.

Joe Koonphool presented a large trophy to the Chiang

Mai captain, and the Stockgrove players all received runners-up medals. By the time they left to return to England in two days' time, all the medals would be individually engraved with the player's name.

At the Nok marquee an hour later, the Stockgrove and Chiang Mai teams were at the post-tournament buffet arranged by their hosts. The teams from Singapore, Hong Kong and America were also present. The weekend had been a resounding success for the brewery. The newspaper and television coverage more than made up for the cost of staging the tournament and the expense of flying the foreign teams to Thailand. The people at the Nok marketing team were already going into overdrive and promotional hats and T-shirts were being liberally handed out. As people enjoyed the sit down Thai buffet, they had the choice of just two drinks: water or Lanna Beer. It was the first time any of the Stockgrove players, excluding Sammy, had tasted the produce of the company that sponsored the team. The beer was only available in supermarkets in Thailand, but negotiations with Tesco in Britain were going well and there was every chance that the beer the players were drinking today in Chiang Mai, would be available before Christmas at their local supermarket back home.

After dinner, the Stockgrove party had two hours of free time to look round the campus and enjoy the festivities. They watched the Thai boxing for a while, and then they spotted it. Opposite the area staging the boxing were a dozen yellow booths. Each one was about the size of an average garden shed and designed to hold a maximum of six people. Once Gary Sweeney realized what they were, that was it; game, set and match.

'*Yes*! We are definitely 'aving a bit of that!'

The rest of the players didn't need too much convincing, and their partners had drunk enough of their hosts' products to be giggling, as they approached the yellow cabins. They could only squeeze ten inside; any more and they wouldn't have been able to operate the machinery. It was still a ridiculous scene as the men were pressed against each other, reaching into their pockets and fumbling to find the seventy baht in coins needed. Gary Sweeney had taken command of the karaoke booth — admiral of the H.M.S. *Gary Oakey* — and not just any karaoke booth. This one enabled the participants to record their own fifteen-minute CD. The other cabins were all busy too, with locals singing Thai pop songs, but there was only one booth with ten people inside and as many more crowded outside. Admiral Sweeney briefly went through some instrumental backing tracks before he opted for the one that came closest to meeting his crew's requirements. He selected a gentle, romantic sounding guitar, which wouldn't hinder the vocal arrangement too much. And then they launched into song. *'Today is gonna be the day . . .'* At the chorus, the door was opened and those outside joined in, *'. . . and all the runs that JC makes are winding, and all the goals that Sweeney scores are blinding . . .'*

Gary was conducting proceedings, keeping everybody together. He had his mates from Stockgrove around him, and even with the singing it was all about teamwork and friendship.

'Hey, hey, we're the Stockgrove
So don't come drinking with us
'Cos we'll drink you under the table
Without any fuss . . .'

The songs weren't taking up too much recording time and Kimberley shouted a suggestion from outside, remembering the night she had been serenaded in the Globe. Woodsy could remember the words this time. Thoughts of diarrhoea, dog bites, Mickey Finn and Dave Pheasant couldn't be further from his mind. He linked arms with the other players in the karaoke booth and sang.

'I don't wanna talk about it . . .'

In between each song there was laughter and chatter as the men discussed which song they'd record next. Sammy Koonphool may have harboured dreams of playing football in the Nationwide, but his singing talent would have got him kicked out of the Abbey National let alone Abbey Road.

Abbey National, Abbey Road, Abbey Days.

Gary took control once more for the last song.

'Right boys, follow my lead. We're singing this one acapulco with no backing track.'

'Fucking hell Gal, what do you want us to do . . . drink a bottle of tequila and dive off a cliff?' said Kev.

The lads were all laughing and it was left to Butch to inform Gary of his mistake.

'Bollocks,' said Gary. 'Whatever it is, a cappella, Acapulco, Acker Bilk . . . just follow my lead.'

He was the only one who knew the words all the way through and the others would join in with the chorus and the other bits they could remember.

'Two little boys had two little toys
Each had a wooden horse . . .'

It must have sounded strange to the Thai people who were beginning to crowd round the Stockgrove booth and look at the crazy farangs singing. The door of the cabin was ajar and the players would have been stunned if they knew how far away they could be heard. That didn't concern Gary Sweeney. This was a song about loyalty and friendship. It didn't matter that the Thai people outside wouldn't understand the lyrics of the song. Rolf Harris himself could have been there, handing out song sheets, riding a kangaroo and speaking in Thai with the locals, 'Can you guess what it is yet?' The Thai audience may not have known the song, but they could see this was a group of friends enjoying themselves — *sanuk* — and they smiled and applauded when Gary and the others emerged from the karaoke booth.

Before they left to go home to England, everybody on the trip would have their own personal copy of the debut CD; The Stockgrove Singers — *Live and Direct in Chiang Mai*. There was as much laughter and talking on the CD as there was singing, but it captured the moment perfectly and Neil and Helen would appreciate their copy when they received it in three days' time.

CHAPTER TWENTY-SEVEN

Two days after the final, the Stockgrove party were on their way back to England. They had all said goodbye to the Koonphool family and thanked Joe for everything he had done. Sammy would be staying in Thailand until the beginning of September before returning to England to start university.

On his final night in Chiang Mai, Stan went out to dinner with Lek and her aunt, who was acting as chaperone. Stan and Lek swapped telephone numbers and email addresses, and he promised he would be back in December. He got a lot of stick from the other players for 'spending his last night with some bird and not his mates.' It had been a strange end to the holiday for Stan. He had only known Lek for a few days and he knew he couldn't have developed real romantic feelings with a woman he hardly knew. And yet, he did have feelings. He didn't believe in that love at first sight nonsense — two divorces had taken care of that — but there was something about this Thai woman. Something about Thailand. Gary Sweeney had given his friend more ribbing than most, but when he spoke to Stan privately he said, 'Good luck to you mate. If you want to come back here, you come back and don't listen to anybody who tells you otherwise. If anybody deserves some happiness it's you.' Stan appreciated Gary's words, but Gary knew he couldn't leave it like that, he had to add something else, 'So . . . have you shagged her or what?'

The day that the Stockgrove group flew back was the same day as Brian Roberts's funeral. He hadn't been a church going man during his life, but he did believe in God. The service at the village church in Essex was well attended by neighbours and many of Brian's former railway colleagues. Eileen Roberts chose the hymns, both favourites of her husband: 'Jerusalem' and 'I Vow To Thee My Country'. Neil Roberts gave a brief but emotional eulogy, and after the service everybody was invited back for beer and sandwiches at the Roberts' family home. There was nothing extravagant; it was all plain and simple the way Brian would have liked it. The forecast rain had held off and most of the guests took their plates of food and their drinks, outside to the patio area that Brian Roberts had built single-handed fifteen years earlier.

As people chatted politely and made small talk, a number of people asked Neil and Helen about their trip to Thailand. The young couple both enthused about the country they had visited and the warmth and hospitality of the people. At the back of his mind however, Neil Roberts kept thinking about the fact that he wasn't there when his father died. He should have been there. He had got back as soon as he could, but he wasn't there with his mother and brother the moment his dad passed away. That couldn't be helped, it was 'just one of those things', his mum told him. Eileen Roberts was right. Who could have predicted anything like that? It wasn't as if Robbo went off on his football trip whilst his dad was seriously ill. It was still a regret for Neil that he wasn't there when his father died, in the same way that he would regret his

276

dad not seeing him marry Helen and have children.

Robbo looked at his watch and switched on his mobile phone. He told Helen he was going upstairs to make the telephone call to Joe Koonphool in Thailand. Helen kissed her boyfriend on the cheek and smiled.

Ladawan Koonphool answered and was surprised to hear Neil's voice. She immediately asked about his father and Neil explained what had happened. The Thai woman passed on her condolences and called her husband to the phone. Joe was already on the way before his wife called him. As soon as he had heard his wife talking in English, Joe guessed it was Neil, and he heard Ladawan offer her condolences. Neil Roberts thanked Joe for everything he had done. Not just for him personally, but for everybody that had been on the trip. Robbo asked if Sammy was there, but the youngster had been to a party with his friends the previous night and had rang to say he wouldn't be back until the afternoon.

Robbo laughed. 'Well it looks like he might have another cause for celebration when he gets back.'

Sammy's sports teacher explained to Joe about the phone call he had received the previous day from Steve Palmer. The man who had recommended Sammy to Reading had joined the coaching staff at Wycombe Wanderers. He was very keen to get Sammy to come and have a look at the set up of the club and do a bit of training with the team. This was a bit more than being invited to a trial. Neil told Joe what George Fielding had said when he rejected Sammy as being too small; '. . . if it was down to Steve Palmer, he'd give him a contract here and now . . .'

Neil Roberts had been delighted when he received the call from Steve Palmer. He didn't think he would be punching the air in celebration the day before his father's funeral, but that's exactly what he did.

* * *

Bill Shankly famously once said, 'Some people believe football is a matter of life and death. I'm very disappointed with that attitude. I can assure you it is much, much more important than that.'

Bill Shankly was a football man, one hundred per cent. One hundred and ten per cent, to use the true football cliché. A Scotsman with a razor wit and a master of the one-liner. He understood footballers and football changing rooms; the banter and the humour, the loyalty and the camaraderie. It exists in the amateur game just as much as the professional game. The playing fields of Hackney Marshes and Anfield may be vastly different in appearance, but some things are the same. If somebody misses a sitter in a match, they will be ridiculed afterwards. Robbo knew that. Just as Willo would always be reminded about his penalty miss in Thailand. Temporarily, he was dubbed 'Wilko.' Kicking a ball that high over the bar, Jonny Wilkinson would have been proud. The lads taking the piss out of each other — the banter from the changing room — Robbo would miss that. It could hardly compare to losing your father, but it was a part of his life that would be gone. And when the team came back and handed him the debut CD from the Stockgrove Singers, he'd hear as much talking and laughing as he would singing. Acapulco style singing. Gary Sweeney would never be allowed to forget that particular gem.

Stroker.

278